ATTRITION

The Great War on the Western Front, 1916

By the same author:

Military History

The Bomber War: Arthur Harris and the Allied Bombing Offensive
The Great War Generals on the Western Front
A Fighting Retreat: The British Empire, 1947–1997
In the Combat Zone: Special Forces Since 1945
By Sea and Land: The Royal Marines Commandos, 1942–1982
The Battle of Normandy: 1944
The Eighth Army
D-Day, 1944: Voices from Normandy (with Roderick de Normann)
The Conquest of the Reich: Germany 1945
The Raiders: The Army Commandos, 1940–1945
The Desert Rats: The Army Commandos, 1940–1945
The Dervish Wars: Gordon and Kitchener in the Sudan
Wellington and Napoleon: Clash of Arms, 1807–1815
The Hundred Years' War
The Wars of the Roses
True Stories of the SAS
True Stories of the SBS
True Stories of the Paras

Travel

The Road to Compostela
Walking Through Scotland
Walking Through Ireland
Walking Through Spain

ATTRITION

The Great War on the Western Front, 1916

By

Robin Neillands

ROBSON BOOKS

First published in Great Britain in 2001 by Robson Books,
10 Blenheim Court, Brewery Road, London N7 9NY

A member of the Chrysalis Group

British Library Cataloguing in Publication Data
A catalogue record for this title is available from the British Library.

ISBN 1 86105 348 7

Typeset by SX composing DTP, Rayleigh, Essex
Printed by Butler & Tanner Ltd, Frome and London

This one is in memory of Colin Fox

'But war's a game, which, were their subjects wise,
Kings would not play at.'

William Cowper,
'The Winter Morning Walk', *The Task*, 1785

Contents

Acknowledgements

A great many people helped me with this book. My thanks go first to those who set me on the trail of this story, the branch secretaries and members of the Western Front Association, for giving me the idea and providing both useful criticism and some very detailed information on different aspects of the Western Front; whatever you need to know, some member of the Western Front Association will have the information, and my thanks to them all.

I must then thank my critical readers, those who read the book in its various drafts, checked the facts, queried my opinions and voiced doubts that I have sometimes been able to answer in the text – a process known as 'Getting your retaliation in first.' My thanks therefore to Group Captain Drury-Bird, Major-General Julian Thompson, Colonel Terry Cave and the late and much-missed Colin Fox. Without Colin this book would not have been started, for he put the idea of writing about the Western Front into my head and was a constant supporter and critic of the work as it progressed.

Beyond that thanks go to Terry Brown, for his company on many visits to the Western Front, especially Verdun and the Somme; to the staff of the Musée Historial in Péronne; the staff and guides on the Verdun battlefield; Simon Robbins and Lawrie Milner at the Imperial War Museum; the Submarine Museum, Gosport; Andy Robertshaw at the National Army Museum; William Spencer at the Public Records Office; the RAF Museum, Hendon and the Wiltshire County Library Service. And, finally, to those many visitors I talked to on the Western Front in recent years, people who walked the ground, visited the cemeteries and raised the great question: *After what happened here, and at such a cost, why was it allowed to continue?* I hope that at least part of the answer is provided in the pages which follow.

About This Book

'It is not for the historian to accuse or defend.
His duty is to establish facts and to marshal
them in the sequence of cause and effect.'
Fritz Fischer, Foreword to *Germany's Aims in the First World War*

It would be pleasant to think that, somewhere in the world, there flows a stream of good, novel and interesting ideas, available to writers seeking a subject for their next book. Alas for authors, it rarely works out like that. Worthwhile, viable ideas are always hard to find, come from a number of sources and often arise from matters touched on in the previous book – or from the comment that book causes.

That is certainly so in this case. The origins of this book lie in a series of lectures I gave to branches of the Western Front Association in various parts of Britain during 1999–2000, talks based on the subject of my previous First World War book, *The Great War Generals on the Western Front*. In that book I attempted to demonstrate that the cause of the disasters on the Western Front during the Great War had a rather wider base than that fixed on by the public at large: the incompetence and callousness of the generals – especially the British generals – charged with the planning and management of the fighting on that front.

This argument was usually well received, but on a number of occasions during these lectures I was asked why Haig and Rawlinson, the overall commander in France and the general most closely concerned with the first phase of the battle, had agreed to attack on the Somme in 1916. Surely, said the questioners, the decision to assault this German bastion and so precipitate a battle which, after a disastrous first day, continued for months and cost so many lives for so little territorial gain, shows that these British generals *must* have been incompetent?

The short answer to that particular question is that the 1916 Somme offensive had been planned as a *combined* offensive by the French and British commanders, Generals Joffre and Haig – with Joffre, the *generalissimo*, as the prime mover – and this offensive was placed astride the River Somme because that was the place where the positions of the French and British Armies met and the French generals, specifically Joffre and Foch, could therefore dictate the progress of events.

However, even as I pointed that basic fact out, time and again during those lectures, I began to wonder if there was not more to it than that. After all, when the German Verdun offensive opened in February and continued unabated into the summer, the French contribution to the combined Somme attack inevitably declined . . . so why did not Haig abandon this 'combined offensive' and switch the British attack to his much-preferred ground in Flanders and the Ypres salient? If that course did not appeal, why, given the nature of the German defences, did Haig not wait until the tank was available to breach them? Clearly, the question of the 1916 offensive needed more investigation . . . but where to start?

One can start by dismissing some of the more absurd suggestions. Liddell Hart has suggested that after the failure of the First Day on the Somme, Haig should have switched his offensive to Messines, on the edge of the Ypres salient some 60 miles to the north. As Major-General Julian Thompson has remarked:

Forget about the political effect of pulling out of an Anglo-French operation. Just consider the logistics. In order to mount the Somme offensive, the British laid 55 miles of fresh railway track, leaving only ten miles of track available and unused. In the event, the Messines offensive in 1917 required the laying of 90 miles of railway track as well as the transport of ammunition for 1,314 guns which, in one week of the Messines offensive, fired 3,258,000 rounds of all calibres.

In short, if the Somme operation was a mistake, that mistake had to be realized long before the men went over the top on July 1;

after the battle was joined it had to be fought until some outcome
was established . . . but what sort of outcome might that be?[1]

The best place to start the study of any particular battle or campaign
is at the beginning, with the decision to attack. This decision is not
always in the hands of the generals, for the politicians will have their
say, but the first question that has to be asked is, was the decision to
attack on the Somme fundamentally wise? Did General Haig even
want to attack on the Somme, which was a new area of operations for
the British Army, on a part of the line only recently taken over from
the French?

If not, then why did Haig agree to the combined offensive in the
first place and, rather more to the point, if he did not want to attack
there, why did he persist in doing so after the German attack at
Verdun made it increasingly clear that his French Allies would not be
able to play their promised part in the battle? Would it not have been
wiser, as so many now assert, to give up the Somme campaign *entirely*
and revert to an attack out of the Ypres salient, where the strategic
advantages – in the event of success – were much more obvious?
Questions, questions . . .

These were good questions, more would follow from them and I
had no idea of the answers. I therefore decided to find out, and the
result is this book. In the course of researching it the project has
expanded somewhat, not least after the discovery, or realization, that
the story did *not* start with the decision to mount a combined
offensive; it started with the *reasons* for mounting a combined offensive
and that had to include a number of other issues, like stopping the war
altogether. To get to the bottom of the problem I would have to go
back to the very start of the war and see how the war and the armies
that fought it had changed, from the time the war opened to the
critical year of 1916.

To find that the object of the work has changed during the research
phase is quite usual. You never know what you are going to find until
you start looking, and it soon became apparent that if I was going to
write about 1916, Verdun and the Somme, I would have to spread my
net much wider than the battlefields. It would have been possible to

spread the search almost to infinity, but one must stop somewhere and in the end, although I have included what I regard as the essential background, I have generally kept the story within the confines of a single year – 1916 – and addressed only those issues which affected the fighting on the Western Front ... though the extent of those issues is surprising.

To keep the Western Front in context, these issues must touch on the reasons nations go to war at all or fail to make a peace when the cost of the conflict gets too high, and why generals change their methods of fighting for others that simply increase the suffering and the losses. Whatever is done, is done for a reason, and that reason has to be understood and explained.

As far as I can discover there has never been a book on the Great War events of 1916. Examine the shelves in any bookshop or library and you will find books on the Great War in 1914, 1915, 1917 and 1918, often in quantity, and by different authors ... yet 1916, *as a year*, is noticeable only by its absence.

This is curious, for 1916 was arguably the most decisive, even the pivotal, year of the First World War. Perhaps one reason for this neglect is that British interest in 1916 has tended to centre on the Battle of the Somme – and especially on the First Day of that terrible, four-month struggle – while French interest has been focused on the ten months of the Battle of Verdun. German interest has been concentrated on both these epic struggles and on the pressing need for the opening of an all-out submarine campaign as a means of bringing the British to their knees.

In view of the massive casualties suffered by all three nations in these 1916 battles, such a concentration is understandable, but it still does not fully explain why the events of 1916 have never been considered in total. That said, it is also true that those books which cover the events of other years tend to concentrate on particular battles – Neuve Chapelle or Loos in 1915, Arras, Cambrai or Passchendaele in 1917, the March Offensive in 1918, for example, rather than on the year as a whole.

This concentration cannot be because there is nothing to write about in 1916, apart from the Somme and Verdun; 1916 was full of incident. It can begin with the sacking of Field Marshal Sir John French, the elevation of Sir Douglas Haig to command the British Armies in France in December 1915, the death of Kitchener, the departure of General Joffre, the rise of General Pétain and General Nivelle, the dismissal of General von Falkenhayn, the events on the Eastern Front, the withdrawal from Gallipoli and the siege of Kut, the Battle of Jutland and the Easter Rising in Dublin, the arrival in France of the New Armies and the Australians, the advent of the tank, pressure for the German submarine campaign, the replacement of Prime Minister Asquith by Lloyd George . . . 1916 is full of dramatic events, and that may be the problem. Perhaps there is just too much to write about and separating out these happenings for individual treatment is no more than sensible. Certainly getting these events into focus and deciding which of them has relevance to the main subject of this book – the war on the Western Front – has proved a difficult task.

And yet there is something to be said for considering these events as a whole, as parts of the 1916 tapestry. A new year always offers the chance of a new beginning; anyone who has ever made a New Year's Resolution knows that. So, possibly, the varied events of 1916 do have some common threads or can be combined to make an interesting picture; we shall see. What can be said, even before the first word of the first chapter is written, is that 1916 was an important year, with effects that live with us to the present day.

After 1916, after the Somme and Verdun, Britain and France were never quite the same again; that 'glad, confident morning' had reached a sunset and, when the sun rose again, it was to shine on a very different kind of Europe, a continent shorn of the best of its young men, in economic ruin, but still riven by rivalries. The Great War shattered several empires and fatally damaged many countries but it taught the political leaders of Europe absolutely nothing; twenty years later they went to war again.

As far as the British were concerned, 1916 was supposed to be the year when it all came good. In 1916 the British Armies in France reached full strength; at last the British generals had an adequate supply of men and *matériel* and were no longer obliged, from a lack of manpower or logistical facilities, to be deferential or even subservient to their ever-querulous Allies, the French. The demands of the French tended to negate the advantages of military technology that were now becoming available but, by the start of 1916, the tank was coming into service, airpower was making its mark and a great offensive – the Big Push – by the Franco-British Armies on the Somme – was going to restore open warfare to the battlefield . . . a breakthrough and victory looked so possible in January 1916.

Alas for all these hopes. By November 1916, the total casualties for that year alone, in the French, British and German Armies, amounted to 1,300,000 men while the front lines had barely shifted and *still* the belligerents would not talk of peace. So the war surged on into 1917 and further slaughter.

This book then is a look at 1916 and how the war was fought on the Western Front: at the hopes and fears, the aims and ambitions, what was tried, what worked, what failed and why. It will also attempt to analyse why a common strategy, the one previously adopted by all three combatant nations, one focused on making a break through the opposing trench lines and restoring open warfare to the battlefield, was tacitly dropped in favour of a doctrine that promised no major territorial gains but ensured great losses among the opposing forces. This was the doctrine of *attrition*, a doctrine that states that the side which can inflict more losses than it sustains must, in the end, win the struggle.

There is, of course, a disadvantage with the doctrine of attrition. It accepts that the losses to one's own side will also be severe and must therefore be justified by victory. It is a doctrine based on exploiting the full brutality of war and since it puts the more appealing military assets, like good generalship, sound tactics and the competent use of all arms in the common struggle, at a discount compared with simple slaughter, it is hardly a policy that any general or politician could hope to justify to the electorate. Attrition is a doctrine of the shadows and it is not surprising that it was first introduced by the chief of the German General Staff, General von Falkenhayn, who did not have an electorate to worry about and only his Kaiser to please.

And yet, as we shall see, before the year ended, all the armies on the Western Front and most of the generals openly or tacitly came to accept that attrition was the only way to bring this war to a conclusion. Von Falkenhayn had no other object but a battle of attrition when he attacked the French at Verdun. Pétain, who came to defend that city, was determined not to give him that kind of fight but Joffre played into von Falkenhayn's hands by appointing Nivelle to the Verdun command – and the actions Joffre proposed and indeed forced on General Sir Douglas Haig on 3 July had no other intention but to get the British involved in a battle of attrition on the Somme.

And, in the end, even General Haig, with victory slipping from his grasp after Flers-Courcelette, went over to the tactics of attrition in October and November of 1916 and lost a great many lives in attacks that were at best fruitless, before winter brought his battle – his 'wearing-out offensive' as he calls the Somme battle in his official despatch – to a close.

This is a point the book will return to, but it is possible to understand the need for attrition, at least on the Allied side; whether it can be justified is another matter. The hard fact is that by the New Year of 1916 the Anglo-French side – the Entente – was not doing well in this war and yet saw no way to end it without making unacceptable concessions to the Germans.

When this book opens, at the end of 1915, the Germans held all the cards. They occupied all but a small strip of Belgium and much of Northern and Eastern France. They had held this territory since the autumn of 1914 and the various attempts to dislodge them, at Ypres, in Champagne, on the Chemin des Dames, at Festubert, Neuve Chapelle, Aubers Ridge and Loos, had been both unsuccessful and most costly in French and British lives. The attempt to outflank the Western Front with the attack in the Dardanelles had ended in failure and the fighting elsewhere, in Russia, the Balkans, Italy and the Middle East, had got nowhere. War had long since lost what little appeal it had in August 1914 and if peace could have been had on acceptable terms, it would have been welcome.

The problem was, on what terms? What could the Allies put on the table to match the cards held by the Kaiser? An offer to swap the German colonies in Africa for occupied territory in Northern France or Belgium would not do it, not least because von Lettow-Vorbeck was making life very difficult for the British in East Africa. Study the options carefully, which will not take long as there are not many of them, and it is clear that peace would not come until Germany had been hurt enough to want peace, and one way to do that – perhaps the only way in 1916–18 – was to kill as many of her young men as possible. That need and that alone, is the only justification for the doctrine of attrition that seized the armies in France in the fateful year of 1916. This book will argue, however, that there were other ways, technological or strategic, of cracking the Western Front problem. That argument, the story of what happened – and what might have happened – in 1916, provides the theme for this book.

Note

1 Letter to the author, 20 July 2000.

A Note on Sources and Military Terminology

One of the oddities of 1916 is the variable nature of the sources. There is a considerable amount of disagreement, even over the most fundamental details, which was at first perplexing and drove me back to original sources in search of enlightenment. For example, in the secondary sources, depending on which account you read, you will discover that the German Fifth Army's first assault at Verdun was on an eight- or a twelve-mile front and was made by either six, eight or nine divisions with, according to Holgar Herwig, 41.5 divisions in the field and with another 14 divisions of infantry in reserve.[1] Finding the actual number of divisions committed to this offensive on a day-to-day basis is not an easy thing to do.

The same variation exists over the matter of German artillery which, according to the account you read, ranges from 800 guns to 1,200 guns to, again in the case of Holgar Herwig, 1,521 'heavy guns' (and, we must presume, a large or small number of lighter ones).[2]

These variations have driven me back to the various official histories and, having no German, I am grateful to the late Colin Fox for his help in finding the official figures in the relevant volume of *Weltkrieg*. Finally, since many people are no longer familiar with military organization, it might be useful to note the following facts.

The British Army. By the end of 1916 the British Expeditionary Force consisted of five armies. Each army was divided into a number of corps, a corps consisting of two, or more, infantry divisions and perhaps a cavalry division. An infantry division in 1914 had three brigades, each brigade containing four battalions, though this was reduced to three battalions in 1918.

Each infantry division contained some 18,000 men, 76 guns and 24 medium machine-guns (two per battalion). The divisional artillery contained 54 field guns and 18 4.5-inch howitzers and was supported by heavy artillery from corps or army units. A cavalry division was smaller, consisting of 9,269 officers and men, 24 guns and 24 machine-guns.

The French Army. A French infantry corps consisted of two divisions, or sometimes three. French divisions were somewhat smaller, containing around 15,000 men, 36 guns, usually 75 mm, and 24 machine-guns, plus some artillery. A French cavalry corps usually contained three divisions, each of 4,500 officers and men and eight field guns.

The German Army. A corps consisted of two divisions, each of around 17,000 men, with 72 guns and 24 medium machine-guns. A cavalry corps had two or three cavalry divisions, each of 5,600 men, with 12 field guns and 6 machine-guns. Reserve divisions were the same size as regular divisions but had fewer guns. German corps also contained a motorized supply element from early on in the war.

It should be added that, while these figures will give the layman some idea of the composition of the main units, these were always in a state of flux and varied continually, in size and composition, throughout the war. They should therefore only be regarded as guidelines.

Notes

1 *The First World War, Germany and Austria-Hungary, 1914–1918*, p. 183.
2 Op. cit.

1

The Course of the War
1914—1915

'The situation with which the Allies were faced at
the close of 1915 was not an encouraging one.'
British Official History, 1916, vol. 5, p. 1

The Great War on the Western Front can be divided into a series of annual phases. The year 1914 was the Year of Movement, with massive German invasions of France and Belgium, the retreat to the Marne and the so-called 'Race to the Sea', that outflanking movement that took the armies from the Aisne to the Belgian frontier and the North Sea. Then came 1915, the Year of Offensives, a series of attempts to break through the trench system, with the German attack at Second Ypres, the French attacks at Artois, on the Chemin des Dames, and in Champagne, and the British attacking at Neuve

Chapelle, Aubers Ridge, Festubert and Loos. Following that disastrous year came 1916, the Year of Attrition where the purpose and nature of the fighting changed. At that point, this story begins.

But wars, offensives and battles do not come in neatly contained packages, firmly sealed at both ends. They arise from what happened previously and contribute to the events which follow, so before examining the events of 1916, it is necessary to study in some detail the events of 1914 and 1915 which led up to the decisions and courses of action adopted for 1916.

The direct development of the 1916 Western Front offensive on the Franco-British side of the line can be dated to 19 December 1915, when Field Marshal Sir John French gave up command of the British Armies in France and was replaced by his dour but well-regarded subordinate, General Sir Douglas Haig. Sir John French had been in command since the British Expeditionary Force (BEF) arrived in France 16 months previously and had therefore presided over both its rapid growth and a series of engagements and disasters unparalleled in British military history. Losses had been considerable and in the fighting of 1914 and early 1915 the old Regular Army, the original BEF, had largely disappeared. This brief litany of loss and disaster should not conceal the fact that 1914 and 1915 had provided some hard-won lessons on this new kind of war.

The British Army that arrived in France in August 1914, though superbly trained and full of professional soldiers, was quite unprepared to take part in a major European war of any kind and was even less prepared for the sort of warfare that quickly developed on the Western Front. The pre-war British Army was small and designed for fighting colonial campaigns around the fringes of the Empire. Only six infantry divisions could be mustered for the original BEF and only four of these, plus a cavalry division, a total of around 100,000 men, went to France in August 1914 to join a struggle in which other armies mustered millions of men from the word go. Nevertheless, though small, the BEF gave a good account of itself in the early fighting.

The small-scale actions fought by the BEF at Mons and Le Câteau were gallant, but inconclusive; the BEF was a minor player in the war at this time and would remain one until the full manpower of the British Empire could be recruited, equipped and trained. Meanwhile the British Regular Army – the 'Old Contemptibles' as they were proud to call themselves – fought on against the odds.[1] The Franco-British forces fell back to the Marne. After the German defeat there in September 1914 and the subsequent series of outflanking attempts towards the north-west made by either side – the so-called 'Race to the Sea' – the original BEF was virtually destroyed in the First Battle of Ypres in November 1914, and in the subsequent winter fighting.

With the Race to the Sea came the establishment of a trench system – the Old Front Line – that by New Year's Day of 1915 ran for over 400 miles across France, from the Channel coast to the frontier of Switzerland. This line could not be outflanked and with the establishment of this trench system a new kind of warfare, *trench warfare*, confronted the armies on the Western Front, a kind of warfare for which all those armies, but especially the British Army, were woefully unprepared.

The causes of that state of unpreparedness can be traced to the fundamental fact that the pre-war British Army had not been designed or equipped for a Continental war. Neither had it received political instruction, or money, to equip itself for such a purpose. Generals did not have a free hand in matters of recruitment or equipment and could not go out and order wire, duckboards or heavy artillery for a war that had not yet occurred, or for which they had no mandate to prepare. The service chiefs operated within political and economic restraints imposed by Government and the British Government of Herbert Asquith had no intention of funding a large army or getting involved in a European war; had it had that intention, money might have been found to equip the army for such a struggle with heavy guns, more men, a trained reserve, an abundance of ammunition and the backing of a munitions industry. All these assets were lacking in 1914 and creating them took time, a fact that the French politicians and generals at times found extremely galling.

French irritation over this British lack of preparation overlooked the fact that although the British Army Staff had been permitted to engage in 'conversations' with the French Army Staff over what the British might do to assist France in the event of a war – 'conversations' that from 1909 usually took place between General Ferdinand Foch and that passionately Francophile officer, Henry Wilson – the British Government had made no firm commitment to assist the French Government and would not do so until after the war had actually broken out, and only then because Germany had violated the neutrality of Belgium. Even pre-war the enemy was assumed to be Germany and the French Government and the French General Staff allowed themselves to believe from these 'conversations' that the British would rush to their assistance immediately on the outbreak of war, and with all the means at their disposal. This the British did, but their means were inadequate and were to remain so for some time.

The French remained unwilling to recognize that even the vast British Empire could not create a large army overnight, not least because, since the pre-war British Army was small, the British munitions and armaments industry was also small. Volunteers could be called to the colours in their thousands but were useless until they were trained and equipped and, until they were equipped with the right weapons of war, they could not be properly trained at all. That meant the creation of a war-scale munitions industry virtually from the ground up; factories built, machine-tools ordered and installed, workers trained, weapons designed and adequate numbers of them produced; it could be done but it took time. As a result of pre-war restrictions, the British Army did not reach an adequate size and state of training until 1916 and, even then, experienced equipment short-ages, especially in heavy artillery.

This belief in instant and adequate support from the British and their empire on the outbreak of war was to be the first of many misunderstandings, accidental or deliberate, made by the French in their relations with the British. The British Government also had a few deep-seated policies which governed their approach to this war. They would not allow any unfriendly or belligerent power, like Germany, to establish itself on the Channel coast; maintaining the balance of power in Europe had been a preoccupation of British politicians for generations, long before the Entente Cordiale patched up centuries of conflict with the French. Britain would also protect the neutrality of

Belgium, a neutrality guaranteed since 1839 by many other countries, including France and Germany. It was the violation of Belgian neutrality, and not any overwhelming desire to assist the French, that sent the BEF across the Channel in August 1914.

The security of Britain, an island nation, rested on the Royal Navy, on which money was lavished. The purpose of the British Army was to fight for the Empire, either to put down rebellion in the colonies or to protect those colonies against incursions from outside. In the 99 years between Waterloo and the Battle of Mons, the British Army fought 17 major wars around the Empire, including one in the Crimea, but most of these wars were on a very small scale and often fought with Indian or Colonial forces. The pre-Great War British Army, with a world-wide empire to protect, could only muster a total of 11 regular divisions, the same as the Balkan state of Serbia, and had light scales of equipment. This army lacked heavy guns, howitzers, a light machine-gun (and an adequate supply of medium machine-guns), large stocks of shells and defensive equipment of every kind, from barbed wire to picks, shovels and duckboards, and offensive weapons like grenades. These requirements soon became apparent among all the nations but the British needed more of these modern weapons – machine-guns to compensate for a shortage of infantry and mortars for either offensive or defensive action among trenches or tumbled ground, because only firepower could compensate for the BEF's shortage of numbers.

The British Army also needed a large, trained and active reserve of soldiers, and should have built this up in peacetime. Britain did have a Territorial Force of young volunteers, but the Territorial battalions were not fully manned or well equipped, or indeed obliged to serve abroad. Their prime purpose was home defence and the soldiers had to volunteer again for service abroad. Volunteering was then the only way of expanding the army at all for, unlike France and Germany, Britain did not have conscription and did not introduce it until early 1916, almost two years into the war.

Finally, the British Army needed to invest in modern technology, especially aircraft, heavy guns and motor transport. Although the British Army had a number of aeroplanes in the infant Royal Flying

Corps, which took 63 aircraft of varying types to France in 1914, and had a useful scale of field artillery, there were few heavy guns capable of smashing defensive systems or levelling trenches. The army did have a small amount of motor transport in the Service Corps, small trucks mainly used for moving supplies of food and ammunition, but otherwise relied almost entirely on the marching power of the infantry, and on the horse. However, the most critical need in 1914 and 1915 was for an abundant supply of artillery ammunition.

This shortage could not be easily or quickly made good. Since the British Army was small, the British munitions industry was small. Even if the means to produce more shells had existed pre-war, the wartime demand soon outstripped any possible supply. When war broke out in August 1914 the British armament and munitions industry not only had to equip the millions of men now flocking into the New Armies and the Territorial Force, it also had to supply the massive and totally unexpected demands made on it by the BEF in France, where the consumption of ammunition and the losses of equipment exceeded the wildest expectations.

This lack of preparation over supply was not confined to the BEF; every other army, including the German Army, was swiftly confronted with the fact that ammunition stocks were totally inadequate for the rate of use demanded by this war, the first intimation that this war was to be unlike any previous war. The French Army expended more artillery ammunition in September 1914 than it had done in the whole of the Franco-Prussian War of 1870–71. Total French production of the 75 mm shell in 1914 amounted to 14,000 shells a day, at a time when one single battery of 75 mm guns could easily shoot off 1,000 shells a day. Nor was arms production concentrated for mass production; French rifles, for example, were manufactured in a dozen different locations – butts here, bolts there, magazines somewhere else – and the weapons were only finally assembled in the government factory at St Étienne.[2]

The root cause of this situation, certainly in the United Kingdom, reflects political caution, not any fault or dereliction of duty among the pre-war General Staff. It also demonstrates the fact that Britain did not live on the brink of war like the French, under a system dominated by a military elite like the Germans, or under a despotism like the Russians. The losses and shortages suffered by the British Army between 1914 and 1916 were a direct consequence of the fact that pre-war British society was liberal, pacific and democratic, unwilling and therefore unprepared for war with its neighbours; for these peacetime benefits and attitudes the soldiers of the BEF would pay a heavy price on the battlefield.

When the war broke out on the Continent on 1 August 1914, the issue of whether or not Britain should go to the assistance of the French was hotly debated over the next three days. Prime Minister Herbert Asquith saw two members of his cabinet resign in protest against British participation before the German violation of Belgian neutrality decided the issue. War was declared on Germany on 4 August, five divisions of the BEF swiftly departed for France and over the next weeks and months millions of men flocked to the colours in Britain, anxious to play their part in this sudden struggle . . . or at least take part in this adventure before it ended.

In August 1914, few people on either side thought that the war would last very long. The ingredients of European conflict – German militarism, French resentment of their defeat in the Franco-Prussian War of 1870–71 and the subsequent loss of Alsace-Lorraine, Austria-Hungary's desire to stamp out dissent in the Balkans, the decline of Turkey, to name but a few – had been simmering for years, but it was generally believed that when war came it would consist of a short campaign followed by a peace conference and some territorial adjustments, rather like the Franco-Prussian War. The popular term of the time in Britain was that the war 'would be over by Christmas', or, as the German Kaiser told his departing troops: 'You will be home before the leaves fall.' The German Imperial Chancellor, Theobald von Bethmann-Hollweg, accepted the advice of the German General Staff that the war would last a maximum of two years, but more probably nine months, and declared that there was therefore no need to mobilize the country for a longer war, telling his colleague von Bülow in July 1914 that he was expecting 'a war lasting three or at the most four months . . . a short but violent storm'.

Even so, men flocked to the recruiting offices; in Britain, more than

75,000 men a week volunteered for service between August and October. By December this had fallen to 30,000 a week and it fell again to 20,000 a week in early 1915, remaining at that level for some months. Volunteers were also joining up in the Empire, in Canada, Africa, New Zealand and Australia. This was more men than the Army could absorb – the kit and the instructors were simply not available – and these volunteers included many men who would have been better employed in their former places of work, the shipyards and the expanding munitions factories. Such men – about 25 per cent of the nation's essential war workers – had to be located, pulled out of the Army and sent back to work . . . and, reluctant as they were to return to civilian life, they were the lucky ones. Sixteen months later, by the New Year of 1916, tens of thousands of those eager young soldiers were dead, there was no sign of an end to the war and millions more young men were being readied for the struggle in the year ahead.

In August 1914 at least two men in Britain did not believe that a European war in the twentieth century would be of short duration or without serious loss: the newly appointed Secretary of State for War, Field Marshal Lord Kitchener, and the then commander at Aldershot and later commander of the BEF First Corps and First Army in France, Lt-General Sir Douglas Haig. Kitchener ordered an expansion of the munitions industry and, since conscription could not yet be contemplated, issued his famous poster – 'Your King and Country Need You' – asking civilians to join the colours. The response surprised Kitchener and amazed the nation; in the weeks following Kitchener's appeal, more than one million men turned up at the recruiting offices, demanding enlistment.

Enlisting, housing, clothing, arming and training these men, the volunteers for what became the Service battalions of the New Armies, 'Kitchener's Armies', stretched Britain's military resources to the utmost. Many men were sent home to await the call but gradually, over the months at the end of 1914 and throughout the spring of 1915, they were called to their units and began training. Given the situation outlined above, this training was bound to be inadequate for the rigours of modern war.

Lt-General Sir Douglas Haig had deep doubts about the first

commander of the BEF, Field Marshal Sir John French. Haig wondered if French was professionally, mentally or even physically, up to the demands of this hard and continuing struggle. French was 64 in 1914 while Haig, at 53, was one of the younger generals. French had made his name in the South African War of 1899–1902 and was one of the few generals to emerge from that shambles with an enhanced reputation. From then on his rise was rapid and although he had resigned from the Army over the Curragh Incident in Ireland in March 1914, when some units of the British Army came close to mutiny over the question of Ulster, the outbreak of war had led to his reinstatement and command of the BEF.

French had commanded the cavalry in South Africa and remained a strong advocate of *arme blanche* (lance and sabre) cavalry tactics and a vocal opponent of mounted infantry, even though the advent of the rifle had made *arme blanche* cavalry all but obsolescent for the last half-century. In 1907 this belief had brought him into direct conflict with a brother officer, Lt-General Sir Horace Smith-Dorrien, a believer in mounted infantry, who came out to command II Corps of the BEF in time for the battles of Mons and Le Câteau, where II Corps was handled with considerable skill. These successes brought Smith-Dorrien only a temporary reprieve from French's simmering displeasure and in April 1915 Smith-Dorrien, now commanding Second Army, was summarily sacked by the Field Marshal.

Small events can have large consequences. This sacking cleared the way to the top for Lt-General Sir Douglas Haig, for Smith-Dorrien was senior to Haig and a good soldier; had he not been sacked, it is more than likely that Horace Smith-Dorrien and not Douglas Haig, would have succeeded French in command of the BEF. Haig's corps had done very little at Mons or Le Câteau but Haig's First Army did well, though at great cost, in the battles of First and Second Ypres and rather less well, also at great cost, at Neuve Chapelle, Aubers Ridge and Festubert in the spring of 1915. During those engagements the generals learned that the war in which they were now engaged was, above all, an artillery war. In January 1915, Field Marshal French stated:

Breaking through the enemy's lines is largely a question of
expenditure of high-explosive ammunition. If sufficient ammunition is forthcoming, a way out can be blasted through the line.
If the attempt fails it shows, provided that the work of the
infantry and artillery has been properly co-ordinated, that
insufficient ammunition has been expended, i.e. either more guns
must be brought up or the allowance of ammunition per gun
increased.[3]

As Field Marshal French and his men were to discover, while breaking
through the enemy front line might be possible, given an abundance
of guns and ammunition, exploiting that break in any useful way was
quite another matter. During the first year of war, up to September
1915, the Regular Army, and those divisions of the Territorial Force
sent to France to reinforce it, were finding out the truth about modern
warfare, learning their trade the hard way, in the harsh school of war.
These battles were unlike anything the generals had anticipated and
all manner of unforeseen problems had to be hurriedly addressed. One
of these was a continuing shortage of shells which led to the 'shell
crisis' of 1915, after the battles at Festubert and Aubers Ridge in May,
when the allegation was made, allegedly from French's HQ, that the
Government was starving the army of necessary ordnance. This
accusation helped in the fall of Asquith's Liberal Government with
which Britain had entered the war. It was followed by a National or
Coalition Government of Liberals and Tories, which retained Asquith
as Prime Minister but allowed the reins of power to slip gradually into
the hands of David Lloyd George, who in 1915 was the Minister of
Munitions.

The problems of equipment and ammunition were solved or
mitigated over time but there were problems with the Army
command, problems that revealed themselves when the expanding but
inexperienced armies were sent into the shambles that came to mark
the battlefields of France. The battles at Mons and Le Câteau went
well because the British commanders and battalion officers were used
to that kind of small-scale struggle, actions involving a few divisions
fighting in open country, battles which called for skill in the handling

of units full of disciplined, well-trained troops, whose weapon and fieldcraft skills had been honed on the firing range and on pre-war exercises.

However, as the Western Front battles expanded in size, duration and violence, this training was found to be inadequate and the professional soldiers on whom so much depended soon faded away. This was bad enough at battalion and brigade level but the root of the command problem was the Staff. The men, the private soldiers, NCOs and junior officers, even those recalled in 1914 or who volunteered from the Territorial Force, could be trained in their duties in a matter of months, but where were the staff officers to come from, to control the brigades, divisions, corps and armies now being rapidly created and sent to the Front? Without trained staff officers – best imagined as the middle management of the army – a modern army simply cannot function.

One reliable estimate[4] states that on the outbreak of war in 1914 the British Army had exactly 904 staff or 'staff qualified' officers,[5] and the pre-war staff course at Camberley took two years. Potential staff officers were soon tracked down and given an all too brief course of instruction but a shortage of trained and efficient staff officers was to bedevil the British Army for much of the war; most of the staff had to 'learn on the job', and if many staff officers were, as Siegfried Sassoon later alleged, 'incompetent swine' there were good reasons for it – though it is arguable that the British staff were nowhere near as incompetent as has been alleged; Army services, handling pay, post, food and medical attention functioned well.

The army that went to France in 1914 was the British Regular Army, a composite of professional soldiers and recalled reservists. By the spring of 1915, after First and Second Ypres, that small but magnificent fighting force had all but disappeared. That alone reduced the effectiveness of the BEF in 1915 but there were other, more entrenched problems, which arose even as the problems of manpower and *matériel* gradually diminished.

Field Marshal Sir John French went to France with two serious burdens around his neck: the political requirements of his government and the demands of Britain's allies, the French. Neither burden can be avoided by any general, especially in an alliance, but these particular burdens proved expensive for they limited French's options. The decision to hang on to the town of Ypres, for example, because it was the only Belgian town still in Allied hands, was a political decision, not a military one. Although Ypres was an important road junction, it was clearly indefensible or could only be held, as it was held, at great cost in lives.

As for the need to co-operate closely with allies, Sir John French was ordered by the British Government to work with and if need be defer to the French commanders, but these instructions were phrased in a contradictory way. On the one hand he was told to 'support and co-operate with the French Army'. On the other hand, the Secretary of State for War informed him that, 'I wish you distinctly to understand that your command is an independent one and that you will in no case come in any sense under the orders of any Allied General'. Advice on how these conflicting instructions were to be reconciled was not provided. These orders would have created a problem for any commander, and French is at fault for not returning them to the War Office for clarification, but at this stage of the war, in 1914 and early 1915, no one fully appreciated just how difficult inter-Allied relations could be.

The crux of the matter lay in the interpretation of the order to 'support and co-operate' with the French Army. Since the French Army, at least in the early days of the war, greatly outnumbered the BEF and had control of all the logistical assets including the railways, Field Marshal French would have been obliged to do that anyway, but the problem went deeper than mere 'co-operation'. The French could be relied upon to push for ever closer 'co-operation' and these orders came to mean that vital matters for any general, like the time, place, weight and duration of his attacks, were subordinated, time and time again, to the wishes of our French allies. In 1915 the battles at Neuve Chapelle, Ypres, Aubers Ridge, and especially Loos, were undertaken when and where they were, to help the French or, as at First Ypres in 1914, with the promise of French support which, in the event, was not always forthcoming. Nevertheless, although the British Field Marshal demurred at some French demands, notably over the site for the action at Loos, orders are orders and, in the end, Field Marshal French usually deferred to the wishes of General Joffre . . . and was always putty in the hands of that silver-tongued French officer, General Ferdinand Foch.

There were other matters, military problems, which time would solve. From the outbreak of war it was clear to the more far-sighted officers and politicians – not an extensive number – that the coming struggle would be a technological one. Among the first units making their way to France in 1914 was a Royal Flying Corps Aircraft Park, a unit so unusual that the military police directing units to their positions had no idea what it was or what to do with it. Within days, however, aircraft were in use at the front, first for reconnaissance and then for artillery spotting, and the Royal Flying Corps (RFC) rapidly expanded. In 1914 the RFC had only 200 aircraft of various types. By the end of 1915 it had 2,000 aircraft, of superior performance, and by 1916 it could put up some 6,000 aircraft of various types. By the spring of 1915, tanks were being developed. Another innovation, armoured cars, made their appearance outside Antwerp in the autumn of 1914.

Artillery expanded in size and quantity and more heavy guns, howitzers and machine-guns were poured into the line. In 1914 the BEF had about 300 medium machine guns. By the summer of 1915 it had 6,000, and by the time the Somme offensive opened in July 1916 it had 33,500 machine-guns, light and medium. Then there were chemical weapons: poison gas. Chlorine gas had been employed by the Germans at Second Ypres in the spring of 1915 and by the British at Loos in September of that year. On 19 December 1915, the day Haig took command of the British Armies in France, the Germans deployed a new and more lethal gas, phosgene. And then there was the submarine, which went into action in the first days of the war, sinking ships and drowning sailors and civilians in the chilly wastes of the Atlantic. Largely thanks to technology, this war would be a terrible one, most expensive in lives, but the problems caused by this new technology were compounded by the fact that its use and effect had not been thought through by those using it, or those enduring it.

It is an oft-forgotten truism that military tactics usually lag behind the technology. Improvements in weaponry are continuous, as steps are taken to improve the existing kit or the men learn to operate it

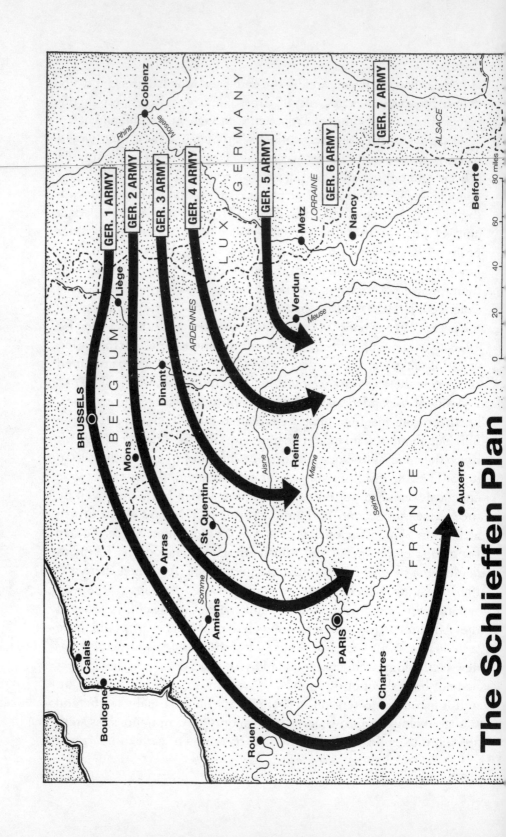

The Schlieffen Plan

more effectively, or new weapons are introduced. This is normal but problems arise when a weapon comes along that makes previous weapons obsolete. This should oblige the commanders to rethink their tactics completely, but this does not often happen. One good example of this time lag between weapons and tactics is provided by the introduction of the Minié bullet to the rifled musket in the 1840s and 1850s. The Minié bullet, which gripped the barrel rifling closely, trebled the range and accuracy of infantry weapons. This should have occasioned a tactical rethink, since the standard tactic of an exchange of volleys at close range – say 100 or 200 yards – before an infantry charge, was rendered impossible. The rifled musket, firing the Minié bullet, could kill men at ranges of up to half a mile.

In the event, nothing much changed. The advance of the Imperial Guard at Waterloo in 1815, of Pickett's Division at Gettysburg in 1863, of the German infantry at Langemarck in 1914, the French at Artois in 1915 and the British on the Somme in 1916 are all examples of the same tactic, which pitted men against metal. As the weight of fire was increased by technology, so the death toll rose inexorably.

The generals were largely responsible for this folly. It arises from a lack of imagination, a failure to realize that things have changed, but generals are both reluctant to adopt change and hard men to argue with. Their experience has been gained on the battlefield, in the hard school of war, not in the classroom, exercise ground or laboratory. They base their actions, decisions and tactics on that experience, even if all they have learned has been rendered out of date by changes in technology.

Another failure, one that can cause continual problems with new technology, is a failure to realize exactly what a weapon can do or what a weapon is actually for. Before 1914, the medium machine-gun was generally seen as an offensive weapon; its defensive potential was not fully appreciated until it started mowing down infantry in the open field and dominating the space between the lines – No Man's Land. The tank was first introduced as an 'infantry support' weapon, and so it remained in the British and French Armies until 1940, when the Germans introduced their blitzkrieg tactics and showed that the tank, if adequately powered and gunned, was actually armoured cavalry, capable of overcoming defensive positions and restoring mobility to the battlefield.

The Great War would become the first truly technological war, and yet one vital aspect of technology, communications, remained almost at a standstill. This led to a great deal of confusion, loss and disaster, because although commanders could use field telephones to contact their subordinates in fixed positions, at least until shellfire cut the telephone wires, once an attack started, the lack of a battlefield radio meant that the commanders had no means of communicating with their troops beyond the front line trench other than by runner . . . and runners did not live long on a fire-swept Great War battlefield. Greater use should have been made of wireless telegraphy, using Morse; WT sets could be carried in aircraft but although WT was used to supply target information to the guns, it was rarely used to provide the generals with information about the progress of their infantry.

In time, most of these problems would be solved, or at least reduced. Armies were raised, armed and trained, the brighter officers were given hasty instruction in staff duties or learned the hard way on the job, and fresh tactics, more suited to the current conditions, gradually came in. New and heavier guns were supplied, aircraft were developed into a formidable arm, and by early 1915 work had started on developing what would become the tank, the one way of breaking through the thickets of wire, shell-churned ground and interlocking machine-gun fire that now marked the Western Front. By the end of 1915 most of this equipment had arrived, but it did not arrive in time to save the reputation or the position of Field Marshal Sir John French.

The losses at Loos in September 1915 marked the end of his time as Commander-in-Chief of the BEF – and the BEF was well rid of him. Not all of what happened in 1914 and 1915 can be laid at his door – he was certainly not responsible for the lack of suitable equipment outlined above – but he lacked the right outlook and failed to adapt his experience to the situation confronting him in France. This may be a harsh judgement, for it may be that French was simply too old when he first went out to France. Modern war is a place for young men, with plenty of energy and flexible minds; French was in his sixties when he was catapulted into a major European war and it is hardly surprising that he found himself out of his depth. He did not speak French, he did not like or trust his allies and he was unenthusiastic about some of his subordinates, especially two competent officers, General Smith-Dorrien, whom he sacked, and General Sir Henry Rawlinson, whom he wanted to sack. His period in command was marked by disaster, and whatever the context of the time and however much the other reasons listed above limited his efforts or contributed to these catastrophes, Sir John French did not handle his men well. There was general relief when he was removed in December 1915 and the command passed to General Sir Douglas Haig.

Douglas Haig cannot be described as a charismatic figure of the Great War; Haig and charisma do not sit well together, but he was undoubtedly one of the most important figures to emerge from that conflict and the myths of callousness and incompetence that have gathered about his reputation since his death in 1926 have little basis in fact. Given the situation outlined above, Alexander the Great would have found it difficult to succeed in forcing a breach in the German line in 1914–1915, and the defeats Haig's armies suffered in 1916 and 1917 – those notorious disasters on the Somme and at Passchendaele – should not obscure the fact that it was Haig who commanded the British armies that spearheaded the Allied victory in 1918 and showed the other armies how this war should be fought; even General Foch admitted that.

Haig had been jockeying for command of the BEF since he first went out to France in 1914. He had commanded I Corps in the retreat from Mons and had commanded the British forces at First and Second Ypres and during the attacks at Neuve Chapelle, Aubers Ridge, Festubert and at Loos, where in spite of using gas and a great deal of artillery, Haig's First Army had sustained terrible losses for negligible territorial gain. Haig learned something in all these engagements – though the cost of his lessons was paid in lives – and had been adamant that it would be folly to attack at Loos, an opinion which proved all too accurate. The débâcle at Loos led to the sacking of French and the elevation of Douglas Haig, so now in December 1915 Haig was in command of the entire BEF, with the weight of the Franco-British alliance on his shoulders.

His appointment, and that of his friend and supporter, General Sir

William Robertson, to the post of CIGS, was popular with the officers and men: 'Those of the old Army who had served under the new chiefs felt that the right men had been put into the right places' but a great deal was expected from him and the obstacles in his path were formidable.[6]

Douglas Haig is the vector for most of the complaints and many of the myths which still surround British generalship on the Western Front during the Great War. It is not too much to say that in certain quarters Sir Douglas Haig is still hated; in 1998, on the eightieth anniversary of the Armistice, there was a press campaign to have Haig's statue removed from Whitehall in London, on the grounds that it should not occupy the same street as the Cenotaph, the memorial erected to commemorate the Great War dead.

The origins of this attitude to the late Field Marshal lie in the memoirs of David Lloyd George, British Prime Minister for the last two years of the Great War, whose antipathy to Haig was almost pathological; in books like Alan Clark's *The Donkeys*; in musicals like *Oh, What a Lovely War!*; and in a host of television documentaries of varying accuracy, including popular television comedies like *Blackadder Goes Forth*, all of which display the Great War generals as incompetent clowns and Sir Douglas Haig as a callous monster.

There is no truth in any of this; Haig will not be numbered among the Great Captains of history but he did well, up to a point, in the circumstances he inherited in 1915 and very well indeed after the March Retreat in 1918. Haig and his generals – and his soldiers – were mainly responsible for the defeat of the German Army on the Western Front in 1918 and it is for that reason – because he defeated the German Army in the field – that Haig's statue stands in Whitehall. Most military historians now agree that Haig has been traduced by history but in the popular mind he is the man responsible for the death of grandparents and great-grandparents and the damage to his reputation goes on.

The battles fought by the British Army in 1914 and 1915 provide an interesting study and display a learning curve for the generals in the rules governing this new kind of warfare. The first two British battles, at Mons and Le Câteau, were little more than skirmishes. Only Smith-

Dorrien's II Corps was engaged and the actions involved little more than a couple of divisions at any one time, the Germans and British colliding in short, sharp encounters, followed by a tactical British withdrawal. Both actions were well handled and the British showed, in their superior fieldcraft and marksmanship, that they had learned the lessons of the South African War, in which many of the men and most of the commanders had taken part.

The two battles at Ypres were much larger affairs and showed the British soldiers, and under this name we must include the Indians and the Canadians, doing what they do best: holding a position they have been charged to defend to the last man and the last round if need be. The British soldier is always superb in defence and the story of these two encounters at Ypres, so expensive in lives and so tenacious in execution, are among the most gallant in the long and glorious history of the British Army.

The next three encounters, the attacks at Neuve Chapelle, which took place before Second Ypres, and at Aubers Ridge and Festubert, were all small-scale affairs, total failures and most costly in lives. They were mounted to show the French that the British were fully committed to the struggle and one at least, Neuve Chapelle, should have been called off before the first shot was fired, as the reasons for mounting the attack had disappeared. From the point of view of tactics, all three attacks had this much in common: they demonstrated that an attack, even on a small scale, if supported by an adequate amount of artillery, could penetrate the enemy line. This much of the lesson was absorbed by Field Marshal French, as illustrated above. The problems arose after the assault phase of the attack was over and the exploitation phase had begun.

At that point, with the enemy line breached, a chronic problem arose: thanks to a lack of communications, there was a loss of tactical control. Add to this the fact that armies could only advance at the speed a laden man could make over muddy, shell-torn ground, and a shortage of reserves and artillery ammunition, and the result is that the advance faltered. The enemy hurried up reserves to seal the breach; the bridgehead gained, a 'salient' or bulge in the enemy line, promptly came under attack from three sides and initial success rapidly turned into failure and loss. The larger attack at Loos, in September 1915, launched over open and totally unsuitable ground at the insistence of the French, simply provided the same lessons on a larger scale. At Neuve Chapelle in March 1915, the British lost almost 13,000 men in three days; at Loos in September, 59,000 men in six weeks, but most of them fell in the first two days; neither attack gained more than a few hundred yards of useless, shell-pitted, corpse-strewn ground.

After these battles in 1915 the fundamental problem of the Western Front stood starkly revealed. Defensive elements dominated the battlefield in the shape of deep trenches, dugouts, barbed wire, muddy ground, machine-guns and artillery. If used in skilful combination, these elements created a defensive system that was proof against penetration by any means yet available to the attacking forces. This problem affected all attacking forces, not just those of the British, a fact that two generations of denigration, both of British generalship and the British Staff, has tended to conceal. During the Great War all armies lost men in quantity in the attack; the Germans at First and Second Ypres, the French in Champagne, on Vimy Ridge, in Artois and on the Chemin des Dames. Everywhere it was the same story: a failure to develop a breach in the enemy defences was common to all armies and, by the end of 1915, French and German losses far exceeded those of the British Empire.

There was, however, a deeper failure, a failure to realize that the current conventional tactics were not working. The focus was on solving the shortages of men and guns and of increasing the weight of attacks – which only increased the scale of loss. The conventional answer might be excusable in 1915 but by the end of that year the losses were too terrible to dismiss.[7] Some fresh thinking should have been applied to the problem . . . as indeed it was – but the problem is that this fresh thinking came up with the wrong answer, on both sides of the front line.

If some national failing is dismissed, then what *was* the fundamental problem of the Western Front and how could it be resolved? To find the answer it is necessary to go back to some basic facts. First, the Western Front was a deep and continuous defence line and there were only two ways to reduce it, either frontally or from the flank. The

Western Front's flanks rested on the Swiss frontier or the North Sea, so there was no way round it there and some wider passage must be found.

An attempt to outflank the Western Front by some far-flung manoeuvre took place at Gallipoli and led to a most expensive failure. Indeed, on 7 December 1915, the British Cabinet approved the evacuation of Suvla and Anzac beaches, and on 28 December the Government ordered a complete evacuation from the Dardanelles; within weeks the Gallipoli fiasco was over and the focus of the war shifted back to the Western Front.

These reduced options left the Allied commanders with only one choice on the Western Front: frontal assault. There were, of course, other theatres where the struggle could be pursued, Russia, Italy, Salonika, Palestine and Mesopotamia, and these were brought forward as alternatives from time to time. Despite arguments between Easterners, who wanted an offensive anywhere but France, and Westerners, who believed that an offensive anywhere else was a waste of effort, it was generally accepted that the Germans could only be decisively defeated on the Western Front, not least because that was where most of them were.

But if a frontal assault was the only viable option, how was it to be conducted, given the inherent advantages possessed by the defence? There were two views on how to conduct a frontal assault and they reveal the basic tactical argument of the Great War. Should the attacker go for 'bite and hold', seizing a small portion of the enemy line and hanging on to it, then bringing up the guns and the infantry before taking another bite, or should he concentrate on going for a full scale 'breakthrough'? It had been proved at Neuve Chapelle that, with sufficient artillery support, it was possible to seize a section of the enemy line and, by digging in quickly, hold it against counterattacks. The problem was that 'bite and hold' did not actually achieve much in terms of territorial gain. It would take a countless number of 'bite and hold' attacks to carry out the BEF's mandate, of driving the Germans out of Northern France and Belgium and, in the meantime, the section of the line seized by 'bite and hold' was under attack from three sides and losses were mounting. Even so, in spite of the drawbacks, 'bite and hold' had its disciples.

The other option was an attack which aimed for a 'breakthrough', a penetration of the enemy line into the open country beyond, followed by the introduction of cavalry through the breach, to create an advance which would balloon out beyond the enemy defences, roll up the enemy line on either flank and restore open warfare to the battlefield. The 'breakthrough' was the ultimate ambition of all the Army commanders during the Great War but only once, in the German offensive of March 1918, was a real breakthrough achieved, though the British tank advance at Cambrai in November 1917 came close. These battles fall outside the scope of this book and were fought in entirely different situations but the fact that four years of calculation, planning and effort produced only two definite breakthroughs is revealing in itself. The generals, British, French and German, were unable to achieve a breakthrough because the defences were always too strong and the facilities available to reduce them were not fully developed, either technically or tactically.

New technology will have a part to play in what follows but the first point to grasp in any study of the Western Front fighting is the second basic fact: the importance of artillery, a point which will arise again and again. The secret of any advance through a well-defended and carefully prepared position in the Great War depended almost entirely on artillery. In spite of the popular image created by TV documentaries and military memoirs, the Great War was primarily an artillery war. Over 60 per cent of the casualties were caused by artillery, and only artillery – heavy artillery – could beat down the enemy defences, flatten the wire, stun his troops, knock out the defending batteries and let the attackers go forward.

The problem, certainly on the British and French side between 1914 and 1916, was a continuous shortage of artillery, especially heavy artillery and a reliable supply of high-explosive ammunition. The French and British were very short of heavy guns and high-angle howitzers, weapons capable of reducing well-prepared defences. On the French side the main artillery weapon was the famous *Soixante Quinze*, the quick-firing 75 mm, a field gun which was highly effective using shrapnel against infantry, but far too light to destroy entrenchments.

The third basic fact was a lack of momentum; an inability of the armies to exploit any breach made by artillery. By the middle months of 1915 all the commanders knew that, given surprise and enough heavy artillery, it was possible to seize a portion of the enemy trench. How big a portion depended on the amount of artillery available to drench the enemy defences with fire, and since there was never enough the gap seized was usually narrow and could soon be sealed off and the resulting salient brought under attack from three sides. Clearly, the attacker had to move on rapidly from this point, 'to exploit the breach' in military parlance, before the enemy could bring up reinforcements and reposition his artillery to seal it off. More use might have been made of surprise, but here again there was a problem; the only way to breach the enemy defences was with shellfire, and this had to be delivered over a period of time, to cut the wire and level the trenches. In that time the enemy became aware that an attack was pending and had time to prepare for it.

The other problem of exploiting an attack after the initial assault, and an apparently insoluble one, was time. The Great War armies were foot-powered armies. They had cavalry, and cavalry existed for just this purpose, for rapid advance over open country, harassing the enemy and exploiting the breach. But horses did not live long on a Great War battlefield and just one machine-gun on the flank could bring a cavalry advance to a halt. Therefore, it came down to the speed of exploitation that the infantry could manage and, given the conditions of the time, heavily loaded men moving over shell-torn ground were doing well if they could make one mile an hour. This was simply not fast enough to prevent the breach being sealed off.

Since it was not possible to exploit a narrow breach, the sort usually taken by 'bite and hold' attacks, the only answer was to widen the breach; if you cannot go forward, you go sideways . . . but that must mean more artillery to create a wide breach . . . and more artillery was simply not available. Impasse, yet again.

There was, of course, another alternative to this endless, pointless killing – peace. Achieving peace depended on a recognition by all the participants that the war was not worth fighting, or that all that could be achieved had been achieved and the argument should be promptly transferred to the conference table. Given the benefit of hindsight and the losses so far, by the end of 1915 this seems the obvious alternative to more slaughter but that was not how it appeared at the time. Just to begin with, there was the question of who started the war – and should therefore offer compensation for the destruction it caused – and what terms would be necessary to achieve a secure and lasting peace.

The object of war is victory. Peace depends on the subsequent settlement. As a result, the achievements of the soldier on the battlefield are all too often squandered around the conference table; the 1919 Treaty of Versailles, which ended the Great War but paved the way for the Second World War 20 years later, is the classic example of this point. It is therefore necessary that the participants in any peace conference first agree on what they hope to achieve and, even before that, on what exactly they are fighting for. Peace negotiations began, or were at least initiated, almost as soon as the war began, but by 1915 they had led nowhere. The nations of Europe were not yet sick of killing and at the end of 1915 there was no doubt in anyone's mind that the fighting would go on.

This meant a renewal of the offensive in 1916 as soon as the ground was dry enough for an assault. The old arguments, over the prospects for a 'breakthrough' or the merits of 'bite and hold', surfaced again at the various Allied headquarters: which of these two tactics to employ, which was the best way for artillery to support the infantry, how to solve the problems of rapid reinforcement by the reserves, what methods could improve communications and so improve control on the battlefield. All these questions and many more were the principal concern of the new British Commander-in-Chief, Sir Douglas Haig, when he took up his command on 19 December 1915.

Four days later, on 23 December, General Sir William Robertson succeeded Lt-General Murray as Chief of the Imperial General Staff. The CIGS is the Army's link with the Secretary of State for War and the Cabinet and General Robertson's appointment demonstrates the falsity of yet another Great War myth, that all the commanders were aristocrats. 'Wully' Robertson was the son of a Lincolnshire postman and had risen from the ranks on merit. Robertson was to prove a stout supporter of Haig in the years ahead, not least in his conflicts with

David Lloyd George, but his appointment was a mixed blessing, for Haig and Robertson were two of the most inarticulate officers in the British Army.

Haig could write lucid notes and detailed instructions but was unable to express himself clearly at meetings or discussions, while Robertson's normal response to any query or criticism was either an explosive grunt or the dour comment 'I've heard different.' This lack of loquacity may seem a small point but it had unfortunate consequences when these officers had to explain their needs or account for complicated operations in front of the Cabinet or around a conference table, especially when the others present, like David Lloyd George and the French generals Nivelle or Foch, were giving their contrary opinions full voice. War was becoming more politically charged and it was necessary to carry the day in committee behind the lines as well as at the Front, especially at the Inter-Allied Conferences which were now being called by General Joffre, the French Commander-in-Chief, in an attempt to provide some overall direction to the war.

This was the background to the events of 29 December 1915, therefore, when General Sir Douglas Haig was invited by General Joseph Joffre to the French Headquarters (GQG) at Chantilly, to discuss the future conduct of the war. Haig had attended many conferences with his opposite numbers in the French Army since 1914, and had one advantage over his predecessor, for he spoke good French. Thus equipped, Haig set out for a meeting that had far-reaching consequences and one that can be considered one of the most fateful meetings of the war.

Notes

1 The name comes from a remark attributed to the Kaiser, directing his forces to sweep aside Field Marshal French's 'contemptible little Army'. This remark may not be quite accurate for the German word can also mean 'insignificant' which, at least in terms of numbers, the BEF probably was.

2 *La Comité des Forge de France, Août 1914–Nov 1918*, Colin, Paris, 1919.

3 Quoted in *British Strategy and Politics, 1914–1918*, Paul Guinn, OUP, 1965, p. 49.

4 The author would like to thank the historian John Hussey for this information.

5 A 'staff-qualified' officer was one who had a sound grasp of staff duties learned and practised in the field but had not completed the Staff Course at Camberley.

6 *Official History, The Great War in France and Belgium*, vol. 5. p. 1.

7 From 1 August 1914 to 31 December 1915, the casualty figures, killed, wounded and missing, came to the following totals: 2.1 million Austro-Hungarians; 2 million Russians; 1.3 million French; 612,000 Germans; 279,000 British (includes Indians and Canadians); 180,000 Italians, plus countless Serbs and Turks. (Figures from *The First World War: Germany and Austria-Hungary, 1914–1918*, p. 172.)

2

Meetings at Chantilly
December 1915–February 1916

'The French had for the time lost faith in the
doctrine of the infallible success of the offensive.'
M. Poincaré, President of France, 1916

The meeting called by General Joffre at Chantilly in December 1915
was only the latest in a series of attempts to bring some strategic
direction to the war against Germany. During 1914 and 1915, in spite
of a measure of co-operation on the battlefield, the two Allies on the
Western Front had been fighting what amounted to separate
campaigns. Each national army, on both sides of the line, tended to
take care of its own interests and in moments of stress the amount of
co-operation they were prepared to offer their ally tended to decline.
Quite apart from the fact that these ad hoc arrangements on the
battlefield did not last and their failure contributed to further losses in
the field, this was clearly no way to fight and win a world war. The
side that first established a unified command and fought the war
strategically would have taken a major step towards winning it.

The Entente Powers, fighting on a wider canvas than the Germans,
Austrians or Turks, certainly needed to take an overall, strategic view
of the war, but such a view did not exist, not least because no one in

particular was charged with having one – there was no Supreme Commander. That problem should have been addressed by the two leading prime ministers, Herbert Asquith and Raymond Poincaré but, although both these politicians and many of their generals were well aware of the need to arrive at some commonly agreed strategic concept of the war, no one had yet come up with a workable, acceptable means of creating one.

The real answer was the appointment of a Supreme Commander, an officer who would work under some central strategic directives provided by an inter-governmental committee composed of representatives from all the Entente Powers, rather as in the Second World War, when General Eisenhower worked under the direction of the Combined Chiefs-of-Staff. Under the stress of war such a measure would eventually come on the Western Front, but not until 1918, and only with limited powers, and only then because the Allies were in extremis. A great deal of misery and loss might have been avoided had such an appointment been made earlier.

A Combined Chiefs-of-Staff Committee could have considered the grand strategy for the war, deciding the theatres to engage in, how to use the Entente's naval strength, how to wage a world war globally, over-riding national interests in the common cause of victory, but those posts remained unfilled. Until there was some overall, commonly agreed strategy it all depended on mutual respect and co-operation between the commanders, a task which took up a great deal of time and, certainly on the British side, considerable amounts of patience, for the French considered that they should have the last say in the conduct of the war. This belief in French prowess on the battlefield was not shared by the British generals, with the possible exception of that strongly Francophile officer Lt-General Sir Henry Wilson, whose admiration for the French in general, and Foch in particular, was little short of obsessive.

Even at the end of 1915, therefore, the appointment of a Supreme Commander seemed unthinkable, which is not to say that the idea was not being thought about. The French generals, especially General Foch, thought about little else. Many of Foch's colleagues were well aware of his ambition, and indeed when he was finally appointed to the Supreme Command at the Doullens Conference on 26 March 1918, the then prime minister of France, Georges Clemenceau told him to his face: 'Well, you've got the job you so much wanted.'[1] And, because the war on the Western Front was being fought on French soil and the French currently had more men fighting it, General Joffre was tacitly accepted as the notional commander, the *generalissimo*, of the Allied Armies in France. As a result, the British Commanders, Field Marshal French and now Sir Douglas Haig, had been instructed to conform to his wishes whenever possible. They did so, not least because everyone was aware that arguments at the Command level could only give comfort to the enemy. Therefore, in July 1915, when General Joffre addressed the matter of a concerted effort by calling the first Inter-Allied Military Conference at his headquarters at Chantilly, the commanders of all the Entente armies duly came to listen.

General Joffre was then Commander of the French Armies in the north-east, but he was also effectively the head of the entire military effort of France, working under the overall direction of the Minister of War. In 1915 General Joffre was still 'the man of the hour', his reputation buttressed by the immense personal prestige he had garnered for his actions on the Marne in 1914, where his refusal to panic in the face of impending defeat prevented the collapse of the French armies and arguably settled the eventual outcome of the war.

Like a number of senior French commanders, including Ferdinand Foch and General Vicomte de Castelnau, Joffre's Chief-of-Staff, Joseph Césaire Joffre came from the Pyrénées. He joined the Army as a gunner in 1870, served in the defence of Paris during the Franco-Prussian War and then transferred to the engineers, spending most of his subsequent career in the colonies, campaigning in Madagascar and on the expedition to Timbuktu. He returned to France in 1904 as Director of Engineers, became a member of the War Council in 1910 and in 1911 became Chief of the General Staff. This appointment owed as much to the desire of the military establishment to get rid of the other candidate, General Michel, as to any great urge to promote Joffre.

General Michel was out of favour with the French military establishment, for he was firmly opposed to the doctrine of all-out attack – *l'attaque à outrance* – which had been propagated throughout the French officer corps in the period after the Franco-Prussian War by the Chief of the Operations Section, Colonel de Grandmaison. By the turn of the century, all-out attacks by hosts of valiant French infantry, rather on the style employed by the Imperial Guard at Waterloo, were the received wisdom in French military circles, and would remain so until the losses of the Great War killed off its adherents and a million or so brave young men. Joffre, a sapper, had no particular views on the merits of *l'attaque à outrance* and was therefore seen by the military establishment as more malleable on tactical issues.

L'attaque à outrance arose out of the reverses of 1871, when the Prussian Army walked all over the French Army and defeated the French nation in a matter of weeks. This defeat called for a great deal of heart-searching among the soldiery and led the French military to recall their finest hours under Napoleon. Napoleon was a gunner and a great general, but the devotees of *l'attaque à outrance* remembered only that the armies of Europe had broken before the onrushing columns of French infantry, attacking with great force and *élan*, driven on by the sound of drums beating the *pas de charge*. What had been done once could be done again; the effect of modern weapons and their vastly increased firepower could be overcome and *la gloire* achieved in abundance if only the men and their officers, especially their officers, had enough *cran* (guts).

This was total tosh, of course, given the awesome effect and range of modern weapons, but the men of the French Army have never been short of guts. Clad in their brilliant uniforms, carrying swords and wearing white gloves, the officers of this gallant army led their men into the German machine-gun fire in 1914 . . . and then war was suddenly not glorious any more. A million men were killed or wounded trying to make this tactic work. Although General Joffre did nothing to challenge this fatal belief in *l'attaque à outrance* in the pre-war years, his time was not wasted. He strengthened the defences on the eastern frontier of France, notably the forts around Verdun and along the border with Germany, increased the number of heavy artillery units, and introduced a universal three-year conscription term in 1913, an action which greatly increased the size of the French Army.

Joffre's principal characteristic was his imperturbability. Whether this arose from a remarkably steady nerve or simply because he lacked sufficient imagination to see how desperate the situation really was remains debatable, but in the late summer of 1914, when the armies of France were falling back on every front, Joffre's steadfast calm saved the French nation from defeat. He waited on the Marne until the flanks of the German invaders were fully exposed, then struck with full force and drove them back to the River Aisne, where the trench system began to develop and the nature of the Great War changed. If Joffre had done nothing else in that war, his actions on the Marne earned him a place in history.

This first Inter-Allied Military Conference at Chantilly ended with the vague and unhelpful conclusion that the various national armies, French, British, Italian, Russian, Serbian, should each fight the enemy on its own front and in its own way, which is what they were already doing. Nevertheless, a start had been made, a step in the right direction, for the governments and the generals did at least begin to consider the war in a broader context. This meeting was followed, in November 1915, with a meeting in Paris between Herbert Asquith and M. Poincaré, at which the two sides adopted in principle the idea of setting up 'a mixed permanent committee to co-ordinate the action of the Allies.'

Following up this idea, Joffre promptly called another Inter-Allied Military meeting at Chantilly on 2 December, which was attended by military representatives from all the Entente Powers. The British delegates were Field Marshal Sir John French, the Chief of the Imperial General Staff (CIGS), Lt-General Sir Archibald Murray, Lt-General Sir William Robertson, Chief-of-Staff of the BEF, and Lt-General Sir Henry Wilson, Chief Liaison Officer with the French Army.

Before the delegates arrived they received a paper from General Joffre, outlining the 'Plan of Action proposed by France to the Coalition'. The plan proposed steps that the Coalition partners – France, Britain, Russia and Italy – might, in their various spheres of operation, take, ranging from 'simultaneous attacks with their maximum forces in their respective fronts' to the accumulation of material, equipment and help towards the training and re-equipping of the Russian and Serbian armies. The list of French proposals goes on for pages and the meeting to discuss them lasted three full days. The conclusion was a unanimous decision that the outcome of the war could only be decided in the principal theatres; that is to say, those in which the enemy maintained the greater part of his forces – in other words on the Russian, Italian and Franco-British fronts.

Until that could be done, the Austro-German forces were to be worn down by attacks from those armies with sufficient reserves, namely those of Britain, Italy and Russia. Gallipoli, where a large force of French, British, Gurkha, Indian and ANZAC troops was achieving very little at considerable cost, would be evacuated. The 250,000 French and British soldiers at Salonika were left outside this calculation, though everyone but Sir John French felt that the Franco-British Expeditionary Force at Salonika should stay in post; Sir John declined to comment on Salonika at this time, on the grounds that he knew nothing of the situation there.

At the end of 1915 the political direction of the war was handled by the British Government through a small committee originally called the Dardanelles Committee, having been established after the setting up of the Coalition Government to handle the situation at Gallipoli. This committee, which later became the War Committee, was headed by the Prime Minister and at its largest contained no more than ten members, most of them directly connected with the conduct of the war on a day-to-day basis – the Secretary of State for War, the Minister of Munitions, the First Lord of the Admiralty, the Foreign Secretary and so on.

When the communiqué from Chantilly was presented to the War Committee in London, the members concluded that Salonika, like Gallipoli, should be evacuated forthwith. However, under French pressure, this not inconsiderable Allied force stayed on in Salonika, achieving nothing, for much of the war. The Russians and French believed that the presence of the Allied force in Salonika exerted pressure on Greece and Romania and prevented these countries joining the Central Powers. In view of the strained relations between Greece and Turkey, one of the Central Powers, such action looked unlikely, but the French and Russians were adamant that the force should stay in place and that the British divisions should remain with it.

It is not the intention of this book to cover the actions taken in other theatres, main or subsidiary, unless and until such actions affect the steps taken on the Western Front, but it should be pointed out that all actions have some effect. Modern battles are not fought in isolation; the deployment of troops, the supply of equipment and transport to one theatre of war, are affected by the needs of other theatres. This, again, is a strategic matter, requiring a decision on where, given the circumstances, it is best and most profitable to prosecute the war.

A case in point is Russia, which had the manpower but was grievously short of modern equipment, from rifles and heavy guns to every kind of ammunition. Germany was anxious to seize territory in the East, as was Austria-Hungary, and had the Entente powers been able to supply more *matériel* to the Tsar's vast armies much might have been achieved, for the Eastern Front was mobile, open, and of vital interest to the Central Powers. Historians should not 'play general', let alone pontificate on the possibilities of different initiatives in the strategic area, but it is difficult not to wonder what the outcome would have been if the Entente had simply held its ground in France and Belgium and tackled Germany and Austria-Hungary by sending every piece of kit they could spare to the Russians – which is not unlike what happened until 1944 in the Second World War.

The problem was that there was no kit to spare; all the nations involved in the Great War entered it with an inadequate amount of kit for the struggle they soon had to face. It was hard for the British and French to equip their own armies and they had very little to spare for the Russians. The point cannot be discussed in detail but the strategic picture should be borne in mind, and the matter of Salonika is another case in point. The French wanted their Allies to bring all possible force to bear against the German Army in France, but the drawback – and there was always a drawback – was that when that wish meant giving up Salonika, the French drew back. This was yet another point on which they clashed with their British allies and another instance of the need for a supreme commander. This failure to concentrate all forces on the main front illustrates another problem for the British – manpower.

On 16 December, two weeks after the second meeting at Chantilly, the British CIGS, Lt-General Murray, placed a memorandum on 'The

Future Conduct of the War' in front of the War Committee. This weighed up the overall situation from the British perspective and made certain recommendations for 1916 based on the principle that the British Army should: 'place every possible division, fully manned and equipped in every respect in France next Spring . . . for we require every man we can find to break the enemy's resistance in that theatre.' Murray's proposal was based on a realization that the British Empire, after more than a year of frantic effort, was finally about to deploy its full strength in this war.

The expansion of the British Army in the first two years of the war was a remarkable feat of organization. In August 1914, the BEF mustered two corps totalling four divisions (plus a cavalry division) from an Army which, at full strength, could muster eleven divisions. When the Battle of the Somme opened two years later, on 1 July 1916, the BEF could muster 58 divisions in 18 corps organized in four armies – the Fourth Army being formed on 1 March. A great deal of that expansion had taken place since the beginning of 1916.

On 1 January 1916, the British had three Armies in France, under the overall command of General Sir Douglas Haig. These armies were deployed between the River Somme and the North Sea. In the north lay the Second Army under Sir Herbert Plumer, deployed around Ypres from Armentières to Boesinghe, with a small Belgian force between their left flank and the North Sea. South of Armentières lay the First Army, currently commanded by General Sir Henry Rawlinson. Then came the French Tenth Army, holding the front from Lens to Ransart, and finally, General Allenby's Third Army, which lay between Gommecourt and the Somme. These British Armies mustered a total of 38 infantry divisions, two of them Canadian in Plumer's Second Army, and five cavalry divisions, two of them Indian. The British Empire's total manpower in France on 1 January 1916 amounted to 987,200 men.[2]

This was a considerable number of soldiers, but the force was still only just sufficient to hold the British section of the line in adequate strength and to harass the enemy with local actions. Even with this number of soldiers in the field the divisions were understrength by about ten per cent of their establishment. To mount a major offensive, or play their part in a combined offensive, the British armies in France needed more men, both to fill out the gradually depleting ranks of the units in the line – where casualties in 'normal' times ran at around 1,000 a day – and to provide the commanders with the essential for any attack, a supply of fresh, trained troops *in reserve*, to follow up the initial attack and reinforce the assault troops now embedded in the enemy line.

There was nothing new in this constant need for reinforcements, which would continue until the end of the war. Divisions, brigades and battalions had been flowing to France ever since August 1914: regular reservists recalled to the colours; volunteers from the pre-War Territorial force; and, increasingly, divisions of the New or 'Kitchener' Armies, which were to make their major contribution to the struggle in the months and years ahead. The first of these divisions had already entered the fray, disastrously, at the Battle of Loos. Every man who could be found and trained had to be committed to the struggle for, even at the end of 1914, the notion that a lack of momentum could be compensated for by weight, or numbers, still held sway in military circles.

Fortunately for the new commander, General Haig, the British force in France was about to be reinforced for the coming campaign. On 1 January 1916, there were 19 divisions in the UK: four New Army formations, thirteen Territorial Force divisions and two cavalry divisions, plus a few brigades – a total of nearly one and a half million men. Other British and Empire divisions were currently deployed at Gallipoli (8), in Egypt (10), in Mesopotamia (4) and in Salonika (5), with single divisions in South Africa and East Africa. All told, including scattered garrisons, there were a further half-million British and Empire soldiers deployed in these theatres, so that in early 1916 Britain had some two million soldiers, two-thirds of her current military strength, either at home or in far-flung places well away from the crucial front in France. General Haig naturally wanted as many of these men as possible in France, where the coming year offered the prospect of victory and the certainty of severe fighting.

There was also the question of how this force could be expanded in the future, or how reinforcements could be provided to make up the inevitable casualties in the coming months. Since August 1914 the prospect of war had lost its gloss and the supply of eager volunteers for front line service had slowed considerably. Kitchener's New Armies were now assembling in France and these divisions of volunteers were eager for the fray but, together with the Territorial Force, they had absorbed most of the patriotic fervour of 1914. Though British losses had not reached the French or German scale they were still considerable. French losses, from August 1914 to 31 December 1915, came to 1,932,051 of whom no less than 1,001,271 were killed or missing. The British total in the same period was 512,420, of whom around 200,000 were killed or missing.

Losses on this scale could not be concealed from the public. Finding more volunteers was not going to be easy and there was currently no way to compel men into the British Army for, unlike the French and the Germans, Britain and her Empire had no conscription; in January 1916, every man in the British Forces, at home or at the front, was a volunteer. The Continental armies, on the other hand, were fleshed out with conscripts. As a result, the French could muster 95 divisions on the Western Front alone, while the Germans had no less than 117 divisions there, regular or reserve, with more arriving every month. Even now, more than a year into the war and with a million men in France, the British were still minor players in this war.

In the Empire the idea of conscription was anathema to the civilian population and therefore to the elected governments. In Britain, though the notion was equally unwelcome, the introduction of conscription was now being contemplated through sheer necessity. With the enemy in such strength and our chief ally so heavily committed, no other course was possible.

The first step to this end had been taken in July 1915 by the National Registration Act. The main purpose of this Act was to discover just how many young men and women Britain possessed, by compiling a register. Then, by deducting those who had to stay in reserved occupations, in munitions or armament factories, on the land, or in shipbuilding, it was possible to make an accurate assessment of the number available for conscription into the armed forces. However, before resorting to conscription, the Government had another scheme. In October 1915, Lord Derby was appointed Director of

Recruiting and at once introduced what came to be known as the 'Derby Scheme', which required all men aged between 18 and 41 to enlist voluntarily; others could also attest their willingness to serve and would be called if needed.

This scheme produced another flood of volunteers and by the time the list closed in mid-December 1915, more than 200,000 men had joined the Army, and more than *two million* men had attested their willingness to serve if necessary. To this can be added the large number of young women who had come forward for war work in the factories, each woman freeing a man to fight – but good as this was, it was still not good enough. A rough calculation showed that a further 650,000 men had failed either to volunteer or attest and, on 4 January 1916, the British Government finally introduced conscription – the Military Service Act – for all able-bodied men between the ages of 18 and 41. At first this was limited to single men but, in May 1916, the Act was extended to married men as well.

With this influx of volunteers and conscripts the manpower situation gradually improved, but it takes time to train soldiers and it was not until May 1916, five months after the first conscripts reached the barracks, that any effect was noticed at the front. From then on the number of men arriving gradually overhauled the wastage at the front, until the Armies were only about 10,000 men below establishment. This did not allow for an adequate supply of trained reserves to make up the inevitable casualties in the big battle which followed on the Somme, but at least the improving manpower situation enabled Haig to form another Army, the Fourth, which was activated on 1 March 1916, under the command of Lt-General Sir Henry Rawlinson.

The point of this general survey of the manpower situation is to underline the fact that when Haig took over command in December 1915 he had barely enough men to cover the BEF's existing commitments. Unless he had more men, and trained men at that, he had no way of making a meaningful contribution to *any* offensive in 1916 . . . and this was without considering the possibility that the Germans might launch an offensive first, which was by no means improbable. In his survey of the options on 15 December, General Murray had examined the courses of action open to the enemy and had come to the conclusion that a major attack in France would pay Germany greater dividends than any successful attack in Russia. Murray's memorandum was duly considered and approved by the War Committee on 23 December, with the rider that the actual plan of attack in 1916 would now be left to the discretion of the commanders in the field. Since Sir John French had been sacked on 19 December, this meant the new Commander of the BEF, Sir Douglas Haig, would need to discuss this matter with the French Commander and *generalissimo,* General Joffre.

The instructions given to General Haig by the British Government at the end of 1915 varied somewhat from those given to his predecessor at the start of the war. Field Marshal French, while directed to 'coincide most sympathetically with the plans and wishes of our Ally', had also been told that his command was an independent one and that he was not to risk his troops in offensives 'where they might be unduly exposed to attack'. General Haig's instructions, while reiterating the point that his was an independent command, concluded that 'the closest co-operation between the French and British as a *united army* [author's italics] must be the governing policy', adding the rider that 'You will in no case come under the orders of any Allied general, further than the necessary co-operation with our Allies referred to above.' It does not take great perspicacity to see that Haig's orders were more specific on the matter of co-operation than those of his predecessor.

On the other hand, these instructions were still somewhat ambivalent, leaving a great deal to the good sense of General Haig and wide scope for interference by General Joffre. The French attitude of bland superiority was summed up in a French memorandum, prepared by General Joffre and presented to the British Government by M. Millerand, the French War Minister, before the 1915 Battle of Loos:

> During the period in which the operations of the British Army take place on French territory . . . the initiative in combined action of the French and British Armies devolves on the French Commander-in-Chief, notably as concerns the effectives to be engaged, the objectives to be attained and the dates fixed for the commencement of the operation.

This Note graciously concludes: 'The Commander-in-Chief of the British Forces will, of course, fully retain the choice of means of execution.' In other words the French would decide where the British would attack, when they would attack and how many British divisions should be committed to the attack. All the British commander had to do was to decide on *how* to attack – and carry the blame if it all went awry. It should be noted that the Battle of Loos, fought when and where the French wished, was a total shambles, costing a great number of British and French lives, but this catastrophe and all the others since the war began had clearly not dented the French belief in their military infallibility.

This belief should have been resisted, for there was little basis for it. At Loos, for example, although Field Marshal French and General Haig were more than willing to assist the French attack in Artois in September 1915, by mounting an attack on the German line, they were adamant that they did not want to attack at Loos, where the flat, open ground was clearly unsuitable. The British generals offered to attack in the Ypres salient or at Aubers Ridge, or to make strong feint attacks at Loos if that would satisfy the French need for assistance. These sensible suggestions were scornfully rejected, Joffre and Foch did not want feint attacks at Loos or full-scale attacks anywhere but at Loos. So the British duly attacked at Loos and the losses were appalling. What the French gained from this slaughter of their Allies is not immediately apparent, but the British generals failed to learn that they must stand up to the French. Throwing away their men's lives simply to bolster French egos or to demonstrate British commitment to the common cause was little short of criminal.

It might be added that superiority of numbers was not, of itself, any guarantee of a command appointment, at least as far as the British were concerned. The British forces in Salonika outnumbered the French by many thousands of men – at the end of 1915 the British had five divisions in Salonika to the French three – but the overall commander was a French officer, General Sarrail, appointed to that post on 31 December 1915. This may have been because the French were far keener on maintaining a force on the Salonika front than the British were or because the French were totally determined that any overall commander, anywhere, would be French.

As we shall see, one conclusion in General Murray's report, that the Germans could profit from a major attack in France, was also the conclusion reached by the German Chief-of-Staff, General Erich von Falkenhayn. That two opposing generals can reach the same strategic conclusion is not surprising. It is usually possible for a general to work out what the enemy general might do, simply by putting himself in the other's place, working out the various courses of action open, and choosing the best one to follow. This process, of guessing 'what was on the other side of the hill' to use Wellington's phrase, is only useful up to a point. It may indicate what the enemy will do, but it will not indicate how or where or when he will do it . . . and he might do something completely different.

As far as the British were concerned, what they might do depended very largely on the French but Murray's report should have received more attention, not least in considering how a German offensive, should it occur, could be turned to Anglo-French advantage. The big lesson of 1915 was that in any battle the attacker lost more men. If Joffre really wanted to 'wear down' the German armies on the Western Front before the 'combined offensive', he should have welcomed the prospect of a German attack and laid plans to exploit it.

General Haig met Joffre at Chantilly on 23 December, six days after taking up his new appointment. Joffre stated that he was not yet in a position to discuss the plan of operations for the coming year, but that he would be glad in the meantime if the British could take over more of the Front Line, especially by expanding to fill the 20-mile gap between the British Third and First Armies, a space currently occupied by the French Tenth Army. Haig hesitated to comply, not least because he had yet to hear what extra strength or reinforcements he might receive in the coming months but, as a gesture of goodwill, he arranged that the British should take over a section of the line near Loos, and directed the commanders of the Third and Second Armies to prepare outline plans for local offensives when the winter eased.

Five days later, on 28 December, the War Committee proposals for 1916 were placed before the entire British Cabinet and approved.

These proposals centred on the belief that the main action in 1916 would take place in France and that all possible strength should be assembled there – including, yet again, the eight Allied divisions currently locked up in Salonika. However, according to the *Official History* no decision on a joint Anglo-French offensive in France was taken at this time.[4] Indeed, a final decision on the summer offensive was not reached until later in 1916, after the German assault at Verdun. When Haig left Joffre's Headquarters after that meeting in December, he certainly did not feel that his Army had been committed to falling in with the future wishes of the French.

Indeed, after his meeting with Joffre, Haig ordered the commanders of the Second and Third Armies, General Plumer and General Allenby, to prepare outline plans for separate offensives on their own fronts, using what power they had available and whatever reserves he could supply. The Third Army was to investigate what might be done with an attack on a ten-mile front north of the Somme, while General Plumer was tasked with considering attacks on the Messines–Wytschaete ridge on the south edge of the Ypres salient, followed by an advance towards Lille and the Houthulst Forest in the east and north of the salient, a plan that has strong echoes of the 1917 Passchendaele offensive. No proposals were invited from the First Army, Haig's old command, which was currently holding the line between Loos and Armentières.

The question of a combined assault on the Somme appears for the first time shortly after another meeting at Chantilly, one called by General Joffre on 29 December, a high-powered meeting attended by the President of France, M. Poincaré, the Prime Minister, M. Briand, the Minister of War, General Galliéni, and the three French Army commanders, Generals Foch, Dubail and de Langle de Cary. Haig attended this meeting accompanied only by some members of his personal staff. The strong French military and political presence is interesting, and although the subjects under discussion mainly concerned the state of Western Front defences, the letter from Joffre that arrived at Haig's HQ next day covered a much wider range of issues.

After declaring that he had directed General Foch to study the possibilities for a powerful offensive south of the Somme, between that river and Lassigny, Joffre went on to state that, whatever the final plan for the employment of the French armies in 1916, the French offensive would be 'greatly aided by a simultaneous offensive of the British forces between the Somme and Arras'. Haig went to his maps and discovered that this amounted to a proposal for a combined Anglo-French attack astride the Somme and probably on a sixty-mile front. Of course, it was not necessary for all British forces north of the Somme to attack but if even one army attacked the others must advance, if only to protect the flanks of the attacking force. This was the thinking behind Joffre's request . . . or was it? Whatever the motivation, if the Anglo-French forces attacked at the same time on such a wide front, this would indeed be a major 'broad front' offensive of unprecedented size and that created a large number of problems – not least that of where all the artillery was to come from to support such a stupendous effort.

Joffre's letter again requested that Haig should take over the positions held by the French Tenth Army, between Loos and Gommecourt, which Haig was already preparing to do. It concluded with the more debatable remark that 'the ground [on the Somme] is besides in many places favourable for the development of a powerful offensive'. Joffre had made similar claims for the ground in front of Loos where the British infantry had been cut to pieces four months earlier, so Haig would have studied this comment with particular care. Joffre also claimed that it would be of considerable advantage to attack the enemy on a front which had been quiet for months. This point is again questionable, for the energetic Germans had used that time to create a comprehensive defensive system on the high ground east of the River Ancre. Although Joffre was asking for a 'simultaneous' offensive, he had not mentioned a 'combined' offensive – the difference lying in the planning and agreement on aims and objectives; the first kind of offensive does not require close co-operation, the second demands it.

Matters then speeded up. On 20 January 1916, Joffre visited Haig's HQ and revealed that he had now been committed by his Government to a series of five attacks along various sections of the French line, but that before these attacks took place it was essential that the German strength should be reduced and German reserves sucked into action by at least one large British attack, preferably on a 20,000 yard (ten-mile-wide) front north of the Somme, on or about 20 April. As usual, this verbal proposal was followed up by a letter, which arrived at GHQ on 23 January. In this letter Joffre requested that 'before the general offensive, the British Army should "wear down" [*usure*] the German forces in the West by a series of powerful offensives, using a minimum of fifteen to eighteen divisions.' This was about half Haig's current strength and one-third of all the divisions he could expect to get by the middle of the year. The idea that Haig should send such a substantial amount of his strength into action in the spring, simply to wear down the Germans before the French attack in the summer, cannot have been a welcome suggestion.

Joffre also suggested that one of these preliminary battles should take place north of the Somme in May and the next in June on some other part of the front. Haig had 38 fully trained divisions under command in France, so this request, if agreed to, would mean the commitment of up to half his force before the British part in the 'simultaneous' offensive opened later on, probably in July.

Haig did not agree to Joffre's proposal and he was right to do so. If he was expected to take part in something even approaching a 60-mile-wide attack at some as yet unspecified date in the near future – and take over a large section of the French line as soon as possible – it would be less than sensible to mount two major attacks in the spring and early summer, and in 1916 an attack on a ten-mile front was a major attack indeed. Such 'spoiling' attacks would probably do more damage to the British attackers than they would to the German defenders. Haig therefore suggested that if a 'wearing down' of the enemy was deemed essential, the same effect could be achieved by a series of trench raids which would divert German attention to the British front.

With plans being laid by the British generals for attacks around the Ypres salient and north of the Somme, and suggestions coming in fast from General Joffre, Haig also had to consider the continuing question of the size and effectiveness of the BEF, the force that must put these schemes into effect. Divisions were now coming out from

Britain and other divisions, including those removed from Gallipoli, were remustering in Egypt but even if the War Committee had agreed to ship as many divisions as possible to France in the coming year, these had not yet arrived and they would need more training and some experience in the line before they were fully effective.

The question of training the BEF battalions is one that constantly interests military historians. The allegation is that part of the reason for the failures in the British attack on the First Day of the Somme, 1 July 1916, was that the men were not properly trained. This begs another question, for by July 1916 these men, the surviving Regulars, the Territorial Force volunteers and the men of the New Kitchener divisions, had all been in the Army for the best part of two years. If they were still badly trained, what had they been doing for all that time? In peacetime, given an adequate supply of good instructors, suitable equipment and training facilities, an infantry soldier can be adequately trained in 12 weeks, very well trained indeed in 18 weeks, and taught how to use a full range of infantry weapons and tactics in 24 weeks; six months should be enough to produce a trained soldier, though one who still needs battlefield indoctrination. The men who flocked to the colours in 1914 and 1915 were the pick of the nation, many of them well educated, all of them willing, even anxious, to become soldiers. The answer, surely, is not that they were badly trained but that they had not been trained for the tasks that confronted them on 1 July and in the subsequent fighting on the Somme. That lack of training is much easier to understand when the experience of the previous two years is taken into account.

Put simply, the British Army that went into action on the Somme had been recruited too quickly for the training and equipment resources of 1914 and 1915. It was months before the men got uniforms and equipment, rifles were in short supply until the middle of 1915, and many other arms, like machine-guns and artillery, which the infantry needed to use or work with were not available at all for training purposes. Nor were the instructors of high quality; had they been really good or young enough, they would have been at the Front. They did their best and taught these eager soldiers all they knew, but not many of them knew much about the new kind of war then developing on the Western Front. That war was static, a *defensive* war, while the fighting on the Somme after 1 July called for an *offensive* war, one requiring different training and tactics.

The 1914 volunteers came in such numbers that training facilities were swamped and Kitchener's decision to form New Armies as opposed to expanding the Territorial Force proved a mistake. For all its limitations, the Territorial Force was a force in being. It had a structure, and better use could have been made of it, not least in the straitened state of the nation's military resources. The root of the problem was that Kitchener had not served in Britain for decades and had no knowledge of the Territorial Force or its young volunteers. He could only recall the elderly, ineffective French 'Territorials' he had seen when he served in an ambulance unit in the Franco-Prussian War 40 years before. Kitchener therefore decided that it would be better to raise new armies from scratch.

Added to these problems were the terrible losses sustained by the Regular Army on the Western Front in the battles of 1914 and 1915. Simply to keep the front line manned, troops had to be sent out as soon as their training was completed – which is not to say that their training had turned them into good soldiers. Indeed, in 1915, Kitchener, as Secretary of State for War, had to resist French demands for sending out troops who were barely trained at all, Kitchener retorting that 'to send untrained troops into battle was little short of murder'.

However, war has its own dynamic. From sheer necessity the men went out to the Front as soon as their training was considered complete. This training was soon found to be inadequate and a large number of Army Schools had to be set up behind the Front to train the men in everything from minor tactics to the handling of new weapons. This training was conducted between spells in the line, where there was very little time for training of any kind. A lot of the responsibility for training came to rest on the individual divisional and corps commanders and some of them, Major-General Ivor Maxse of the 18th Division being one notable example, trained their men at every available opportunity, even when the men were in trenches, for Maxse maintained that a certain amount of training could be conducted even there, provided the will existed.

Even so, two difficulties remained. First of all, much of the training the men received on arriving in France concerned trench warfare: the day-to-day routine of living and surviving in trenches. This required a number of skills: wiring, digging and repairing trenches, sniping, night patrolling, trench raids. All this was useful, but life in the trenches tended to give the men a defensive mentality. Although their commanders were determined to resist this and did not let the British soldiers turn their trenches into comfortable, secure billets, as happened with the French and on the German side, the inevitable result was that the men were only well trained to fight the war as it was – in the trenches.

Though the idea of 'the offensive' was not allowed to wane, and it was constantly made clear to the troops that the British trenches were only for temporary occupation, pending an advance on and through the enemy line in the not-too-distant future, the British soldier needed training in assault tactics, trench clearing and fire and movement, before he could be expected to advance quickly over open ground. What was sorely needed before the 'Big Push' of 1 July was more training in 'open' warfare, in such essential skills as advance to contact, fire and movement, the use of grenades, working with artillery support, communications and signalling, in the 'mopping-up' of enemy positions after capture, in digging-in to resist a counterattack and, especially at the command and staff level, in the speedy forward movement of reserves and supporting artillery to renew or maintain the advance. The British infantry tended to go forward, seize a position and then dig in to hold it, when it might often have been better, and less costly in lives, to push on and keep the battle fluid.

For all these reasons these skills and that attitude were not widely developed. This was a new kind of war, much larger and more technical than all previous wars; the staff and commanders needed further training in handling the all-arms battle, on those aspects of the military art that transform a defensive situation into an offensive one. This, however, is easy to say 80 years later, and when disregarding many of the practical difficulties – the most fundamental of which was that the Great War armies, even those capable of mustering great strength in men and artillery, were very slow moving.

The basic infantry tactic employed for the forward movement of troops under fire in 1914, and in 2001, is known as 'fire and movement', which should now be briefly explained. 'Fire and movement' can be employed by bodies of men ranging in size from a section (10 men) up to a company of 200, but is usually employed by bodies of platoon size (30 men), a force which can develop enough firepower from their own weapons to keep the enemy's heads down while part of their platoon, or another platoon, moves forward, goes to ground and maintains fire on the enemy until the other platoon moves up. So, by a process of 'fire and movement', the troops advance on the enemy. As we shall see, 'fire and movement' was not widely employed on 1 July, not because the men did not understand it, but because it had been decided, for reasons that seemed good and sufficient at the time, that the normal infantry formation on this occasion would be an advance in line. It should be added, however, that many units rejected this formation on the day and went forward in whatever formation the local commanders considered best suited to the ground.

These issues came to a head at 0730 hrs on 1 July, when the infantry went over the top to open the four-month tragedy of the Battle of the Somme, but they must be considered now, at the start of the year, months before that fatal day, because it takes time to decide on the tactics for a particular battle and train the men in their application. The theatre of war is not like other theatres; without training and rehearsal, it will not 'be all right on the night.' It is necessary for a commander to work both forward and back from H-Hour, the moment of the attack. 'Forward' to know where his attack is supposed to be going; 'back' to ensure that all the preparations necessary for a successful offensive have been carried out before it starts. That, indeed, is where the commander truly shows his skills, in giving his men the best possible chance of success and survival before the battle begins. Once the troops go 'over the top' his part in the battle is over and, for a while at least, the issue depends on the training, skill and fortitude of his men.

In January 1916, while Haig was anxious to carry out the spirit of his orders and support his ally, he also had a great deal to do in drawing up plans and getting his soldiers properly trained for whatever operations the summer might bring. Fortunately, Joffre was still feeling his way with Haig, and when it became clear that Haig would not go along with his *usure* scheme, but would support a simultaneous or combined attack, he reverted to that proposal. On 14 February, Joffre therefore abandoned his plan for preparatory offensives – one wonders if such a plan really existed – and it was agreed that a 'combined offensive' should take place, on or about 1 July, astride the River Somme.

The *Official History* alleges that Joffre's decision to mount the main 1916 offensive on the Somme was taken solely because at that point the British would be obliged to take part in it.[5] This becomes even more relevant when the reasons for such an attack are examined more carefully. Again, the *Official History* of the period, published in 1931, 15 years after the battle, is in no doubt:

> The reasons advanced by General Joffre hardly bear examination. It was certainly true that the sector had for long months, about twenty, been a quiet one; but that it was so had merely given the Germans time to elaborate their defences. Joffre's phrase that 'the ground is in many places favourable to the development of a powerful offensive' would have applied equally to almost any part of the front.

The *OH* concedes that the ground around the Somme and the Ancre offered scope for observation, but states that, on the other hand, the chalk downlands, where deep dugouts could be excavated by the enemy, made the sector particularly strong for defence 'in fact it might be considered the strongest [on the Western Front]'. However, the most damning part of the OH's conclusion, over the reasons for the Somme offensive, is that: 'The Somme offensive had no strategic object except attrition.'[6]

Since those words were written in 1931, long after the battle, they may have been the result of hindsight. What evidence is there that at the end of 1915 Joffre had decided that an all-out offensive, another attempt at a breakthrough, was not going to succeed and the only alternative was attrition? If he had, was this fact obvious to General Haig and did he concur with the new objective of this battle, always assuming that there was one?

Joffre's views can be considered first. A fair conclusion would be that a battle of attrition on the Somme was indeed what he had in mind, using the British as bait. This allegation is supported in the memoirs of the French Prime Minister, M. Poincaré, which state that Joffre believed that the 1916 offensives offered not a decisive victory but 'a war of attrition which must chiefly be carried out by our [France's] allies, England, Russia, and even Italy.'[7] Poincaré added (p. 157) that 'no single general, not excepting Foch, has any more faith in the offensive proving successful. He [Foch] no longer talks about offensive, but now says that the war will be long, indeed very long, and that we must exercise patience and dig ourselves in solidly.' It can therefore be said, on the evidence provided by the French themselves, that they were willing to engage in a battle of attrition in 1916, provided the British fought it.

It has been alleged – the comment appears frequently in Hankey's memoirs[8] – that in 1915 Lord Kitchener wished to engage the Germans in a battle of attrition and had suggested to Field Marshal French that the German Armies on his front should be encouraged to launch attacks that could be used for this purpose. This allegation, if true, had no perceptible effect. The Germans only launched one major attack in 1915, the Second Battle of Ypres, and they launched that because they calculated that the use of gas would surprise and demoralize the British and Canadian troops and lead to the capture of Ypres. That attack was eventually beaten off, and, for the rest of the year, or even before at Neuve Chapelle, it was the British who attacked.

There seems to be no evidence to support the allegation that Field Marshal French ever attempted to draw the Germans into a battle of attrition. On the strategy for 1916 the *OH* remarks cautiously that: 'The British leaders, having fought both offensive and defensive battles in 1915, were inclined to think that under certain conditions an offensive might succeed', but there is no mention of attrition. Finally, when Haig took command at the end of 1915, there is plenty of evidence that he still believed that a breakthrough was possible, not least in his instruction to the commanders of the Second and Third

Armies that they should prepare plans for 'offensives' with clear objectives on the ground. Indeed, even after the Battle of the Somme, there are indications that Haig still believed in the possibility of a breakthrough. Writing in his memoirs about the Passchendaele campaign of 1917, General Gough states:

> I have a very clear and distinct recollection of Haig's personal explanations to me, and his instructions when I was appointed to undertake the operation. He quite clearly told me that his plan was to capture the Passchendaele ridge and to advance as quickly as possible on Roulers. I was then to capture Ostend. This was definitely viewing the battle as an attempt to breakthrough and moreover Haig never altered this opinion till the attack was launched, so far as I know.

However, at the regular weekly conference of his Army commanders two weeks after the Messines operation ended in 1917, i.e. before the Passchendaele offensive began, Haig also told Gough: 'The object of the Fifth Army offensive is to wear down the enemy, but at the same time to have an objective. I have given two: the Passchendaele–Staden ridge and the coast.' This last remark is an uncanny echo of von Falkenhayn's scheme for Verdun, that the object was attrition – the 'wearing-down' of the enemy forces – but that the men fought better if they were fighting for some clearly defined objective. At Passchendaele, Haig was apparently seeking some strategic gain or even a breakthrough, but was willing to settle for a battle of attrition.

Attrition is a dangerous game to play, for attrition is at best a gamble. The player is betting that his resources are larger or better organized than those of the enemy and that he can afford to take heavier losses than the enemy can, and so win the day. In the final analysis, it is simply a battle of resources, but the risks are high: the enemy may not want to play and may stay behind his fortifications. He may be a better player and husband his resources – the lives of his soldiers – more efficiently. Attempts to lure the enemy into a battle of attrition, using your artillery against his men, may not work either – he may have more artillery, or better fortifications. All too often, therefore, a battle of attrition descends into a slogging match, a zero-sum game. The two opposing armies simply fight it out until, like exhausted prizefighters, they can fight no longer. Only then is the full cost of the struggle revealed in lives lost and ground gained – and the final balance is rarely favourable to either party.

The fighting on the Western Front usually involved three main forms of loss. There was the steady drain of men in the day-to-day course of trench warfare, men killed or injured by snipers or shell fire; the BEF average for the first six months of 1916 was 35,000 battle casualties a month.[9] There were also local attacks and trench raids to seize a position or dominate No Man's Land – the area of tumbled, shell-pocked, rat- and corpse-infested ground between the trenches. Lastly, there were the major offensives which, in 1916, were specifically the Battle of Verdun and the Battle of the Somme. All of these engagements took their toll of soldiers, but in spite of these steady losses the size of the Armies was increasing, their reserves slowly filling up the ground behind the front, in that area poised between peace and war that came to be known as the Zone of the Armies.

Civilian life went on in the Zone of the Armies. The farmers still ploughed their fields, the factories still worked and the daily routine in the towns and villages continued, only interrupted, close to the Front, by the occasional burst of shelling which shattered houses and pocked the roads with craters. In these towns and villages though, another life went on as well, one that almost submerged the old, quiet, peacetime ways that the French civilians left in residence, mostly women, old men and boys, were trying hard to maintain. The barns gave shelter to thousands of resting khaki-clad troops; the roads and tracks gave way under the feet of marching men and the steady erosion of wagon wheels. Fields were given up to ammunition and food dumps, the tents of field hospitals, and lines of picketed cavalry.

In the Zone of the Armies there was no rest, by day or night; men were always marching to the Front or coming back, tired and muddy, into reserve. Wagons rumbled up the line with supplies, mining and wiring parties moved forward at dusk. The industry of war worked a 24-hour shift, preparing for further offensives or simply holding the line. In the Zone of the Armies, the soldiers were trained and prepared for further spells in the line or future offensives. Believing that these offensives were well planned, feeling they were well trained, they could view the prospect of another offensive with confidence, even optimism. The grinding waste of attrition would not have instilled confidence into the troops or attracted the support of their brigade or battalion commanders.

However, in early 1916, one general, Erich von Falkenhayn, the Commander-in-Chief of the German Armies, did believe in the doctrine of attrition. In December 1915 he laid out his thoughts on a war of attrition in a memorandum to Kaiser Wilhelm II, the 'Supreme War Lord' and, two months later, on 21 February 1916, he launched an attack which had attrition as its only purpose, an attack in great force towards the French fortress city of Verdun.

Notes

1 *Memoirs of Marshal Foch*, p. 300.
2 *Official History, 1916*, vol. 1, p. 18.
3 Ibid., p. 16.
4 Ibid., p. 11.
5 Ibid., p. 30.
6 Ibid., p. 31.
7 Poincaré, *Memoirs*, p. 309.
8 *The Supreme Command, 1914–1918*, Lord Hankey.
9 *Official History, 1916*, vol. 1, p. 153.

3

Von Falkenhayn's Plans
December 1915–February 1916

'Within our reach are objectives for which the French General
Staff would be compelled to throw in every man they have. If
they do so the forces of France will bleed to death.'
General Erich von Falkenhayn,
Chief of the Imperial General Staff, 1915

The origins of the German offensive at Verdun in 1916 can be traced
to another conference, this time at the Headquarters of the Supreme
War Lord, Kaiser Wilhelm II, in December 1915. When the fighting
of 1915 petered out in the aftermath of Loos, renewing the offensive
on the Western Front in the following spring was not the only
preoccupation of the German Imperial Staff. A number of officers
suspected that Germany's chance for outright victory in this war had
ended with the failure of the Schlieffen Plan and Germany's
subsequent defeat on the Marne in the autumn of 1914. Their
experiences in the following year only tended to confirm this

suspicion, for Germany had lost a grievous amount of manpower in the Western Front fighting and had very little to show for it in terms of territory.

After the Battle of the Marne Germany faced a long war for which the country was not prepared. Holgar Herwig notes: 'Few leaders, civilian or military, in Austria Hungary or Germany had given much thought, prior to 1914 to the eventuality, much less the conduct, of a protracted war',[1] while Alfred von Schlieffen had written in 1909 that 'A strategy of attrition will not do if the maintenance of millions [of men], requires billions [of marks].' Though the economic argument was sound, there was more to it than money; Germany's entire plan for the war had been based on the need to avoid fighting a war on two fronts, one in which Germany would be squeezed between the armies of France and Russia.

The need to avoid that situation lay at the root of Germany's military policy, and the Schlieffen Plan was a scheme by which Germany could crush France in six weeks, while the massive but ponderous Russian armies were still mustering. Then, with France defeated, Germany could use the advantage of interior lines, and her superb railway network, to rush her forces east and complete the task by destroying the armies of Russia. After those two short, successful campaigns, Germany could obtain a peace on her own terms. However, there is usually a snag in military affairs and the snag here was a big one – the Schlieffen Plan did not work.

Count Alfred von Schlieffen always believed that his Plan was the only way in which his country stood any realistic chance of winning a major European war. After the Plan failed, it had to be asked if fighting on was feasible, or whether Germany would do better to take her not inconsiderable gains on the Eastern and Western Fronts to the conference table and see what sort of bargain could be hammered out there. In 1914 the only alternative to peace was a long and costly war, and von Schlieffen's doubts were echoed by his successors soon after the conflict began.

On 6 September, barely five weeks into the war, the German Chief of Staff, Helmuth von Moltke, wrote to his wife: 'Things are going badly and the battles east of Paris will not be decided in our favour.

This war, which began with such hopes, will go against us and we must be crushed in the fight between East and West.' Such pessimism, however accurate, did not go down well at the Imperial Court and led to von Moltke's replacement by the Prussian War Minister, Erich von Falkenhayn, who became Chief of the Imperial General Staff, or 'Chief of the General Staff of the Army in the Field' as he calls it in his memoirs, on 14 September 1914. In this position von Falkenhayn, who also remained Prussian War Minister, at least for a while, was in direct charge of the German land forces, but he also exercised a dominant voice in all war activities; the admirals usually deferred to his wishes and aligned their plans with his.[2] Government policy, on the other hand, especially in foreign affairs, rested with the Imperial Chancellor, Theobald von Bethmann-Hollweg.

Two months later reality had spread still further. In November 1914, von Falkenhayn informed von Bethmann-Hollweg that the war could not be won in the conventional sense – by defeating the enemy forces in the field, capturing their capital and imposing a peace – and nothing had happened by the end of 1915 to change his mind; 15 months into the war and the situation was a stalemate. One solution to the 'encirclement' – war on two fronts problem was to sign separate peace treaties and divide the Entente, but Russia would not make a separate peace in 1915 even after the defeats at Tannenberg and Gorlice-Tarnow. Meanwhile German casualties were massive and mounting and the war was drifting rapidly into a battle of attrition, one in which military expertise and trained manpower was being overtaken by the power of the guns. There seems little evidence that attrition was a definite policy in 1915 but if the offensives of 1915 achieved nothing else they killed a quantity of soldiers. This fact cannot have escaped the attention of the generals, and an awesome thought – that maybe attrition was the only way to victory – could hardly have remained unthinkable.

Von Falkenhayn certainly had his doubts about the final outcome of the war, but he was too discreet to broadcast them widely. Erich von Falkenhayn was in many ways a political general. He was also one of the younger Great War generals, just 53 when he took up his new appointment. He had been the Prussian Minister for War since 1913 and had done much of the planning for the initial assault on Belgium. Although an efficient officer, with war experience in China during the Boxer Rebellion of 1900–01, he owed much of his subsequent promotion to the personal favour of the Kaiser, who had greatly enjoyed von Falkenhayn's despatches from Peking. As Chief-of-Staff, von Falkenhayn had not done too well in the war to date. His first orders to the German Armies in France, immediately following his appointment to the High Command, that they should renew the offensive in the West and attempt a re-run of the Schlieffen Plan, had led to the First Battle of Ypres, terrible losses among the German units committed to that attack, and no territorial gains.

This was not entirely von Falkenhayn's fault. Like the French and British Great War generals, his plans were inhibited by a lack of suitable pre-war preparation, not least in the matter of supply. At First Ypres, for example, he lacked guns and he lacked shells. 'Every single shot had to be counted,' he wrote . . . 'the failure of a single ammunition train or any stupid accident threatened to render whole sections of the line defenceless.'[3] As with the Franco-British generals, these deficiencies in equipment could not quickly be made good; for example, the German field gun, needed in 1914 to match the French 75 mm, did not come into service until 1916.

Since that time, apart from the gas-supported attempt at a *coup de main* in the Ypres salient in April 1915, an attack which developed into yet another bloodbath, the Second Battle of Ypres, von Falkenhayn had let the British and French do the attacking and had concentrated on holding the ground taken in the West, while his rivals and subordinates, Generals von Hindenburg and Ludendorff, had worked with the Austrian armies and dealt with the Russians in the East. The British and French Armies in the West had therefore spent 1915 hurling their soldiers against a trench system which seemed to be unbreakable.

On 2 January 1915, Field Marshal Kitchener wrote to Sir John French:

We must recognise that the French Army cannot make a sufficient breach in the German line to bring about a retreat into Belgium. If that is so, then the German lines in France may be looked on as a fortress, that cannot be carried by assault and cannot be completely invested, with the result that the lines may be held by an investing force while operations proceed elsewhere.

In the event, the only major 'operation' conducted 'elsewhere' that year was at Gallipoli, a campaign which rapidly collapsed into stalemate and disaster, while on the Western Front the French and British assaulted the German lines continually until the end of the year, always at terrible cost and without gaining a yard. Various authorities have stated in their memoirs that these Allied assaults in 1915 were the start of a 'campaign of attrition', but while there is some documentary evidence to support that view, the physical evidence is scanty. During 1915, the Allied Commanders in the West – French, Foch, Joffre – certainly lost a great many men for no territorial gain, but these men were lost in 'offensives' that aimed to penetrate the enemy line and restore open warfare to the Western Front.

They hoped to do this by achieving the right combination of artillery and infantry to make a breach, followed by rapid commitment of reserves and the insertion of cavalry to expand the breach. Exactly what this right combination was had yet to be discovered. Every battle showed a slightly different combination, with the use of new elements like gas, but by the end of 1915 the magic formula leading to a breakthrough remained elusive. The enemy line could be penetrated briefly, as at Neuve Chapelle, but a breakthrough was something else again.

Field Marshal French thought the magic ingredient was shellfire. In January 1915 he wrote a minute stating:

> Breaking through the enemy's lines is largely a question of expenditure of high explosive ammunition. If sufficient ammunition is forthcoming, a way out can be blasted through the line. If the attempt fails, it shows, provided the work of the infantry and artillery has been properly co-ordinated, that insufficient ammunition has been expended i.e. either more guns must be brought up, or the allowance of ammunition per gun may be increased.[4]

Even the experience of attempting half a dozen fruitless and expensive attacks by the end of 1915 had not caused Field Marshal French to appreciate that breaking the enemy lines with artillery and infantry alone might be much more complicated . . . or even impossible.

The battles of 1915 were not attempts to 'write down' the enemy forces by engaging in battles of attrition, though by the end of 1915, the French Army alone had lost almost two million men, killed, wounded and missing, and losses on this scale could not be maintained. It is hardly surprising that, by the end of 1915, General Joffre thought it high time the British Armies took on more of the fighting and played the largest part in the 1916 offensives.

Though 1915 had not presented either side with any useful territory gain, it could be argued that the forces of the Central Powers had emerged from the year in better case than those of the Entente. The German campaign in the East against the large but poorly equipped Russian armies had gone well, with a massive victory over the Russians at Gorlice-Tarnow in the summer of 1915. Following the success of this offensive the Germans again attempted to conclude a separate peace with Russia, but to no avail.

Turkey had joined the war on the side of the Central Powers in October 1914 and the Entente Powers had then got another bloody nose from the Turks at Gallipoli. Thanks to French insistence, they were also tying up hundreds of thousands of men in Salonika, while in East Africa, the German General von Lettow-Vorbeck was running rings around the British and South African forces and was to remain unsubdued until the end of the war. Then there were the battles in France, where the Entente had lost a great many men to no great purpose.

Most of the losses of 1915 were endured by the French and the Russians. The British Army was still not fully in the field, although it had suffered heavy casualties in several Western Front battles and would clearly become a major force in the near future. As for the Royal Navy, its activity was somewhat restricted by the watchful presence of German submarines and the Grand Fleet usually remained in port at Scapa Flow, though by doing so it tied up the German High Seas Fleet. This may have been useful but, by flatly refusing to introduce the convoy system, the admirals were providing plenty of merchant ships for destruction by German commerce raiders and U-boats. All in all, Germany could regard 1915 as a score draw, with good prospects for the offensives of 1916, if the right decisions were made on the strategic conduct of those offensives.

In his memoirs, General von Falkenhayn states that the German Army in the West would have to be satisfied with holding the ground it had won, while in the East, the successes, if substantial, had still not included the total destruction of the Russian Armies.[5]

Unlike the fighting on the Western Front, the war in the East was one of movement. Since May 1915, the German and Austrian forces had advanced over 300 miles, inflicted some two million casualties on the Russian forces and captured more than 3,000 guns; had this campaign been pressed to a close, as von Hindenburg and Ludendorff wanted, Russia could probably have been driven out of the war and Germany could then have turned her full might on the Western Allies. As it was, the German advance to a line 150 miles east of Warsaw was finally halted by the onset of winter and stubborn Russian resistance and, during the winter of 1915–1916, the Russians had had time to regroup. In December 1915, von Falkenhayn turned his attention to the Western Front where matters were more evenly balanced.

Von Falkenhayn made his appraisal of the prospects for the coming year in a report delivered to Kaiser Wilhelm at the end of December 1915. His survey began by blaming the failure to defeat the Entente in 1915 on a lack of support from the Austro-Hungarian forces, but concluded that the year had provided some solid gains, not least the new alliance with Bulgaria, the latest addition to the Central Powers, and the destruction of the army of Serbia. Von Falkenhayn then gave some consideration to leaving nine German divisions in Galicia (Poland), which would release some Austro-Hungarian divisions for an offensive against Italy, a former ally and the newest member of the Entente.

On the outbreak of war Italy had opted for neutrality. Then, on 24 May 1915, Italy declared war on Austria-Hungary, but not on Germany, which continued to trade with Italy via Switzerland. This abandonment of neutrality was motivated largely by an interest in the possible spoils, notably by taking the port of Trieste and the Trentino region from Austria, an aim hindered by the mountainous terrain in which such a campaign must be fought. Italy's campaign did not go well and it was soon realized that the Austrians could contain the Italians but not the Russians, for which help was needed from the German Army. Quite apart from the fact that Italy and Germany were not at war, von Falkenhayn saw any diversion of strength to help the Austrians as a misuse of resources. Though the German Imperial Staff had no great confidence in the military prowess of the Dual Monarchy – one German general stated that being allied to Austria-Hungary was 'like being chained to a corpse' – it was considered better to let the Austrians and Hungarians fight it out with the Italians and reserve German strength for the main theatres, the Eastern and Western Fronts. Other theatres needed watching, but von Falkenhayn had no doubt that the decisive field of battle in this war lay in the West. He stated as much in his Christmas report to the Kaiser which begins with a summary of the situation as he saw it:

> The Russian armies have not been completely overthrown but their offensive powers have been shattered . . . the Army of Serbia can be considered as destroyed, Italy would probably be only too glad to be able to liquidate her adventure in any way that would save her face . . . and France has been weakened almost to the limits of endurance both in a military and economic sense – the latter by the permanent loss of her coalfields.[6]

That left one major enemy, Great Britain, the arch-enemy, as the Kaiser and von Falkenhayn saw it, on the Western Front and one looming problem, the possible intervention of the United States of America if submarine warfare was pressed in the Atlantic. On Britain, or England, as the Germans were prone to call the United Kingdom, von Falkenhayn pointed out: 'We have indeed succeeded in shaking England; the best proof is her imminent adoption of universal military service. But that is also proof of the sacrifices England is prepared to make to attain her end . . . she is staking everything on a war of exhaustion. We have not been able to shatter her belief that it will bring Germany to her knees. What we have to do is dispel that illusion.'

Revealing the cunning schemes of the British always played well with the Kaiser, and von Falkenhayn stated: 'England's plan, which is daily becoming clearer, is to win the war with a combination of starvation and attrition.' Von Falkenhayn's memoirs were written in 1918 and this passage clearly benefits from hindsight: von Falkenhayn was the only general openly planning a campaign of attrition at the end of 1915, and his attempt to prove that he was not alone is not supported by the facts.

The way to dispel the illusion, said von Falkenhayn, was with a relentless campaign by land and sea, specifically by winning a major battle against the French on the Western Front and by loosing Germany's submarine fleet on the Merchant Navy and starving Britain out of the war. Von Falkenhayn therefore intended to concentrate on a campaign on the Western Front, since he believed that after Gornice-Turnow the Russian armies were in no state to renew the fight. Even so, he acknowledged that the German armies were faced with an extraordinarily difficult problem in bringing the British to battle on the Western Front.

This was partly because of the nature of the ground in the British sector of the Front. The terrain gave considerable advantage to the defence, and it was also judged impossible to muster enough divisions and concentrate them on one section of the Front for an attack leading to a massive breakthrough; the Germans had learned all about the difficulty of breaking the trench lines from watching the efforts of the French and British armies in 1915. To attack either in Flanders or north of the Somme – in other words on the British section of the front – said von Falkenhayn, would require an attacking force of at least 30 divisions and yet 'even if we collected a few more divisions from the German sectors in Macedonia and Galicia, the total reserve in France would not amount to more than 25 or 26 divisions. When all these are concentrated for the one operation all the other fronts are denuded of reserves to the last man.'

At the same time, when defining his aims for 1916, von Falkenhayn insisted that these must amount to nothing less than a resolve to drive the English from the Continent and force the French back behind the Somme. If these strategic objectives were not attained, the attack would have failed. And yet, even if the attack succeeded, von Falkenhayn continued: 'England may be trusted not to give up, and further, France herself would not have been very hard hit', and a second attack would be necessary. On balance, while the main opponent was Britain, it would not be advisable at this time to attack the British Armies directly. The main military blow for 1916 should therefore be struck against her ally, France.

There is a tendency in Great War studies to assume that Germany, a nation of 66 million people in 1914, had an unlimited supply of manpower. This was not the case. Certainly Germany had a demographic advantage over the French, who mustered 37 million people in 1914 and therefore needed assistance from the British Empire to maintain the war at all, but Germany was fighting on two fronts and against the combined armies of France and Britain along a 400-mile front line in France. To maintain this Front ate up vast quantities of troops and to mount a major attack in any one point, of a weight and width sufficient to ensure success, was beyond Germany's power, if she was at the same time to fight in the East and maintain a stout defence elsewhere. Germany did not have the means either to fight a war on two fronts or maintain a war over a protracted period. That was now the looming prospect, so the best option, as von Falkenhayn saw it, was to launch an attack so shattering that it would drive one of these nations out of the war. With hindsight this seems a tall order, but at the time it seemed possible.

Here was the crux of von Falkenhayn's problem. He had identified Britain as the main enemy, the prop of the Entente; knock that prop away and the Entente would collapse and Russia and Britain would leave the war. The problem was that the British front in France was too strong for a direct attack, an offensive strong enough to guarantee success. Therefore, von Falkenhayn continued: 'Her [Great Britain's] real weapons are the French, Russian and Italian armies.' The chief of these 'weapons' was the French Army, which must be destroyed but again, how?

Von Falkenhayn concluded that the strain on France had almost reached breaking point after the battles and losses of the last 16 months. Though he gave no reasons for reaching that opinion, it led him to his next point, that it was necessary to open the eyes of the French people to the fact that in the military sense they had nothing more to hope for. If that could be done, the breaking point would be reached, the French Army would collapse and 'England's best sword would be knocked out of her hand.'

This insight into the mind and thinking of a German general is most interesting, not least for the methodical way in which the path is gradually cleared through the options towards a logical, definite conclusion. This conclusion would be proved right or wrong, depending on the accuracy of the original premise, but von Falkenhayn had no doubts about the accuracy of his premise and went on inexorably to his next point, that a major offensive, with its inevitable heavy casualties, was probably beyond Germany's present strength. However, he continued, such an offensive was unnecessary if the right ground was chosen for the attack, ground where a shortage of men could be made up by an abundance of artillery. Like Field Marshal French, von Falkenhayn was placing his faith in the power of the guns but he intended to use them for an entirely different purpose, not to blast a breach in the enemy line, but to kill a massive number of enemy soldiers.

Von Falkenhayn was proposing to engage the French in a zero-sum game. If the French Army did not succeed in stemming the German onslaught and the German Army took its as yet undeclared objectives, the political and moral effect in France would be tremendous. If the French held these positions, they could only do so at a great cost in lives. Either way the French Army would sustain unacceptable losses. And the objectives that would provide these advantages to the German guns? 'The objectives of which I am speaking,' wrote von Falkenhayn, 'are Belfort and Verdun.' Of the two, he preferred Verdun, a city close to the Argonne forest, set on a narrow front astride the River Meuse. At that point in von Falkenhayn's report, the Kaiser's eyes must surely have turned to the map and whatever information he had on this French bastion.

The town of Verdun on the River Meuse in eastern France is neither large nor greatly noted for its architectural charm. For the French

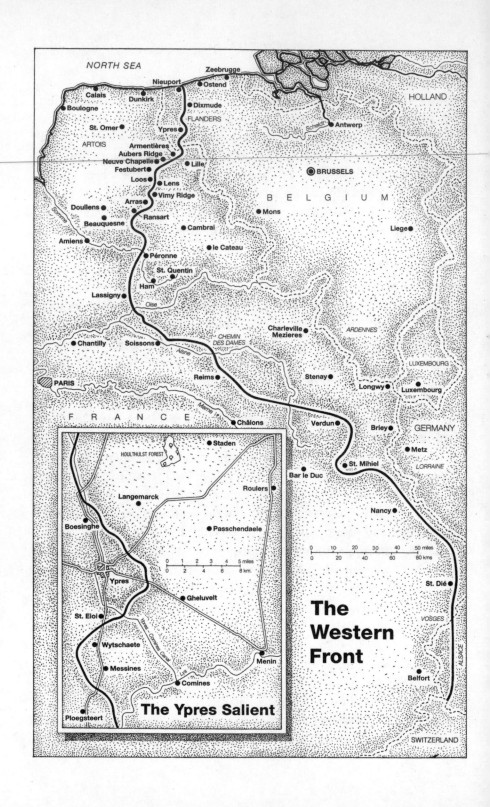

NORTH SEA

HOLLAND

Zeebrugge
Nieuport
Ostend
Calais
Dunkirk
Dixmude
Boulogne
FLANDERS
St. Omer
Ypres
Scheldt
Antwerp
ARTOIS
Armentières
Aubers Ridge
Neuve Chapelle
Lille
BRUSSELS
Festubert
Loos
Lens
BELGIUM
Vimy Ridge
Doullens
Arras
Mons
Liege
Beauquesne
Ransart
Amiens
Cambrai
Somme
le Cateau
Péronne
St. Quentin
Ham
Lassigny
Oise
Charleville
Mezieres
ARDENNES
Chantilly
Soissons
Aisne
LUXEMBOURG
PARIS
Reims
Stenay
Longwy
Luxembourg
F R A N C E
Marne
Châlons
Verdun
Briey
GERMANY
Metz
St. Mihiel
LORRAINE
Bar le Duc
Nancy

0   10   20   30   40   50 miles
0   20   40   60   80 kms

St. Dié

**The
Western
Front**

VOSGES

ALSACE

Belfort

SWITZERLAND

HOULTHULST FOREST
Staden
Langemarck
Roulers
Boesinghe
Passchendaele
0 1 2 3 4 5 miles
0   2   4   6   8 km.
Ypres
Gheluvelt
St. Eloi
Wytschaete
Menin
Messines
Comines
Lys
Ploegsteert

The Ypres Salient

people the attraction of Verdun lies in its history. It was at Verdun in AD 843, that Charles the Bald and Louis of Germany had divided the empire of Charlemagne and set up the kingdom of the Franks. It was at Verdun in the seventeenth century that Vauban had constructed one of his defensive citadels with which Louis XIV nailed shut the eastern frontier of France. It was at Verdun in 1792, during the Revolutionary War, that Danton had called for *'l'audace, l'audace et toujours l'audace'* as the qualities needed to save the French Republic. Whenever the Republic was at risk, Verdun was a pillar of strength. In the Franco-Prussian War of 1870–71 Verdun had been the last French fortress to surrender, and it was here, at Verdun in 1914, that the French Army had halted the direct German thrust on Paris. To the French people, Verdun was a symbol, not just a city.

In 1916, the front line lay a few miles north of the city, curving round in a massive salient astride the River Meuse, a salient created in 1914 when the German armies, avoiding Verdun's fortified positions in accordance with the Schlieffen Plan, directed most of their weight on to their right flank and swung north around the Argonne forests and into Belgium. After August 1914, Verdun, though only 80 miles from Paris, had departed from the headlines. That said, Verdun was, as von Falkenhayn predicted, a city the French would pay any price to hold, rather as Ypres had become a symbol for the Belgians and the British. Their soldiers had shed much blood to defend these places and they would not willingly give them up.

However, there were other, more practical reasons for the French belief, not only that Verdun should be held, but that it could be held, whatever the Germans sent against it. Verdun had been heavily fortified after 1871 and was protected by a string of fortresses, all linked by a trench system and supplied with heavy guns. These fortresses had already proved their worth in 1914 when the army of the Kaiser's heir, Crown Prince Wilhelm of Prussia, had battered against their walls without effect. What had been done once in this war could surely be done again.

Von Falkenhayn was not concerned with, or bothered by, the Verdun defences. Indeed, they formed part of his overall plan, which was not to take the city of Verdun but to destroy the French Army. A rapid collapse of French resistance in this sector would not achieve that end. Von Falkenhayn saw the Verdun forts, not as obstacles in his path, but as rocks for the French soldiers to cling to while his artillery battered them to pieces. But quite apart from those emotional and national arguments which would force the French to defend Verdun at all costs, there were some sound military reasons for mounting a German attack in this sector.

First of all, in a war in which success largely depended on artillery, it was useful that the French lines lay no more than 12 miles from the nearest German railhead. This put the railway beyond French artillery range but put the railhead close enough to the German artillery positions to ensure a constant supply of shells. Then there was the terrain itself. In 1916 the country around the Meuse valley was well wooded, providing cover for the assault infantry and the positioning of heavy guns before the attack, though in January and February, while the attack was being prepared, the trees were bare and concealment largely depended on the German Air Force keeping control of the skies. Finally, the front here was narrow and divided by the River Meuse, which thereby created an area on either bank where the French forces must concentrate. By so doing they would provide a ready and vulnerable target for the German guns. Von Falkenhayn's battle at Verdun would be an artillery battle, a mincing machine for the French infantry. These tactical and terrain considerations also applied to the sector around Belfort, but von Falkenhayn had already made his decision. Historic and emotional reasons tilted the scales, and his preference was for Verdun.

Von Falkenhayn's plan did not depend entirely on a successful battle of attrition at Verdun. He had his eye on wider, strategic considerations and, to supplement the Verdun offensive, he proposed an intensification of the German submarine campaign against British shipping. 'We should ruthlessly employ every weapon that is suitable for striking against England on her home ground,' he wrote. 'Such weapons are the submarine war and the conclusion of a political and economic union between Germany and not her allies only, but all states which are not yet under England's spell.' This latter thought looked back to the nineteenth-century Zollverein, or Customs Union, which had started the Prussian domination of the German States before 1870, and forward to the hoped-for war aim of Mitteleurope, by which Germany would dominate Central Europe politically and economically, and even to the European Federation now planned for the twenty-first century.

Von Falkenhayn was proposing total war on Britain by sea and land, not just another battle against one of the Entente armies in the west. In coming to this conclusion, he was introducing a strategic element into a war in which such wide visions had previously been conspicuous by their absence. Von Falkenhayn was also echoing the views of von Tirpitz, Chief of the Naval Staff, and the other German naval commanders – that if the Kaiser and von Bethmann-Hollweg stopped prevaricating and gave the admirals their head, a campaign of unrestricted submarine warfare would drive Britain out of the war in 1916. This offered Germany the possibility of victory by land or by sea, or by a combination of both; it is hardly surprising that the Kaiser accepted von Falkenhayn's plan with enthusiasm.

One of von Falkenhayn's principal personal characteristics was his love of secrecy and, while a commander is usually wise to be close-mouthed on his intentions, there are limits to this policy. Before Verdun, von Falkenhayn not only concealed the preparations for this major offensive from his fellow Commander-in-Chief, the head of the Austrian Armies, Conrad von Hötzendorf, he also concealed the offensive's aim from the commander of the force tasked with making the attack, Crown Prince Wilhelm of the Fifth Army. As a result, the Crown Prince and his Chief-of-Staff, General Schmidt von Knobelsdorf, believed their task was to capture Verdun by a *coup de main* and laid their plans accordingly. In fact, as von Falkenhayn informed the Kaiser: 'It is immaterial whether we reach our goal. The main objective is to bleed the French Army to death [*Blutabzapfung*].'

Von Falkenhayn was a typical *Junker* but he was also a professional Prussian soldier and he was not a fool. He was well aware that this offensive, indeed any offensive in this war, carried considerable risks to the attacking force, and he covers this point carefully in his memoirs: 'Our precise problem is how to inflict heavy casualties on the enemy at relatively little cost to ourselves. But we must not overlook the fact that previous experience of mass attack in this war offers little inducement to imitate them. It would almost seem as if the problems of command and supply in these attacks was insoluble.' Later in his book, he claims that the loss of two Germans for five Frenchmen was a reasonable ratio – an estimate that fell far short of what actually happened.[7]

In these post-war memoirs, von Falkenhayn later admitted, or at least claimed, that he never actually intended to capture the city of Verdun. Indeed his orders to Fifth Army call only for an offensive 'in the direction of Verdun', but it is hard to see how he could hope to engage the French Army in a battle of attrition unless he mounted a serious threat to their most famous bastion; vague feints 'in the direction of Verdun' would not do it.

If all went well following the Crown Prince's first assault and Verdun was seriously threatened, the French leaders, obsessed with the need to defend the city, would commit more and more troops, and keep on committing them regardless of casualties, and von Falkenhayn's primary aim would be achieved. From the destruction of the French Army before Verdun much might follow, not least the collapse of French political will, which was already creaking after the losses of 1915. Here again we see the strategic element: the aim of the Verdun offensive was arguably far wider than a simple battle of attrition (*Ermatungstratagie*), for the destruction of 'England's best weapon', the French Army, might also lead to the collapse of France.

It would be a mistake to regard the Battle of Verdun in isolation or forget that its primary aim, albeit at second hand, was to attack Britain. Battles like this do not take place in isolation. Even if they do not form part of any deliberate strategic plan they must be related to actions on other fronts, which they must surely affect, and they are, or should be, part of an overall strategy for total victory. To that end, all efforts were in part directed, and the most hopeful contributor to the overall strategy focused on Verdun was submarine warfare around the coast of the United Kingdom.

Britain is an island. While that encircling moat has enabled the British to survive defeats and disasters that have overcome other nations, it presented the British Government with an ongoing problem during the Great War. With a population too large for Britain's internal agricultural resources, how were the people of Britain to be fed in the event of a blockade? The one sure way to prevent a blockade was the existence of a Navy powerful and skilled enough to drive off any blockading vessels from any two other nations, and the Royal Navy had been constructed to that 'two-nation' size and standard. This faith in the Royal Navy to keep the sea lanes open had worked during the Napoleonic Wars and seemed firmly in place at the start of the Great War, when the Royal Navy ushered the BEF to France without losing a single man. That honeymoon did not last, for a new weapon, the submarine, soon intervened in this increasingly technological war and put Britain's survival at risk.

France could feed itself, so the submarine campaign, to be launched at the same time as the race to Verdun, was largely aimed at the British, as was the aerial bombing. Attacking British civilians and British industry with Zeppelins and bomber aircraft and starving the British into surrender by submarine warfare were all part of the German war plan; the Great War in the West was not fought only in the trenches.

Germany justified this extension of the war at sea by references to the effects of the British naval blockade, alleging that Britain was waging 'a war of starvation which had been inflicted on the non-combatant population of Germany, including old men, women and children, by the British declaration of the North Sea as a war zone'.[8] Von Falkenhayn added that 'the submarine war is a weapon in itself.'

The weakness with this second part of von Falkenhayn's strategy was a political one: the attitude of the United States, whose reaction to the sinking of the *Lusitania* in 1915 had caused the suspension of the first U-boat campaign. The Germans had anyway intended to reintroduce unrestricted submarine warfare in February 1916 but, in January, von Bethmann-Hollweg demanded a delay until April for further negotiations with the United States Government, so that the use of submarines be carefully presented in a way that satisfied President Woodrow Wilson. This delay provoked a row between the Chancellor, the admirals and General von Falkenhayn. On 1 January 1916, Admiral von Tirpitz had stated categorically that if unrestricted submarine warfare began in February, Britain would have to surrender within two months. This delay in pitting his U-boats against the Merchant Navy infuriated him.

Von Bethmann-Hollweg's worries were political and deep-seated; he was being invited to gamble with the future of his country for, according to the admirals, even if the introduction of unrestricted submarine warfare brought the USA into the war on the side of the Entente, Britain could be starved into surrender before the USA could intervene or, if it did, the U-boats could sink the transports bringing American troops to France. This calculation on what the U-boats could do was seen by the chancellor as a very high-risk gamble indeed and he had no hesitation in urging the Kaiser to reject it.

The delay was not directly opposed by the Chief of the Naval Staff, Admiral Holtzendorff, who thought that starving Britain to her knees would actually take four months, because he believed that the delay in opening the submarine offensive until the spring would be more than compensated for by the greater number of U-boats which would by then have entered service. Therefore, the current limits on submarine activities, which restricted attacks without warning to armed enemy vessels, could still apply. Under these terms submarine warfare, but only against armed enemy shipping, was resumed on 29 February 1916, one week after the battle opened at Verdun.

The argument over submarine warfare presented the German High Command with a classic dilemma. On the one hand, unrestricted submarine warfare might bring Britain to her knees; on the other hand, it might bring America into the war – although this was by no means certain. The United States was strongly neutral and isolationist and it was arguable that accidental sinkings of American vessels would not cause her to enter the war, where far higher losses in manpower were inevitable.

On the other hand, perhaps it would be better for Germany to assume the worst-case scenario: that if Germany introduced unrestricted submarine warfare, the United States would enter the war. This being so, could the Imperial Navy drive Britain out of the war before the United States could intervene in any substantial way? Given this situation, von Bethmann-Hollweg was more than a little interested in the political aspects of the assault on Verdun. If it succeeded, if France dropped out of the war and the British, now isolated, saw the need to sue for peace, then there would be no need to attack neutral shipping and risk the intervention of the United States. In this way, the strategic nature of the battle, as proposed by von Falkenhayn, was subtly changed; the generals and admirals wanted a two-part, simultaneous offensive, by sea and land. The politicians preferred to see if the land campaign worked before launching the politically far more risky submarine campaign.

Any account of the battle at Verdun, or indeed of any battle, should begin with a description of the ground. At Verdun this is complicated by the fact that the battle eventually took place on both banks of the Meuse, the river that flows through Verdun, out to the north and into Belgium. Descriptions of the fighting and German thrusts at Verdun refer constantly to positions on the 'right' or 'left' bank of the Meuse; this is taken from the direction of flow, to the north in this case, so the 'right' bank lies to the east and the 'left' bank to the west. Confusion can arise because descriptions of the German attack, coming from the north, would seem to reverse these positions, so a careful study of the map on page 136 will be useful at this point.

The battlefield at Verdun is not large and centres on the city of Verdun itself. This lies to the south of the battlefield and is divided by the Meuse, which is around 50 metres wide as it flows through the city. North of Verdun the river meanders somewhat and the valley widens, with wooded hills on the right bank and higher, rather more open country on the left bank, where the prominent features are two hills or ridges known as the Mort Homme and Côte 304. The significant fact about the left bank is that it overlooks the ground on the right bank, though the defences on both banks were designed for mutual support.

In 1916 the right bank had entrenchments, dugouts, plenty of barbed wire, deep concrete blockhouses, and a double ring of fortresses, 60 in all, of various sizes, most of them on hilltop positions dominating the surrounding countryside. This is rolling and well wooded, with plenty of dead ground in which small bodies of troops could move unobserved. The Verdun terrain was, in short, ideal for infiltration but a death trap for soldiers caught in the open by plunging artillery fire. Each fort was sited to offer an interlocking field of fire over the neighbouring forts and the ground in between. The highest of all, at 1,300 feet and dominating the entire battlefield, was Fort Douaumont.

Each fort contained an infantry garrison ranging in size from 30 to 300 men and their concrete casements were equipped with a variety of machine-guns and artillery, some of the guns set under steel hoods or carapaces, rather like tortoises, and some of them retractable. The roofs of these fortresses were up to eight feet thick and the reinforced concrete was covered with a further dense layer of well-turfed soil. Around the forts ringing Verdun was a further ring of trenches and emplacements, more than two miles deep in places. When all these factors are taken into account it seems to put von Falkenhayn's reasoning at a discount; surely, any army attacking this immensely strong position was certain to get a bloody nose?

Alas, no. One of the lessons of the Great War is that a military campaign has few absolutes. Nothing is exactly what it seems, and so it was here. The stout defences of Verdun were largely an illusion, for in 1916 the great concrete fortresses were neither strongly garrisoned nor adequately equipped with guns. And the cause of that situation can be laid at the door of the *generalissimo*, General Joffre, the engineer who did not believe in fortresses. Recent experiences tended to prove him right. When the German armies swarmed into Belgium in 1914 they faced, here and there, forts and defences that rivalled Verdun, most notably at Liège. These Belgian forts had been built to buy time and deter invasion but the Germans had anticipated this long before the war and, when the garrisons of these Belgian forts declined to surrender, the Germans promptly wheeled up massive 420 mm and 380 mm howitzers, whose plunging shellfire shattered the Belgian defences in a matter of days. This artillery then moved on to do equally dreadful work on a bastion of the French line at Manonviller. The rapid reduction of these forts was a great shock to the French command and a seeming endorsement of the Grandmaison doctrine that defensive positions and tactics were a waste of time, that the only answer to an attack was to counterattack or, better still, to attack first. The word spread that these forts were nothing better than man-traps, places where the troops could be penned up, surrounded and then battered into surrender.

Military men sometimes see only what they want to see and ignore facts that dispute their views, and so it was here. The defences at Verdun held the Germans off in 1914 and were still acting as a deterrent 18 months later but by that time they were largely a sham. The French Army entered the war with a great shortage of heavy artillery and, by early 1915, there seemed no reason to keep a large number of heavy 155 mm guns at Verdun when they might be more usefully employed supporting attacks on other parts of the Front. So, slowly and secretly, the fortifications of Verdun were dismantled. This secret was kept from the enemy but it was also kept from most of the French commanders.

By the time the Crown Prince launched his offensive in February 1916, the Verdun forts only retained those guns that were in fixed positions and could not be removed; more than 80 per cent of their artillery had been taken away. No attempts were made to replace it, even in the New Year of 1916, when rumours began to circulate from neutral countries, and from French spies on the Berlin cocktail circuit, that the Germans were planning a massive strike against the city of Verdun.

German preparations for the attack – the movement of guns, the establishment of ammunition dumps, the construction of concrete dugouts (*Stollen*) to protect the infantry before the attack – should also have been visible to reconnaissance aircraft, since the trees were currently leafless, but at this time the French did not have air superiority over the Western Front. The Fokker, with its forward-firing machine-guns, currently dominated the skies and, with the assistance of poor weather, managed to keep the Crown Prince's preparations from prying eyes. The few aerial photographs that were taken revealed a number of artillery positions but showed that the Germans had not dug any forming-up trenches, places where the infantry would normally be assembled for the attack, along their front line. This reinforced GQG's view that no attack was pending, though the absence of these trenches simply indicated that the German infantry were planning a new kind of attack.

Von Falkenhayn reinforced the Fifth Army for this offensive. By early February, the Crown Prince's force mustered five Army Corps, III, V (Reserve), VII (Reserve), XV and XVIII, which together had nine divisions in the front line and more in reserve. Eight of these divisions would spearhead the attack on the French line and this attack would go in without the usual days of prior bombardment. Surprise was considered more important than days of wire-cutting, but the German infantry were to have a more than adequate amount of artillery support. The theory was that weight of shot would replace length of bombardment, with the narrow French front on the right bank suffering nine hours of constant shelling from 1,200 guns before the attack went in.

In mounting this attack, von Falkenhayn introduced a number of new tactics. Instead of attacking at dawn, he was attacking at dusk, and instead of sending in lines of infantry, his attack would be spearheaded by small parties of men acting as scouts, or infiltrators, followed by fighting patrols in platoon strength (30 men), to seek out and destroy any French machine-guns and strongpoints that the artillery barrage had failed to knock out; only then would the main body of assault infantry go in, swamping the French line.

Von Falkenhayn was also flying in the face of established doctrine by attacking on such a narrow front, a mere eight miles on the right bank of the Meuse. As stated, Western Front doctrine currently held that an attack on a narrow front might achieve some initial penetration, given surprise and sufficient artillery support, but before the reserves could come forward, over the dead and wounded and the shell-torn ground, the defenders would be able to seal the breach off, or stem the advance and bring those inside the existing salient under heavy fire from three sides. Narrow-front attacks had been tried again and again in 1915 – narrow only because of a shortage of artillery – but all had failed miserably.

For all these reasons, Joffre, Haig and most other generals favoured a wide-front attack. So did Crown Prince Wilhelm and his Chief-of-Staff, General Schmidt von Knobelsdorf, who were both currently under the impression that the task of Fifth Army was to capture Verdun. They had proposed an attack on a wide front of at least 20 miles and on either side of the Meuse, but von Falkenhayn had ordered an attack on a narrow front and on the right bank only and this attack was not supposed to take Verdun. Its purpose was to serve as bait for the French Army and lure it within reach of Fifth Army's artillery.

To oppose Fifth Army's thrust the French could only muster a single corps, XXX, which had three divisions of varying quality, very little of it first class. The exception was two battalions of Chasseurs, commanded by Lt-Colonel Émile Driant, units which occupied a front-line position in the Bois des Caures at the tip of the Verdun salient where they would bear the first brunt of the German assault. With the Verdun forts denuded of artillery, the defenders had some 270 guns of various calibre, most of them small, all of them short of ammunition. The officer directly responsible for the defence of Verdun was General Herr, the Governor of Verdun, an elderly gunner officer who took up his post in the autumn of 1915 and soon discovered that the Verdun position was almost untenable.

Herr's predecessor, General Coutanceau, had been sacked in August 1915 for protesting about the stripping of the Verdun defences, and Herr's attempts to restore the situation were fraught with equal difficulty. He lacked troops to man the forward positions and pioneers to dig trenches; every time he asked GQG for more artillery, a party of sappers would arrive and remove more of those guns he still had. Again believing what they wanted to believe, GQG assured Herr that Verdun would not be attacked because the Germans did not know it was virtually defenceless. This was true but, as we have seen, the supposedly strong defences of Verdun were part of the attraction for General von Falkenhayn. Defenceless or not, the French would still try to defend the city and the surrounding forts, and their lack of prior preparation and the dismantling of the pre-war batteries would simply lead to higher losses. Abandoning these positions was not an option.

Herr's complaints eventually reached the ear of General Joffre, where they were duly ignored, but Joffre was not able to ignore the protests of that redoubtable officer now serving at Verdun, Lt-Colonel Émile Driant of the Chasseurs. Apart from being an infantry colonel and a serving officer, Émile Driant was a politician, the Deputy for the city of Nancy. Colonel Driant and his men had been at Verdun since the autumn of 1914, holding a section of the line to the north of the city in the Bois des Caures. They had spent the last weeks listening to the sounds of trains bringing men and shells up behind the German line and watching the steady crumbling of the positions to their rear. Driant was in no doubt that an attack was coming and was well aware that Verdun was in no state to withstand it.

None of this was new. In the summer of 1915 Driant had written a letter outlining the situation at Verdun and stating that, in his not-inexperienced opinion, if the city was attacked, it could not be held. Weeks passed without reply, but this letter eventually landed on the desk of the Minister for War, General Galliéni, another officer-politician and no fan of General Joffre. Galliéni sent a delegation to study the defences of Verdun; it confirmed that the situation there was every bit as bad as Driant had stated and Galliéni sent the report to Joffre, asking what he proposed to do about it.

Joffre did nothing. His main reaction to the report was to start a witch-hunt against Colonel Driant, a hunt which, but for the opening of von Falkenhayn's offensive, would have taken Driant before a court martial for, as Joffre wrote to Driant: 'Bringing before the Government, by channels other than the hierarchic channel, complaints or protests concerning the execution of my orders . . . action calculated to disturb profoundly the spirit of the Army . . . nothing justifies the fear which, in the name of the Government, you express in your despatch.'

This letter was penned in December 1915 and very little was done to improve the defences of Verdun in the two months before Fifth Army opened its attack. In that time the German Army made a massive logistical effort to ensure the attack's success. On 12 January, more than 200 ammunition trains began hauling shells up to the railhead, from where they were transported to great dumps hidden in the woods, close to the artillery batteries. By 1 February there were some 1,500 guns of various calibre dug into the woods around Verdun and by the time the battle opened some 3,000,000 shells were lying under the trees, with more at the railhead, the shell dumps being constantly replenished or expanded by ammunition trains. To protect the infantry and stormtroopers, German pioneers had constructed more than one hundred massive concrete waiting rooms (*Stollen*), bunkers half-buried in the ground, roofed with reinforced concrete, covered with grass and branches and soon hidden under the snow.

Building the *Stollen*, moving up the shell supplies, digging the gun positions, all the various steps needed to mount this massive attack on Verdun, took just six weeks. This is a marvel of organization and staff work, especially when compared with the British attack on the Somme, which took seven months to prepare and could have taken longer had it not been for the pressure exerted on Haig by Joffre. The Verdun attack was all ready to go on the morning of 12 February. Then on the night of 12–13 February, it began to snow and by dawn a thick white blanket masked the hills. This in itself was not a problem, but the snow was accompanied by a thick mist and blizzard conditions, which might have given useful cover to the advancing infantry but reduced the activities of the German artillery observers flying over-head and spotting for the guns.

This change in the weather presented the German commanders with a difficult decision. The infantry were already in their forward positions and set to advance; leaving them there for days, in the freezing cold and damp, would not improve their health or fitness, but artillery support, in plentiful supply and precisely delivered, was the most important factor in any Western Front attack. So the offensive was put back, and then back again, for nine days. Day after day the snow fell, and the temperature fell with it, freezing the French infantry in their half-constructed dugouts and crumbling trenches, inhibiting the forward movement of ammunition and supplies, while the German stormtroopers tasked with the first assault waited in their dank and chilly *Stollen*, which soon became knee-deep with icy water. Finally, on the morning of 21 February, the skies cleared, the guns lifted their iron snouts into the air and, at 0700 hrs, the first shells began to blast the French positions around Verdun.

Those shells marked the opening of the 1916 campaign on the Western Front but they marked something else as well. They mark the point at which this war changed, at which all possibilities of a negotiated peace and all the harsh lessons of the previous year and a half were abandoned, first by the Germans, then by the French and finally, sometime during the Battle of the Somme, even by the British.

From now on only victory counted. All other attempts at finding peace were put aside until one side obtained a clear victory over the other. Perhaps that course of action was inevitable in this new kind of war but before we follow the events of this battle at Verdun and the Battle of the Somme which followed it, it is necessary to look at why this war was so different from all previous wars and why it proved impossible to stop it.

Notes

1 *The First World War, Germany and Austria–Hungary, 1914–1918,* Holgar Herwig, p. 271.

2 See *General Headquarters 1914–1916 and Its Critical Decisions*, p. 4.

3 Ibid., p. 44.

4 Quoted in Guinn, *British Strategy and Politics*, p. 49.

5 *General Headquarters 1914–1916 and Its Critical Decisions*, p. 193.

6 Ibid., p. 209.

7 Ibid., p. 237.

8 Ibid., p. 69.

4

Towards Total War

1914—1916

'The political object of war can be of two kinds; either
totally to destroy the adversary, to eliminate his existence
as a state, or else to prescribe peace terms to him.'
Karl von Clausewitz, *On War*, 1804

There is a tendency for books on the Great War to concentrate on the
campaigns, the battles and the suffering of the men at the Front. This
is understandable, for the campaigns were always costly, the battles
were frequently catastrophic and the sufferings of the troops quite
appalling. However, in discussing what happened at the Front, many
commentators have overlooked the reasons why it happened, and
what was happening elsewhere.

These aspects of the conflict also deserve consideration, if only to
put the front-line fighting in context. This chapter will therefore
consider some other, wider issues – the rising importance of air power,
the effect of submarine warfare, naval blockade, starvation, political
reaction in the USA, the problems of military doctrine and much
more. All these factors affected the outcome of the conflict in various

ways and therefore deserve analysis. That analysis must begin with the recognition that while the Great War differed from previous wars in many ways, two factors in particular stand out.

Firstly, this was a technological war, involving equipment that was either in its infancy or had not even been invented when the war began. It can be argued that it is impossible to understand fully the complexity of the Great War without some knowledge of the military technology used to fight it. Secondly, it has to be appreciated that the conflict that began with a political assassination in the summer of 1914, and was supposed to be over by Christmas, escalated from Bismarck's 'small affair in the Balkans' into a 'total war'.

This total war was fought in three dimensions, land, sea and air, and spread quickly over large areas of the world. Total war is war without limits; it involves political, economic and social conflicts, a constant battle for the supply of vital war materials – steel, coal, tungsten, even food – and is the kind of war that bears down hard on civilians.

The Great War was a war between states, not just between armies and it was not the kind of war the politicians or the public had in mind when they entered it in 1914. They had imagined a short campaign on the lines of the Franco-Prussian War, one followed by a peace conference and some territorial adjustments. What they got was a war that destroyed empires and shook the existing world order to its foundations.

When the drums beat and the bugles blew in 1914, it is fair to say that very few people on either side, political, military or civilian, realized exactly what sort of war they were getting themselves into. By December 1915 they had been provided with ample opportunities to find out, for the 'butcher's bill' from the Western Front alone was staggering.

To get a grip on the nature of this war it is necessary to think widely. It could be argued that the fighting on the Eastern Front, between Germany, Austria and Tsarist Russia, was equally important and that the tendency to concentrate on the Western Front, then and now, is a mistake. The Eastern Front certainly saw more swings in fortune and much greater movement as one side or the other fell back or forged ahead. As Holgar Herwig points out, the Eastern Front featured a classic war of movement on a grand scale, ranging from the Masurian Lakes in the north to the Carpathian mountains and Serbia in the south, while the Western Front remained stagnated in a deadly killing ground.[1] On the Western Front, gains of a few hundred yards were celebrated as victories; in the East, advances were counted in hundreds of miles. Failing to exploit these gains, failing to recognize the potential for victory in the East, was a military and political mistake.

In 1914, the Germans, after some initial reverses, had obtained the advantage in the East, culminating in the victory at Tannenberg. During 1915, when they left much of the fighting to the Austro-Hungarians, the advantage at first went to Russia but in August Germany won the battle of Gorlice-Tarnow after a summer-long campaign which cost Russia 151,000 soldiers killed, 683,000 wounded and no less than 895,000 taken prisoner-of-war. It was this victory, and the resulting belief that Russia would not be able to come forward again for some time, that encouraged von Falkenhayn and the German High Command to turn their attention to the Western Front, where the Allied options and room to manoeuvre were more limited.

Whether the German Supreme Command were entirely wise to give the Russians this breathing space is debatable, but the Great War was a *world* war. It was fought in the Balkans, in Arabia and Mesopotamia, in various parts of Africa, in Turkey and Italy, Poland and Russia as well as in Western Europe. But for most of the conflict the various national armies fought what amounted to private wars and, in the West, they used a great range of new weaponry, much of it created by the nineteenth-century industrial revolution.

This revolution had created an industry capable of designing and producing a range of conventional armaments far more destructive than those produced at any previous period in history, plus many weapons which were entirely new. Aircraft, poison gas, flame-throwers, machine-guns, submarines and tanks, all either came into use or became fully effective for the first time during the Great War. It was this battle, the struggle of flesh and blood against industrial technology, that caused most of the casualties at the Front.

The application of science and technology to military might also enabled the politicians and their commanders to move the battle off the battlefield. Before 1914, civilian populations, which lived far from the battlefield or kept away from the path of armies, had thought themselves safe. They lost their menfolk, certainly, but the day-to-day horrors of war were largely confined to the soldiers at the front. This illusion of civilian security was quickly shattered after 1914. The new technology was deployed to increase the killing, both on the battle-field and behind the lines.

The most immediate demonstration of this aspect of military technology was provided by aircraft. The first heavier-than-air flying machine was flown by the Wright Brothers in 1903. In 1909, Louis Blériot flew across the English Channel, a brief, 20-mile flight that sent a shiver of apprehension through the more thoughtful British politicians and military men, for that wide moat which had protected Britain for a thousand years, seemed suddenly vulnerable. Some nations quickly realized that the aeroplane had military possibilities: in the year of Blériot's exploit, Germany allocated the then substantial sum of DM100,000 for military aviation. Much of this money went on airships, which had been in existence for several decades. Airships seemed to offer greater potential for development than the fragile, heavier-than-air flying machines and before the Great War some of the best military minds either failed to recognize the potential of the flying machine or dismissed this new invention out of hand.

General Foch, then Chief of the École Supérieure de la Guerre, thought that the aeroplane was 'good for sport but not for war'. In 1911, the Chief of the Imperial General Staff, General W.G. Nicolson, stated that 'Aircraft are a useless and expensive fad, advocated by a few individuals whose ideas are unworthy of attention.' On the other hand, the Italians, who took an early lead in adapting new technology to war, used nine bombers in Libya during their war with the Turks in 1912. In that year, the British Army formed the Royal Flying Corps (RFC), which came into existence by Royal Warrant on 13 April.

This move did not represent any sudden appreciation of aircraft potential on the part of the War Office; Army officers wishing to become pilots had to pay for their own lessons and a pilot's licence cost £75, though this was refunded if the officer managed to survive the course and was accepted into the RFC. The British Army therefore had the RFC and a core of pilots, mechanics, aircraft and balloon detachments before the war began, but full recognition of aircraft capabilities in war had still not struck the High Command in August 1914, by which time the RFC could muster 113 machines of various types.

Fortunately, once the RFC started to operate in France, the generals soon found that aircraft could be very useful indeed, especially for reconnaissance. RFC aircraft were soon a familiar sight, droning over the battlefields of France. As their role developed, RFC aircraft were used for 'scouting' (fighting other aircraft), reconnaissance, artillery spotting and, before long, bombing. The aircraft were fragile, their engines unreliable, and air tactics had yet to be developed, but under the pressure of war change and progress were rapid. It was soon realized that military aviation offered much more than an increase in the range of firepower or a replacement for the reconnaissance role previously held by the cavalry. Air power offered the possibility of removing war from the battlefield entirely and bringing pressure to bear on areas and targets far from the battlefield and beyond the range of guns – on arms dumps, railway lines, munitions factories   even on civilians.

The first bombing raids on civilian targets were carried out by German Zeppelin airships, which dropped bombs on the east coast of England in January 1915 and killed or injured 20 people, most of them civilians. These Zeppelin raids were to continue, but two years later the Germans deployed the long-range Gotha bomber, which operated from bases in Belgium and first appeared over Britain on 25 May 1917. The Gotha was a formidable machine capable of carrying a 500-kilo (1,100 lb) bomb. The first Gotha raid was on Folkestone, a port through which troops were shipped to France; 300 people were killed or injured in this raid, only 116 of them soldiers.

Tactically, the Folkestone raid achieved nothing and the trooping ferries continued to cross to France but the bombers soon extended their range and choice of targets. In 1915, Zeppelins were attacking targets in the coastal towns and London. Air attacks on Britain by Zeppelins and Gotha bombers continued until almost the end of the war and in that time bombing killed or injured some 2,000 people. Only a third of the victims were connected in any way with military operations and the effect of these raids on industrial production or civilian morale was negligible; it would take another war to reveal the awesome potential of the strategic bomber.

Over the battlefields of France it was another matter. Aircraft were soon playing a useful tactical role in support of the ground forces, one limited only by the current state of aviation technology, which improved rapidly as the war progressed. In 1914, for example, the fastest German aircraft had a top speed of 80 mph. In 1916, 14 months later, every German aircraft type was faster than this and the Fokker E3 Scout could cruise at 95 mph. The 1916 French Morane was even faster, at 102 mph; the Nieuport 13 could manage 105 mph; while the British Vickers FB 12c fighter had a top speed of no less than 130 mph. These later aircraft were also more mechanically reliable and carried more armament than their 1914 predecessors.

The tactical use of aircraft in support of army operations took very little time to begin but some time to develop. The main reason for the delay was a lack of suitable technology; the early machines simply could not deliver what the air power disciples visualized as the true potential of air power until the air battles over the Somme in 1916.

By that time the RFC Commander in France, Major-General Hugh Trenchard, who had been appointed GOC, Royal Flying Corps, in August 1915, had 27 front-line squadrons, mustering over 400 aircraft. This compares with the 12 assorted RFC squadrons available for the battle of Loos in September 1915. Nor was the improvement confined to numbers; the aircraft of 1916 were better designed and more strongly built than all previous machines, and the DH 2, FE2b and Sopwith 'one and a half-strutter' were able to match, if not overcome, the newer German machines like the Fokker monoplane, which dominated the skies over France from mid-1915 until the spring of 1916.

Technology only becomes truly effective when it is matched with efficient organization and, since 1914, there had been a large number of organizational and operational changes in the RFC. In 1914 all RFC squadrons, whatever their role, used the same aircraft for bombing, reconnaissance or scouting, and a squadron might contain a range of different aircraft types; it all depended on what types were available, with the squadron commander and the senior pilots getting the best aircraft. By 1916, however, a squadron usually had aircraft of the same type, which greatly reduced the problems of spare parts, maintenance and training.

The squadron also had distinct roles, as fighter (scout) squadrons, artillery-spotting squadrons, which also supported the front-line infantry in battle by flying 'contact patrols', or bomber squadrons. The first true British 'fighter', or scout, squadron was No. 24, flying de Havilland DH 2s, which arrived in France in February 1916; from then on, air power developed at an ever-increasing rate.

Many of these rapid changes and improvements in aviation technology arose from the experience gained in months of hard, unrewarding work over the front lines. Aircraft were seen by the Army commanders as very useful, not least in taking over the reconnaissance role of cavalry after the development of the trench system made horse patrols impossible. From this role other tasks developed: aerial photography of the enemy defences, air patrols searching for enemy troop movements and, most significantly, the use of aircraft equipped with wireless telegraphy (WT) to control artillery fire or spot for counter-battery work.

All these tasks became RFC functions and they all had one fundamental aim: to improve the killing power of new weaponry. By 1916 the various air forces had become effective parts of their national military establishments and were to play a large part in the war, though air superiority depended far more on technical performance than on the number of machines an air force could put into the air. As in so many other aspects of this war, air power depended on technology.

The early aircraft were fairly primitive flying machines and very few of them were apt for war. The first machines were not designed to carry machine-guns or drop bombs, and steps to equip the aircraft for combat often arose from private enterprise, either by the squadron mechanics or from individual pilots. In 1915, a French pilot, Roland Garros, greatly improved the killing power of fighters when he found a way of accurately directing machine-gun fire at an enemy aircraft. Up to that time, aerial combat had consisted of the aircrew engaging each other with pistols, rifles or cockpit-mounted Lewis guns, but the need to 'aim-off' to allow for the speed of the machines as they passed made even machine-gun fire very inaccurate. The way to solve that problem was by pointing a pair of machine-guns forward and then aiming the aircraft at the enemy – but forward-firing guns could shoot off the aircraft's propeller. Garros tackled this problem by fitting his propeller with a shield of metal plates, and then promptly shot down five German machines inside two weeks.

Unfortunately, on 19 April 1915, Garros was brought down by engine failure behind the German lines. Although he tried to destroy his machine his invention was soon in the hands of the inventive Dutchman Anthony Fokker, an aviation genius who was currently working for the Germans. Fokker taught himself to fly in 1911 when he was 21 and, in 1912, foreseeing the potential for military aircraft, set up a factory in Germany and began producing fighters. This was a wise move: when war came the Netherlands remained neutral, while Fokker's German factory went on to produce no less than 40 different types of aircraft, most of them biplanes, for the German Air Force.

Fokker took Garros's invention back to his factory and was preparing to put it into mass production when he was introduced to a far better device invented by a Swiss engineer, Franz Schneider. This was an 'interrupter gear', a device which synchronized the gun mechanism with the engine revolutions and stopped the weapon firing when the whirling propeller blades were in line with the muzzle. This device, far superior to Garros's invention, was in a matter of days being fitted to German fighters in the front-line squadrons.

Largely thanks to Anthony Fokker's aircraft and the forward-firing machine-gun, by the end of 1915, German pilots had the upper hand on the Western Front and, for a while, the Franco-British machines, the BE2c, Gun Bus and Morane Parasol were widely regarded as 'Fokker fodder'. Losses mounted steadily and, by the spring of 1916, the RFC and the French Air Force were in serious trouble. But then new types turned the air war in the Allies' favour, and by the time the Somme battle opened the British and French had a three-to-one superiority in numbers – 386 aircraft to the German 129. Air superiority was now seen as essential and the battle to control the skies went on continuously, both in the air and in the engineering workshops, as one side or the other came up with better machines or new tactics.

The ability to fire guns directly at enemy aircraft had other effects. It led to the introduction of the single-seater fighter, making the air-gunner role superfluous, at least in scouting aircraft. This changed the status of the pilot; before this time the pilot had been the 'driver', whose main task was to get the machine into a position from which his passenger, the 'observer', could engage the enemy with the Lewis gun or observe the ground. The gunner, or observer, was then the captain of the aircraft but from 1916 on the focus switched to the pilot, where it has since remained.

The RFC was also to lead the way in solving, or at least mitigating, another chronic military problem – communications. It was no longer possible for a general to know what was going on all over the battlefield, and, even if he had known, he had no rapid means of communicating new orders to his subordinates or of influencing events.

When fighting in fixed positions this did not matter too much; communication between the commander and his forces in the front-line trenches could be maintained by field telephones. Millions of miles of telephone wire were strung across the Old Front Line support and communication trenches into the front-line trench, and repairing and extending this field telephone system, and digging deep, narrow trenches to protect the lines from shellfire, was a constant task for the sappers, the battalion signallers and the pioneers. When the wires were not cut by shellfire or carelessly driven artillery caissons, this field telephone system worked well enough, but problems arose when an attack was ordered and the infantry moved forward, outrunning their communications. Within minutes all control was lost and, when matters went awry – and in battle matters usually do go awry – there was little the commander could do to rectify matters.

The problem was two-fold. The first solution had to be a radio, a 'wire-less' apparatus. This had to be small and light enough for a man to transport across tumbled ground. This last requirement was never met during the war, for one enduring facet of technology was, and is, that the early versions of any technical device are both heavy and large; people who now use laptop computers should remember that the first computers were big enough to fill an entire room. Weight and size were the main factors inhibiting the development of battlefield communications, because a workable 'wire-less' system already existed and had been tested by the British Army as far back as 1912.

Technical matters like signalling were then in the hands of the Royal Engineers, and in 1912 a sapper officer, Captain H.P. Lefroy, was placed in charge of the Army's 'wire-less' development programme. Lefroy got round the transportation problem by installing the early, heavy and bulky wireless sets in airships. These were not voice sets; communication was by Morse code. The main aim of pre-war developments and experiments was to increase the range of wireless transmissions, and this was still the broad thrust of development work when the RFC went to France in 1914. Then it was discovered that what the soldiers really needed was a short-range 'wireless' with which flying artillery observers could communicate with gun batteries on the ground below and direct their fire on to targets.

Spurred on by the evident need, work on this project commenced and by December 1914 the task of developing artillery spotting and wireless communication skills was in the hands of No. 9 Squadron, RFC, which was based at St Omer and commanded by an RFC-trained sapper officer, Major Herbert Musgrave. No. 9 Squadron attracted some elite personnel; among the aircrew were the future Lord Brabazon of Tara, a leading figure in the British aircraft industry for the next 50 years, and a future marshal of the Royal Air Force, Major Hugh Dowding, commander of RAF Fighter Command in the 1940 Battle of Britain.

The development of artillery-spotting techniques owes much to these men, for almost every improvement and development came from practical, on-the-job attempts to solve a technical problem or answer a definite need. For example, since the gunners on the ground and the observer in the air had different perspectives on the fall of shot, some commonly understood means of giving corrections had to be developed: 'up a bit and left a bit' clearly would not do. The answer came in the form of a standard artillery grid, mounted on a flat board and common to both observer and gunner, on which corrections could be accurately calculated and given in degrees and hundreds of yards. Another benefit of this development work was that the size and weight of the wireless sets slowly decreased; by 1916 most 'wireless aircraft' carried the lighter and much more reliable Sterling wireless. These aircraft experiments proved of great benefit later, when it became possible to put wireless sets in tanks. Ever-improving communications technology gradually increased the accuracy and power of artillery, the most potent killer of the Great War.

Another new weapon, one which gave naval commanders a fresh tool for waging total war, was the submarine. This extended twentieth-century warfare into a new element, though the submarine was not an entirely new weapon. The first recorded use of a submersible craft in war dates back to the American War of Independence when, in 1776, Sergeant Ezra Lee went out in a 'submersible' to attack a British frigate off the coast of Maine. The attempt failed because Lee could not find any way of attaching an explosive charge to the ship's hull. In 1801, during the Napoleonic Wars, another American, Robert Fulton, attempted to demonstrate the effectiveness of his five-man submarine – propelled by oars – to the French admirals by attacking a British frigate at anchor in Camaret Bay in Brittany. Fulton's craft was about to reach the frigate when the British warship weighed anchor and sailed away but attempts to develop a submarine weapon continued throughout the nineteenth century.

These efforts were aided in the 1880s by the development of electric motors and, by 1914, there were submarines in service with many of the world's navies, some of them displacing 700 tons, capable of travelling at 10 knots when submerged, and carrying a crew of 35. The larger submarines had a considerable range and were equipped with a most effective undersea weapon, the torpedo, invented by Robert Whitehead in 1866. By 1914 Whitehead torpedoes had a range of over one mile, a speed of 30 knots and a warhead capable of sinking a capital ship. There was no scientific means to counter the submarine but, again, technology came through quickly. Rising shipping losses led to the speedy invention of the 'depth charge', which entered service with the Royal Navy in 1915.

The introduction of submarines placed surface fleets in immediate jeopardy. As a result, the use of submarines was deplored by many naval officers as both uncivilized and unsporting. As early as 1901, Admiral Sir Arthur Wilson, Controller of the Royal Navy, wrote to the First Sea Lord proposing that 'the crews of all submarines captured should be treated as pirates and hanged'. This proposal did not halt the pre-war development of the submarine weapon and the German admirals certainly saw the submarine as a way of combating British naval superiority.

After the war began, fear of submarine attack certainly inhibited the movements of the Grand Fleet, especially after German submarines managed to sink a number of British warships, including HMS *Aboukir*, *Cressy* and *Hogue*, which were sunk by one submarine, the U9, on one day, 22 September 1914, with the loss of over 1,400 men. Between August and December 1914, German submarines sank nine British warships for the loss of five submarines but Germany mainly used the submarine to attack merchant shipping, first in coastal waters around the British Isles and in the Western Approaches and then, as new and larger submarines entered service, farther afield.

Attacks on the Entente's merchant shipping by submarine proved more effective than German attempts to match the strength and efficiency of the Royal Navy's surface fleet. In spite of all pre-war attempts to expand the German High Seas Fleet, the Royal Navy was still far ahead in number of ships and fighting efficiency, though the German warships were technologically more advanced and German gunnery was far superior to that of the Royal Navy. Another step towards total war came in November 1914, when the High Seas Fleet battlecruiser squadrons bombarded several of Britain's coastal towns, killing or injuring some 500 civilians. Some use was also made of commerce raiders, but apart from the Battles of Coronel and the Falkland Islands in November and December 1914, a small action off Heligoland at the end of August 1914, when three German cruisers were sunk, and another cruiser action off the Dogger Bank in January 1915, the surface ships of the German Navy engaged the Royal Navy in a major action only once, at the Battle of Jutland on 31 May 1916.

This engagement was inconclusive; the Royal Navy lost more ships and men but, except for one more foray in August 1916, when they were nearly caught by Admiral Jellicoe's squadrons, the High Seas

Fleet stayed at anchor from 1916 until the end of the war, the ships deteriorating and the seamen increasingly mutinous. The naval war against Britain was left to the submarine, which the Germans were to find a distinctly two-edged weapon, beneficial in war, if they had enough of them, but perilous politically.

The Kriegsmarine – then the Kaiserliche Marine, or Imperial German Navy – entered the Great War with 28 U-boats in service and a further 16 almost completed. Submarines were regarded by the Naval Command as a defensive weapon, a way of preventing Royal Navy incursions against German naval bases or into their training waters in the Baltic. On the outbreak of war these submarines went over to the offensive but it was swiftly revealed that the German submarine force contained only a fraction of the number required to maintain an undersea offensive against Great Britain. Before the war, a German naval officer had calculated that Germany would need more than 200 submarines to maintain a blockade of Britain. Germany had nowhere near that number, the boats in commission were far from ideal and, in order to rest the crews and service and resupply the boats, only about one-third of the submarines in commission could be at sea at any one time. This number proved insufficient for an effective blockade.

Kriegsmarine actions were also inhibited by its attack doctrine, Article 112 of German Naval Regulations, which stated that a U-boat could not sink merchant vessels indiscriminately or without warning. To comply with Article 112, a U-boat must surface and stop the enemy vessel, either by signalling or with a shot across her bows. A boarding party must then go on board, inspect the cargo manifest and establish whether the ship belonged to a belligerent or neutral country and whether the cargo could legitimately be regarded as war material. Only when satisfied that the vessel was either of the enemy nation or carrying war contraband could the vessel be sunk – and only then after giving the passengers and crew time to get into the boats and pull away.

It was clearly impossible for a small, cramped vessel like a submarine to take any of the crew or passengers on board but the U-boat captains were obliged to do their best to see that the crews of the ships they sank were safe. This is what happened in October 1914, when the U17 sank the British coaster *Glitra* off Norway. The U-boat captain not only gave the crew ample time to abandon ship, he also towed their lifeboats to within easy rowing distance of the Norwegian coast. This humane and gentlemanly way of waging war could not last; it received its first reverse in November 1914 when the British Government declared that the entire North Sea was a 'war zone' where any German vessel could be stopped, searched or sunk, an action taken to enforce the British blockade of German ports.

The problems of mounting a successful blockade during the Great War were complicated by the Declaration of London, a treaty drawn up in 1909 by the major powers, including the later Great War belligerents, which defined the terms under which warring nations might impose a naval blockade. This restricted the blockade to military materials only; it specifically excluded food for the civilian population or the supply of non-military supplies through neutral ports, unless such supplies were on the 'contraband list' or destined for onward transmission to the enemy, on 'continuous voyage', as the Declaration called it. The Declaration distinguished three kinds of goods: absolute contraband, conditional contraband and free list goods. 'Absolute contraband' was easy; arms, munitions, uniforms, petrol – even if destined for a neutral port – could be seized or destroyed under the 'continuous voyage' proviso. 'Conditional contraband' was more tricky; this included non-warlike goods, but items which could be used for war use or to support the enemy economy: food, forage, oil and clothing could be confiscated if considered suitable for military purposes. The 'free list' goods could not be considered contraband at all and largely consisted of raw materials for basic industries, wool and fertilizers being two examples. The Germans could, and did, evade the blockade by routing essential supplies through neutral ports in Holland and Denmark, or sending them overland via Switzerland, so it was only sensible to seize 'absolute contraband' and 'conditional contraband' cargoes at sea wherever possible.

The declaration of the North Sea as a war zone was part of an overall Franco-British strategy aimed at tightening the naval blockade of Germany and imposing hardship on its civilian population. Britain was thus able to stop and search vessels heading for neutral ports in Holland or Denmark and to detain cargoes destined for onward transmission to Germany. One effect of this blockade was the slow starvation of the German people, whose food was being rationed by the end of 1914 – another indication that the Central Powers had not anticipated a long war.

Germany's submarine warfare and Britain's naval blockade both had political risks, not least from the possible reaction to these activities in the USA. If German submarines sank American ships, or American citizens were drowned in the sinking of neutral or British ships, US public opinion might be brought to bear on the President and nudge the United States closer to war on the side of the Entente. Equally, when the Royal Navy stopped and searched American ships on the high seas, this was seen in the USA as a violation of US sovereignty, which it clearly was, and exactly the kind of imperious behaviour that had brought the US and Great Britain to war once before, in 1812.

Restricted submarine warfare, though humane, also limited the operational effectiveness of the U-boat. After Britain declared the North Sea a war zone, Admiral von Pohl and his commanders started to push for the introduction of 'unrestricted' submarine warfare – the sinking of merchant ships without warning. In 'unrestricted' warfare, the loss of life in submarine attacks tended to be heavy, as there was little or no time for the crew and passengers of torpedoed ships to take to the boats before the stricken vessel sank. Apart from this humanitarian problem there was a political dimension; how could the submarine captains guarantee that their attacks were solely concentrated against warships or merchant ships of the belligerent power without surfacing to check?

It was often hard to tell through a periscope whether a ship was British, French or from some neutral nation, and in war accidents will happen. On the other hand, submarines were only effective when they remained undetected, and surfacing to check the identity of a targeted vessel in crowded coastal waters was rarely practicable. This meant that neutral vessels were also sunk, which caused an outcry from the nations concerned. Even so, after resisting the admirals' pressure for some months, on 1 February 1915 the German Chancellor agreed to the introduction of unrestricted submarine warfare in the North Sea.

Implementation of this decision was delayed until 19 February, to enable neutral ships to get clear of the North Sea, which Germany now also declared to be a war zone, in which any ship of any nation was liable to attack. This declaration drew warnings from the USA that Germany would be held responsible for the lives of any Americans lost but German submarines sank many ships in the next few months, including a number of neutral vessels. These attacks brought Germany a great deal of odium and did little to restrict Britain's food or armaments supply.

British and French warships were obvious targets and ships of the British Merchant Navy, then the largest in the world, totalling 49 per cent of world tonnage, were most at risk. Legally and morally there was no problem here; the problem arose when neutral ships, profiting from the war by carrying cargo to Britain, were attacked by German submarines. Following American protests, the Germans directed their captains to surface when possible and check the identity of any neutral vessel, its cargo and the ship's destination. If it was found to be carrying war supplies to Britain or France, or the ship was a British vessel flying neutral colours, the crew were ordered into the boats and the ship was sunk. This did not make Germany popular with the shipowners or the Governments of neutral nations, but it was generally accepted as a legitimate practice in time of war.

Surfacing to check the identity of merchant vessels, however, exposed the submarines to attack, not least from British 'Q' ships, armed vessels disguised as merchant ships, and frequently flying the flag of neutral nations, which would engage German submarines with gunfire when they surfaced. These 'Q' ships did not actually sink many submarines, but they certainly inhibited the actions of the submarine commanders. Obliging submarines to surface before attacking also took away the invisibility that was their principal asset and 'stop-and-search' was a difficult and dangerous policy to apply in well-patrolled coastal waters. The U-boat captains were advised by their superiors that should they decide not to surface, and neutral ships were sunk, 'they would not be held responsible if, in spite of great care, mistakes were made'.

The risks of this policy had been pointed out from the start by von

Bethmann-Hollweg, and his objections were borne out on 7 May 1915, when a German U-boat sank the British liner *Lusitania* off the south coast of Ireland. Among the 1,198 passengers drowned were 118 American citizens; the USA promptly threatened Germany with the severing of diplomatic relations, the first step towards war. Before this tragedy had been resolved, another liner, the SS *Arabic*, was sunk on 4 August and four more American lives were lost. Further protests by the US Government led to a suspension of 'unrestricted' submarine warfare, at least for a while, on 18 September 1915, though British and French merchant ships were still attacked and sunk without warning.

The storm created in the US press, and protests from President Wilson after these sinkings, enabled von Bethmann-Hollweg to pressure the Kaiser into banning any further extension of submarine warfare, though the fact that the Kriegsmarine only had a few submarines with limited range was another, sounder reason for delay. Why stir up opposition from a large neutral country, argued Bethmann-Hollweg, when the achievements of German submarines were limited by numbers and technical factors? At this time, the risk of the USA entering the war was not balanced by any possible gain.

As time passed, however, and the U-boats increased in number and improved in performance, and German losses mounted on land, cries for the reintroduction of unrestricted submarine warfare were heard once again. If it was impossible to drive Britain out of the war by a land offensive, why not let the submarines show what they could do? These voices grew louder in the winter of 1915–16, urging von Falkenhayn to launch an all-out submarine campaign in February 1916, just before the attack on Verdun.

This proposal was immediately contested by von Bethmann-Hollweg and the start of the unrestricted submarine campaign was therefore delayed. Von Bethmann-Hollweg came out firmly against it at the Imperial Council table on 4 March and informed the Reichstag that, in his opinion, Great Britain could not be starved into submission by the present submarine force, certainly not in time to prevent the USA entering the war, which it would most certainly do if the campaign led to further losses of American lives. Von Falkenhayn's plan was duly rejected, though the sinking of Allied merchant shipping went on.

As a weapon of war the submarine was highly effective, and had the Germans had more of them in 1914 or 1915, they might have altered the outcome of the war. They certainly sank many ships – 800,000 tons of British shipping between August 1914 and September 1915. However, since the Merchant Navy was then the largest mercantile fleet in the world, with over 12 million tons of registered shipping, such losses were fairly easily absorbed and were soon made good by purchase or hire of ships from neutral nations and by the expanding shipyards of the Clyde and Tyne. As more submarines entered service though, the number of vessels sunk increased and by the end of 1916 the submarine was making a great impact on the war. So too, if less dramatically, was the British blockade of Germany.

Germany began to feel the effect of the British naval blockade in early 1915. The supply of fodder for farm animals was in short supply by the autumn of 1914, much of it having been taken by the Army or left to rot in the fields because farm workers had gone off to the war. The blockade took time to work, but it slowly strangled Germany's food supplies. During the Great War tens of thousands of German civilians died of malnutrition and starvation because of the British naval blockade; the accepted estimate is that between half a million and one million people died of hunger in Germany between 1914 and 1918, a fact about which most military histories are strangely silent.

By the winter of 1915–16, many goods had disappeared from German shops, fats and sugar were almost unobtainable and meat and butter were only available on the growing and thriving black market. Austria introduced food rationing in April 1915, and three 'meatless' days a week were imposed on German restaurants in November 1915, with bread rationing added to meat rationing later. Matters were made even more serious by the poor harvest, when many crops were not properly gathered in. In October 1915, there were food riots in Berlin, and in January 1916 bread riots in Vienna. Germany acted to head off similar demonstrations by rationing bread to five pounds per person per week. By the spring of 1916, the basic weekly ration for most German people consisted of black bread, sausages, three pounds of potatoes, one egg and a few pounds of turnips. And, by the summer, many Austrian and German civilians were coming to rely on soup kitchens for the bulk of their daily food and, when winter arrived, a shortage of coal for the central-heating boilers added cold to their other privations.

For the moment, these restrictions did not apply to the Army. German soldiers ate well, although finding sufficient food to feed them became increasingly difficult. One estimate states that in a single week of 1916 the German Army consumed 60 million pounds of bread, 131 million pounds of potatoes and 17 million pounds of meat, increasingly horse meat.[2] A single army corps ate 1,320 cows, 1,100 hogs and 4,158 sheep every week. This level of supply could not be maintained in the face of poor harvests, a declining amount of livestock – and the British blockade. The tightening of the blockade over the coming years was to prove a major factor in the Allied victory of 1918 when, with her Armies defeated on the battlefield and her women and children dying of hunger in the streets, Germany had no option but surrender. A book on the Great War which concentrates solely on the death toll on the Western Front is leaving out much of the tragedy.

On the battlefield, losses had been immensely increased by technology, but if technology had improved the killing power of conventional weapons it had also greatly increased their cost and therefore restricted their supply, at least to begin with. The problem facing the British and French Armies until 1917 was not only a shortage of guns but specifically a shortage of *heavy* guns – especially howitzers, guns with a high, plunging trajectory that could drop a high-explosive round into the enemy trenches and strongpoints and destroy them before the infantry attacked.

The British Army did have the 4.5-inch howitzer as early as 1909, but did not have enough of them in the first months of the war; field artillery, designed to support the infantry, was too light to destroy emplacements. Eventually more heavy guns became available and it was artillery, its weight and quantity, that largely determined the outcome of the battles of Verdun and on the Somme . . . and killed a great number of soldiers.

Important as artillery was, the Great War armies had other, perhaps more terrible weapons, notably poison gas, which also killed many soldiers and wrecked the lungs of thousands more. Gas made an impact on the popular imagination far in excess of its actual effect in the field, for gas was a two-edged weapon, often as dangerous to those using it as to those it was deployed against. Poison gas was also an 'illegal' weapon; the 'diffusion of asphyxiating or harmful gases' being banned by the Hague Convention of 1899. Germany had experimented with poison gas before 1914 and the first major use of gas on the Western Front was by the Germans at the Second Battle of Ypres in April 1915. This was chlorine gas and, although the immediate result was the headlong retreat of the French Colonial troops holding part of the Ypres salient, the effect of such gas was swiftly limited by the introduction of a reliable gas mask.

War destroys morality, and by September 1915 the British were also using poison gas. Haig used chlorine gas at the Battle of Loos and it quickly became standard practice to add a mixture of chlorine and tear-gas shells to artillery bombardments. If it failed to kill, the gas would certainly cause discomfort, oblige the enemy to don gas masks and reduce their fighting efficiency. In 1916, the Germans introduced phosgene gas at Verdun and later on the lethal mustard gas. Gas was distributed either from containers in the trenches or by shellfire; either way it was dangerous to the attackers for it could, and frequently did, drift back into their own trenches or lie in clouds across the path of their attacking infantry. Wounded men who crawled into shell holes where gas, being heavier than air, tended to collect, often died of asphyxiation. Others died in the open, shot to death while entangled in a more prosaic but highly effective invention, barbed wire.

Barbed wire was invented in the USA in the last decades of the nineteenth century as a way of containing cattle on the open ranges in the far West. The first patent was taken out by Joseph Glidden in 1874 and the use of barbed wire produced a number of small-scale range wars in the USA as it spread across the West in the next two decades. The first use of barbed wire in the military role came during the Russo-Japanese War of 1904–5, when the combination of barbed wire covered by machine-guns made a decisive impact on the attacking infantry. This fact was not widely noticed in the Western armies before the outbreak of the Great War but, by early 1915, thousands of miles of barbed wire were being strung along the Western Front, greatly improving the defences. It is worth noticing that some of these belts of wire were up to half a mile thick; Great War barbed wire was not just a few rolls of wire hung across No Man's Land, but a formidable defensive screen, especially when covered by the interlocking fire of automatic weapons.

Machine-guns came into use during the later stages of the American Civil War (1861–5) when Richard Gatling's gun was employed by the Union Armies. Another automatic weapon, the Reffye machine-gun, was used by the French during the Franco-Prussian War. At this time the machine-gun was seen by the generals as an artillery weapon, rather than as an infantry-support weapon, or for defensive fire. Both these early models were prone to jam; the great leap forward came in the 1880s, when Hiram Maxim invented his semi-automatic, 7.69 mm calibre, water-cooled machine-gun, which had a cyclic rate of fire approaching 550 rounds a minute. The British Army bought these Maxim guns and Kitchener used them in the Omdurman campaign of 1898 and in the Boer War which followed, again in the artillery role. It was not until the Russo-Japanese War that the machine-gun was allowed to display its defensive potential.

The main lessons of the Russo-Japanese War – that modern weapons like the machine-gun and massed artillery would massively increase the casualty rate – were largely neglected by European military experts in the years before 1914. The European yardstick was the brief Franco-Prussian War, when automatic weapons were a rarity, and when the Great War began, all the armies entered it with a scale of two machine-guns per battalion. This number could not be rapidly increased when the machine-gun began to display its prowess, for the facilities to produce more guns were simply not available.

By now the British had adopted the Vickers medium machine-gun, the MMG, a modified version of the Maxim firing the standard British infantry .303 inch round, a weapon with a range of 3,700 yards – more than two miles – or up to 4,500 yards with special ammunition. In October 1915, the British Army removed these guns from the infantry battalions to form the Machine-Gun Corps, which used the Vickers

gun in quantity to support attacks, defend positions and provide
harassing fire at night on positions far behind the German lines. As a
replacement, the infantry battalions received the Lewis light machine-
gun, a drum-fed platoon weapon which was heavy to carry at 15 lbs
and reluctant to function in mud, but was very useful for close support
of the infantry in the attack and for 'fire and movement' tactics. The
French Army also introduced an air-cooled machine-gun, the Hotchkiss.

What these automatic weapons had in common was increased
range and rate of fire through developments in manufacturing
technology. With such weapons war did not become impossible; it
merely became more efficient. Casualties soared on the Western Front
in particular because the weapons of defence dominated the battlefield and the side that attacked would inevitably pay a heavy cost in
lives for any gain in territory.

What was needed was not another way to kill soldiers – by 1916 the
Powers had enough of those – but some way of overcoming the
defensive technology – technology that stopped attacks after a few
yards and killed thousands of soldiers on the wire or in the tumbled
wastes of No Man's Land. *Defensive* technology – emplacements, wire,
machine-guns and artillery employed in combination – had made the
Western Front a hard nut to crack, and the only sensible way to crack
it was by the invention and use of *offensive* technology. The finest
example of offensive technology was the tank.

The armoured fighting vehicle, or AFV, was not entirely new in
1914. The Simms armoured car appeared as early as 1900, and the
Italians used armoured cars in their war against the Turks in Libya in
1912. In 1914, armoured cars – actually civilian Rolls-Royce cars
covered with armoured plate – were used to scout in the Belgian
countryside around Antwerp and armoured cars were used to good
effect by Allenby's army in Palestine in 1917.

Armoured cars are road-bound or can only operate on firm ground
and open terrain. After the development of the Western Front the
great need, and one which was quickly recognized, at least by the
British, was for some device or machine which could operate over
rough ground and defy the defensive combination of barbed wire,
machine-guns and artillery – though the British saw such a machine as

an infantry support weapon, not a separate arm or armoured cavalry capable of opening up the front. The search for such a weapon was under way by early 1915 and resulted in the creation and development of the tank. It is worth noting that throughout the Great War the British led the way in the development of the tank and tank tactics. The Germans, who were fighting a defensive battle until March 1918, never appreciated the need for a tank, although they built several models, including a massive tank, which weighed 30 tons, carried a crew of 17 and appeared on the battlefields in April 1917; generally, though, the Germans preferred to use captured British machines. The French developed light tanks, manufactured by Renault or used British light tanks, Whippets, or full-sized British machines. The tank took time to reach its full, tactical potential and, meanwhile, the killing went on.

The point of this chapter is to demonstrate that the losses of the Great War were largely caused by the introduction of modern technology, not only on the battlefield but also at sea, and in the air and against civilians. It will also be apparent that while the means to cause casualties had vastly increased, the means to reduce them had yet to be thought of This applied in particular to the attack, because the armies, all the armies, were fighting a twentieth-century war with nineteenth-century tactics – even though the new technology had made those tactics either obsolescent or positively dangerous.

New technology changes things, but not everything: cavalry survived the long bow and the musket and stayed in use with armies until well into the last century, and battleships, though vulnerable to air attack, are still useful for shore-bombardment and were so used by the US Navy in Korea and the Lebanon. The marginal application of obsolescent equipment enabled the supporters of outdated methods to state a case – and many of them were senior officers who had learned their trade on the battlefields of previous wars and were therefore hard men to argue with. They believed that the Great War could be won on the battlefield if only the right combination of *matériel* and tactics could be found. In the end, in 1918, the range of *matériel* they had available had been greatly increased and improved by the introduction of more guns, tanks and aircraft, and tactics had been developed to make the best use of these new weapons, but between 1914 and 1917 this adherence to outdated methods was lethal.

It should have been apparent by 1916 that until some technological means could be found to overcome the defensive combination of trenches, barbed wire, machine-guns and artillery, and until the communications problem was solved, the war could not be won on the battlefield by conventional means, except at a terrible cost in lives. This leads us back to the point made at the start of this chapter, that even those who saw a European war coming in the years before 1914 had no conception of what sort of war it would turn out to be.

There was failure at every level: failure to see what was coming; failure to estimate how long the war would last; failure to set up a supreme command to fight the war strategically; and finally failure extended to the battlefields. Whatever their size, in terms of doctrine, the armies of 1914–1916 were nineteenth-century armies. Even the German Army, the product of a national military system, well commanded by professional generals and equipped with a great quantity of the most modern weapons, was still commanded by officers deferring to the Kaiser – whose grotesque title, 'The Supreme War Lord', says a great deal about the nature of command at that time.

It might be argued, though not by this writer, that since no one foresaw what this war would be like, no one can be blamed for not forecasting the nature of the fighting. Politicians who lead nations into war should, at the very least, know what kind of war it is likely to be – limited or total – and either prepare for it properly or avoid it at all costs.

It might also be claimed that the generals cannot be blamed for failing to read the future in 1914. No one asked them to read the future, but professional military men surely ought to understand the potential of new weapons before they are introduced – or else why introduce them? They should also have been able to draw sensible, professional conclusions from the evidence that rapidly accumulated once the war began, before their eyes in many cases, but for more than three years they did not do so. The generals were certainly not to blame for all that went wrong in the Great War but they were not entirely free of blame either.

Until 1916 many generals, and most politicians, in most countries, were still convinced that the war could be won by the application of superior, conventional strength *on the battlefield*. There were some exceptions to this rule. General Sir Ian Hamilton had been the British Official Observer during the Russo-Japanese War and came home stating firmly that the day of horse cavalry was over – a statement that made him extremely unpopular with people like Sir John French. He also noted and reported on the large number of heavy guns possessed by the German Army when he attended their manoeuvres in 1909 but, again, little account was taken of his report or what it might portend. Hamilton was using his common sense and looking ahead; it is a great pity that his colleagues did not listen.

The concept that victory could only be obtained by a clash of arms on the battlefield was entirely outdated by 1914. The war the nations entered in 1914 was a total war, one where the outcome would depend on the productive capacity of industry, on the brains and skill of economists and scientists, on the courage of civilians and their willingness to endure privation at home, as much as on the skill of the generals or valour of the troops on the battlefield. It was a war requiring the use of strategy as well as of tactics – but, above all, it was a war that could only be won by the use of superior technology and superior skills in command.

By any measurable standard, the Great War was a human catastrophe on a massive scale and, as with any catastrophe, when it is over there is a search for the cause and a place to lay the blame. In Britain, and in many parts of her former Empire, the blame for the death toll is generally laid on the incompetence and callousness of the Great War generals, especially the British generals. In France, they blame their politicians; in Germany, historians blame the Kaiser.

Popular opinion is often at least partly right, but it would probably be more accurate, far more fair, and more useful to posterity, to blame the nations at large for drifting into this war without any true understanding of what a modern war would be like. The excuse that they did not know may – just – be valid for 1914, but by 1916 it should have been very clear, certainly to the political leaders, that the war could not be 'won' in any meaningful way.

The cost of victory, whoever gained it in the end and whatever it might mean in those circumstances, was already too high. This being so, one has to ask now why the national leaders, confronted with this situation and with the prospect that the killing would continue, did not insist on peace negotiations. There were reasons for this failure and therefore, before we move on to the battlefields, we should briefly examine the progress of peace.

Notes

1 *The First World War, Germany and Austria–Hungary*, 1914–1918, p. 172.

2 Ibid., p. 284.

5

War Aims and Peace Proposals
1914—1916

'. . . Peace hath her victories
No less renowned than war.'
John Milton, 1652

A war that cannot be won should be ended. That much may be obvious but the problem confronting the powers for much of the Great War was that of how this particular war *could* be ended and on what terms. This was the crux of the matter but the starting point for any move towards peace has to be a realization that the war cannot be won; the losing side must appreciate that eventual defeat is inevitable, the victors that victory can only be achieved at terrible cost, since Pyrrhic victories in the modern world tend to be extremely expensive.

The second point competing parties have to decide is exactly what they hope to achieve in the war – their war aims. From that point it is possible for the peace party, if any, to argue that all that can be achieved has been achieved, or that more will never be achieved, and that to continue the struggle is therefore pointless. These logical points seem clear enough with hindsight, in times of peace or to outside parties, but are often less apparent to the contestants at the time. The contestants either entered the war with some clearly defined aims, or have committed so much in blood and treasure to the struggle already that the thought of it all being for nothing is too dreadful to contemplate.

These points were abundantly clear to the combatant nations by the end of 1915. This is not to say that they were freely admitted in Government circles, though attempts to stop the war had begun even before it started, and increased very significantly in the autumn of 1914 as the German armies moved on Paris. These first attempts were initiated by the British Government, which offered to negotiate between the parties in July 1914. The issue was taken up soon after the war broke out by the President of the United States, Woodrow Wilson, who sent his great friend and roving ambassador, Colonel E.M. House, on a peace-finding mission to Europe in September 1914.

Colonel House visited the chancelleries and government offices of Europe, urging a cessation of hostilities, but these offers of negotiation were firmly rejected by the German Government. With its armies flooding into France, Germany believed that victory was within its grasp and that within days the Kaiser would, like his grandfather, be dictating another stern peace to the French at Versailles.

The next US intervention came in mid-September through Oscar Strauss, a former US Ambassador to the Sublime Porte in Constantinople, who suggested to the German Ambassador in Washington that, since France had clearly lost the war, the time had come for the USA to call an ambassadors' conference to discuss mediation. The Germans said that they would agree to discuss mediation only if the other belligerents did so as well. The French Government rejected this proposal, as Germany had hoped, since the French now realized that the battle on the Marne was turning their way; they did not want a cease fire which would leave Germany in possession of most of northern France and therefore in a strong negotiating position. Their aim was to drive the German armies back across the Rhine, so peace was no longer attractive. These two rejections of mediation illustrate another point that peacemakers have to bear in mind: nations do not talk peace when they think they are winning.

When consulted by the Americans, the British explained that they had entered the war to protect Belgian neutrality and that the

Germans had offered no unequivocal guarantee that Belgian
sovereignty would be restored. Any real hope of continuing the
Strauss initiative collapsed on 16 September, when Germany
announced that it was not interested in negotiation but that it would
accept and consider an application for peace from the Entente. This
statement was met by the British Foreign Secretary, Sir Edward Grey,
with the suggestion:

> When Germany really wishes peace she should approach all the
> Allies or make her wish for mediation known to President
> Wilson, who could then communicate with all the Allies fairly
> and straightforwardly, and who together would take the
> situation into consideration.

For the moment, therefore, the war would continue, but peace terms
cannot be separated from war aims. Lloyd George later declared that
the nations of Europe 'stumbled into war' in 1914, but there is ample
evidence that all the nations entered the war deliberately – and most
of them were determined to get something out of it, either in terms of
territory or in the elimination of some perceived pre-war threat. It is
therefore necessary to discuss, briefly, why the various nations entered
the war and what they hoped to gain from victory. This is not easy,
for the issues are not clear-cut and the various national war aims
changed as time passed.

As a starting point, it must be appreciated that what developed into
the Great War might have remained a small spat on the Danube but
for the interlocking series of alliances drawn up by the European
nations in the latter decades of the nineteenth century and the early
years of the twentieth in a determined bid to prevent a European war
breaking out at all. These alliances had been drawn up since the
Franco-Prussian War, and their source can be traced to fear of the
growing economic and military power of Germany and the belligerent
provocation offered to Europe at large by the third Kaiser, Wilhelm II.

The first of these alliances was the 'League of the Three Emperors',
between Germany, Austria-Hungary and Russia, a pact created in
1872 by the German Chancellor, Prince Bismarck, to protect his

recent creation, the German Empire of the first Kaiser. In 1882 Bismarck created another grouping, the Triple Alliance, which linked Germany to Italy and Austria-Hungary; this alliance was renewed in 1887. Bismarck had no interest in further German expansion inside Europe or, indeed, in the wider world; his main concern was the security of the German Empire from French aggression and the expansion of Prussian hegemony over the German-speaking parts of Central Europe. By the time he was dismissed by Kaiser Wilhelm II in 1890, he felt he had achieved both these aims.

France shook German belief in this collective security in 1893 by concluding the Franco-Russian Pact, a military convention which stated quite openly that either nation would come to the other's aid if attacked. The potential enemy was clearly seen by both parties as Imperial Germany, which had been the major European power since 1871 and had been rattling sabres loudly since Wilhelm II mounted the Imperial throne in 1888. The Kaiser and his ministers saw this pact as a Franco-Russian attempt at 'encirclement', an aggressive move that threatened Germany with war on two fronts in the event of hostilities. The Schlieffen Plan, which was finally adopted in 1905, was seen as Germany's way of breaking out of this encirclement and striking down both opponents in a matter of weeks.

The seeds of the future war were sown by these various alliances. Russia was in dispute with Austria-Hungary over the Balkans, partly because both hoped for territorial gains there when the Turkish Empire in the Balkans finally collapsed, but also because Russia saw herself as the natural protector of the Balkan Slavs, especially the Serbs, who were seeking freedom from Austrian domination. This was the tinder box awaiting the spark, and war therefore came to Europe in 1914, as Prince Bismarck had always predicted, over a minor affair in the Balkans.

The fragile edifice of European peace collapsed after Serb nationalists shot the Austro-Hungarian heir, Archduke Franz-Ferdinand. The Austrians then demanded that Serbia admit responsibility and allow Austrian police to intervene in Serbian territory to seek out and punish the assassins. Russia offered Serbia aid against these Austrian demands, so Austria looked to Germany for help against Russia. Germany then offered Austria an unconditional guarantee of support in the case of war with Russia – the so-called 'blank cheque' – and Russia promptly looked to France, calling in the marker of the Franco-Russian Pact.

So, at first gradually and then with increasing speed, tension mounted across Europe, armies mobilized and finally, between 1 and 4 August 1914, the European nations went to war. Each nation had a reason for doing so, some immediate, like the British determination to defend the neutrality of Belgium, some long-term, like France's desire to repossess the provinces of Alsace and Lorraine, lost in the Franco-Prussian War more than 40 years before. In the early months of the war, survival was the main aim of the Entente Powers – France, Britain, Russia at this time – and victory via the Schlieffen Plan the main aim of Germany. Only when the original crisis had passed did the politicians begin to look ahead to where the war might lead.

The prime cause of British participation was German violation of Belgian neutrality, a neutrality first guaranteed by a number of European nations, including France and Germany, as long ago as 1839. In 1871, Germany took on the neutrality guarantee given by Prussia when the Belgian State was created, and Germany's dismissive reference to this guarantee as 'a scrap of paper' horrified and disgusted the British Government and led to a declaration of war against Germany. However, not all the reasons for Britain's commitment were quite so high-minded. The Foreign Secretary, Sir Edward Grey, argued in Cabinet that Britain had to maintain the nineteenth-century balance of power in Europe by aiding France, or face the prospect of a continent dominated by a German confederation. Only four members of the Cabinet accepted that argument, but they included the Prime Minister and the First Lord of the Admiralty, Winston Churchill.[1]

There were also questions of national security. Britain was well aware of the envy felt by the Germans, and especially by the Kaiser and German admirals like Tirpitz, towards the British Empire and the Royal Navy, then the world's largest maritime force. Britain needed the Navy to protect her sea lanes and merchant shipping and guard her world-wide Empire. Germany had no such need, so the British saw the creation of the German High Seas Fleet as a direct challenge to British naval supremacy, which it undoubtedly was, and regarded the building of the Kiel Canal, through which German naval units could proceed unhindered from the Baltic to the North Sea and Atlantic, as a step towards eventual war, which it also was.

The Germans are excellent soldiers and superb tacticians, but their grasp of strategy, certainly at the geo-political level, is often weak. In threatening British naval supremacy, the Germans drew British attention to their long-term plans, which is the last thing they should have done. As a result, when war loomed in 1914, the British were determined that, whatever else happened, the Germans must not gain naval bases on the French and Belgian coasts, from which they could directly threaten the east coast of England and the naval base at Chatham.

Such strategic considerations alone did not guarantee Britain's entry into the war. There was also the economic argument against entry – could Britain afford a Continental war? – and the British fear that crushing German power, at considerable cost, would simply allow some other power, like Russia, to arise in its place. The British Government, declared David Lloyd George, was: 'Dead against carrying on a war of conquest to crush Germany for the sake of Russia.'[2] Before long the British Government became determined that when victory came they should be in a position to impose terms, not only on the defeated enemy, but also on their victorious allies.

France had been anticipating a war against Germany since her humiliation in the Franco-Prussian War and the consequent loss of Alsace and Lorraine. *Revanche* (revenge) for this defeat and loss had been woven into the fabric of French political life for 40 years, and another war with Germany had long been seen as inevitable. France had therefore been making plans for war for decades, building up her Army and forging alliances, notably with Russia. Such alliances were necessary for, with a population of 37 million as compared to the 60 million of Germany, France could not hope to defeat Germany on her own.

Russia, the other major player among the Entente powers, was in no state to go to war in 1914. War meant instability and Russia was already unstable enough, riven with political faction and teetering on the brink of that revolution that would finally break out in 1917. Russia entered the war ostensibly to protect the Slavs and see off the expanding Austrian dominion of the Balkans. However, on 12 September 1914, one month into the war, Sazonov, the Foreign Minister, gave a hint of further Russian war aims when, in a conversation with the French Ambassador, he stated that when the war ended he hoped that Russia would acquire the Polish-speaking parts of Silesia and the mouth of the River Nieman on the Baltic, adding that the Austro-Hungarian Empire, Russia's rival in the Balkans, should be broken into three parts – Austria, Hungary and Bohemia – while Russia's client state, Serbia, should gain Bosnia, Hercegovina and a large area of the Dalmatian coast on the Adriatic. Since the main burden of fighting Austria-Hungary currently fell on Russia, Sazonov felt that these acquisitions were a fair return for Russia's contribution.

In September 1914 Sazonov suggested that one way to counter the possibility that the Germans, pressed by a war on two fronts, would try to detach the Allies from each other was to put the Entente relationship on a firmer footing. He proposed that the main players in the Entente should agree not to conclude a separate peace with Germany and to record this agreement openly, in a published Note. Sazonov made this suggestion before the German advance was repulsed on the Marne, when he was clearly worried that if Paris fell the French would surrender. If that happened, the British would probably retire to their island and Germany's entire might would be turned against Russia. The French and British accepted this proposal and the agreement, the Pact of London, was signed on 5 September.

The Pact of London was both wise and timely. By November 1914, Germany had realized that a quick victory via the Schlieffen Plan had eluded her and that a war on two fronts was inevitable. Peace feelers were duly extended to France and Russia, urging them to break with the Entente and to conclude a separate peace on some reasonable, negotiated basis. This was no longer an appealing prospect. Now the Allies thought they were winning and the Germans were being driven back, but German hopes rose again on 5 November, when Turkey entered the war on the side of the Central Powers.

The German public began the war firmly believing that they were fighting a war of self-defence against an aggressive combination of

France, Russia and Britain. This line played well in the towns and villages of the Reich, where Kaiser Wilhelm II's relentless belligerence in the pre-war years had been seen in Germany as simple statements of fact – that Germany too needed 'a place in the sun', colonies in Africa, and a high place in world affairs. Many historians still cite Lloyd George's previously quoted comment that the European nations 'stumbled into war' as evidence that no nation was entirely free of guilt for the conflict, but a careful analysis of German plans and ambitions in the pre-war years by the German historian Fritz Fischer confirms the popular opinion that the root causes of the Great War were German militarism and political ambition – and that these roots had been established for some time.[3]

An opinion need not be wrong just because it is popular. Although there were plenty of other contributory factors behind the outbreak of war – the pre-war Continental arms race, the French desire for revenge for Alsace-Lorraine, Austria-Hungary's desire to crush the Serbs, Germany's fear of 'encirclement' by France and Russia – all of which had a part to play – it is now generally accepted that these issues were subordinate to the fact that Germany had been planning a European war for a long time and seized on the Balkan issue in 1914 as the excuse to provoke one.

This case can be argued even at second hand; if it had not been for the threat presented by German militarism it would not have been necessary for the alliance between France and Russia, which led to the alliance between Germany and Austria-Hungary, which in turn led to the Russian guarantee to the Serbs. These alliances spread the war, and these alliances can all be traced to German militarism. This, however, was not how the Germans saw it.

At the Versailles Peace Conference in 1919, the Allied insistence on Article 231 of the Treaty, which imposed war guilt on Germany alone, was strongly resisted by the German delegates. According to the German version of events, Germany had been attacked in 1914 and was therefore obliged to defend herself against the 'encirclement' of Russia and France, whose act was swiftly supported by the arch enemy, England. This rather ignores the basic fact that it was Germany that declared war on Russia, France and Belgium; only one country, Great Britain, declared war on Germany, and that was after the German violation of Belgian neutrality, a neutrality which Germany had agreed to respect.

Personal matters also contributed to the war. German attitudes to Britain were strongly influenced by jealousy among the officers of the German High Command and in the Imperial Household. The Kaiser, though a grandson of Queen Victoria and therefore close to the British Royal Family, was almost insanely jealous of British power and influence and had a particular detestation for his late uncle, King Edward VII. When King Edward's charm and influence defused six centuries of Anglo-French rivalry and led to the signing of the Entente Cordiale in 1904, the Kaiser saw this as yet another cunning British attempt to unite Europe against Germany. This jealousy of Britain was not restricted to the Kaiser and his immediate circle. German politicians envied Britain's possession of a world-wide network of colonies and dominions, and influential naval officers like Admiral Tirpitz envied the size and reputation of the Royal Navy.

When the war began, Great Britain gave further unwitting cause for dislike in the first days of August by offering to mediate between Germany and her opponents, and then withdrawing the offer when it became apparent that Germany had invaded Belgium. The idea then got about in Germany that Britain was the major player in the Entente and was using the other Entente powers – France and Russia, and eventually Italy – to pursue her deep-seated aim of destroying Germany as an economic and political rival.

The Germans declined to participate in talks, initiated twice by the USA, having decided that they would get more out of separate peace deals with their individual opponents than at a general peace conference chaired by President Wilson. But Germany's ambition to divide the allies was thwarted by the Entente Powers' adherence to the Pact of London.

In the spring of 1915, the German Chancellor agreed to meet Colonel House, who was again touring the European chancelleries in an attempt to find grounds for a peace conference. On this occasion the Entente Powers demanded that suitable terms for negotiation must include German evacuation of Belgium and reparations for the damage caused there; Germany again found the terms unacceptable. The question of Belgium was to remain the sticking point in efforts to start negotiations, but American impartiality over the peace terms issue became rather less certain after the sinking of the *Lusitania* in May 1915.

By now Germany had drawn up some war aims of her own, specifying what she expected to get out of the war and her terms for agreeing to peace. These terms constantly expanded but, by 1916, they included a wide range of demands, territorial, industrial and political. Just to begin with, Germany's existing territorial integrity must be guaranteed, so Alsace and Lorraine would be retained. Germany would also annex the Belgian city of Liège and the French industrial basin of Longwy-Briey. Above all, Germany must be the centre of a new economic and political grouping – Mitteleurope – a grouping not unlike the present European Community, the descendant of the nineteenth-century Zollverein, which had provided the economic base for the rise of Prussia in the previous century.

Germany's Mitteleurope concept was not new. It had first been bruited abroad in the aftermath of the Franco-Prussian War, a conflict that had created the German Empire, but not a unified state. The first German Empire, or Reich, was a federation composed of no less than 24 units including four kingdoms – Prussia, Bavaria, Württemberg and Mecklenburg-Schwerin – six principalities, six duchies and three free cities – Bremen, Hamburg and Lübeck. Many more German people, or at least German-speaking people, lived in Austria, or within the boundaries of Poland or the provinces of the Austro-Hungarian Empire. The King of Prussia was the Emperor of Germany because Prussia was the largest state of the federation, and because he was recognized as the Head of State by the other German rulers. This political federation needed an economic base as well, and the aim of Mitteleurope was for Germany to dominate Europe as Prussia dominated Germany, politically as well as economically.

Sooner or later this aim was bound to cause conflict with France, a country with her own long-standing claims to European dominance. As far back as 1812, the Emperor of the French, Napoleon Bonaparte, declared: 'The picture as yet exists only in outline but there must be one code, one court of appeal, one coinage, for all Europe. The States of

Europe will be melted into one union and Paris will be the capital.' The German Emperor's ambitions at the start of the last century differed from this aim only in scale and both nations had elected to pursue their aims not by economic domination or political means, but by war.

The establishment of Mitteleurope was one of Germany's fundamental war aims long before 1914, though it was put into its final form in a programme put forward by the Pan-German League, a powerful political body, in August 1914. This Mitteleurope, once complete, would be dominated by Germany and resemble a European superstate, one able to compete on equal terms with Russia, the USA and Britain.

The visionaries of Mitteleurope foresaw no small-scale undertaking. Belgium must be annexed or subordinated to Germany and either way Germany was to have access to the Belgian ports. The French mining and iron ore district of Longwy-Briey and the French Channel coast as far as the Somme must be given to Germany. German troops must occupy France in a line drawn from the Somme estuary to the fortress of Verdun, and the port of Toulon must be handed over to Germany as a naval base in the Mediterranean. The French population of these towns and districts was to be evacuated and replaced by Germans, possibly by Germans currently living outside the Reich in eastern Europe. In short, this German-dominated superstate in Europe would contain such currently independent nations as Austria, Bulgaria, Romania, the Netherlands, Denmark, Norway, Sweden, Finland, even Switzerland.

In the east, Russia was to shrink to the territory occupied in the eighteenth century, well east of the Nieman river, losing large areas of territory in Poland as well as the Baltic provinces, and ceding Courland and Lithuania on the eastern frontier of Germany to provide *Lebensraum* (living space) for Germany's expanding home population. The Entente Powers must pay the full cost of the war and Germany would also expect to be compensated for her war expenditure with a large colonial Empire in Africa, including the French and Belgian Congos, where another superstate, Mittelafrika, would provide Germans everywhere with their 'place in the sun'. These war aims, if and when realized, would have the effect of either rewarding German aggression or confirming her in possession of the territory conquered in 1914.

This list of acquisitions was by no means the end of Germany's dreams. Further demands were drawn up by the German Army and Navy, the Colonial Office, by financiers and industrialists; people came running from all over the Reich to get their snouts in the trough of anticipated post-war spoils. German industrialists and bankers, Krupp, Thyssen, Rathenau and the rest, demanded the annexation of French ore and coal districts; the land owners of Prussia wanted access to the grain fields of Poland; the generals and admirals demanded the winding up of other fleets and armies and the ceding to Germany of foreign territory and fortifications. Once that had been done, they declared, resistance to further German demands would be impossible. These ambitions grew with anticipation and soon extended world-wide, to embrace even the nickel fields of New Caledonia in the Pacific, but the broad thrust of the Mitteleurope concept was political and European.

In September 1914, von Bethmann-Hollweg drew up a draft – the 'September Programme' – which stated that this new body aimed to create a unified economic union in central Europe . . .' by the means of joint customs agreements. This union, which must stabilize Germany's hegemony over central Europe, would probably not have a joint constitutional executive and its members, while ostensibly enjoying equal rights, would in fact be under German leadership.' The German Chancellor regarded this entrancing prospect as a 'moderate' position.

Germany clung to these Mitteleurope aims throughout the war but never more firmly than in 1916, though her allies, Turkey, Bulgaria and Austria-Hungary, were less than fully enthusiastic about this ambitious scheme which appeared to offer them, in return for their support in the war, the chance of being first dominated by Germany and then absorbed into the German superstate.

This was possible anyway, not least because of Germany's central and powerful economic situation. As Marshal Foch points out in his memoirs:

The Germany of 1914 would never have resorted to war if she had properly estimated her own interests. No appeal to arms was necessary. She had only to continue an economic development that was already penetrating every corner of the world. Who would have dared oppose her? Her trade and commerce were moving forward with steady strides that left other nations behind. There was no need for Germany to resort to war in order to conquer the world.

All that is very true, but it overlooks the fundamental nature of the German state. The Kaiser's Reich was a militaristic oligarchy, dominated by generals, not economists. Aggressive militarism permeated every corner of the state and to it can be added the character of the Kaiser himself – the Supreme War Lord. Throw in the fear of French revenge for 1870–71, which led to those pre-war treaties, and it now seems inevitable that Germany saw her way forward towards the security of European domination as a path cut out with swords. Germany included these ambitions in any response to calls for peace, and it is hardly surprising that the Entente Powers found them totally unacceptable.

Even so, there was a problem. The hard fact was that Germany had made extensive territorial gains in 1914 and was now in possession of all Belgium and large parts of northern and eastern France. In territorial and therefore in political terms, Germany held most of the cards and, until the Entente had something to put on the table in response, there was no reason for Germany to compromise. German military power was certainly waning, for the combined populations of the Entente promised armies that would, in time, outnumber and overcome those Germany could put in the field – even without the hoped-for participation of the United States – but that was still a long way in the future.

The German Chancellor did attempt to find the basis for a negotiated peace with at least some of his country's enemies but soon discovered that France and Russia would not discuss peace while German troops remained on their territory. Moreover, between December 1914 and February 1915 the French Prime Minister, M. Viviani, declared in a series of speeches that France would continue fighting until it had driven Germany from Alsace and Lorraine, obtained satisfaction for the losses in life and property in the fighting so far, restored Belgian independence and destroyed Prussian militarism once and for all.

Though belligerent, this seems to have been the sensible approach.

Apart from Germany's main war aims, an indication of the terms she would have wanted had peace talks begun before her forces were beaten can be estimated by those she extracted from Russia in the 1918 Treaty of Brest-Litovsk. In return for peace, Germany stripped Russia of 34 per cent of her population, 32 per cent of her agricultural land, 85 per cent of her sugar beet production, 54 per cent of her industrial capacity and 89 per cent of her coal.

Viviani's fighting talk cleared the air for the moment but another attempt at a negotiated peace had already begun. In November 1914, the Italian Government, which had elected to stay out of the war for the moment, offered to mediate between the Powers. The offer was promptly rejected, but another offer from the United States was treated with more consideration. This came in December 1914, when the German and Austrian ambassadors in Washington asked President Wilson to send his emissary, Colonel House, back to Europe again to see if he could find any basis for mediation among the Entente.

As a sweetener to this proposal, the ambassadors suggested that Germany might agree to withdraw from northern France and Belgium before any negotiations actually took place, which seems unlikely in view of the Mitteleurope ambitions, but the prospect of Colonel House's mission was not well received by the Entente. There was a feeling about that the USA had nothing staked in the war and was now treating the Entente and the Central Powers as if they were equally to blame for starting the conflict – and Sir Edward Grey did not believe for one instant that Germany really intended to withdraw from Belgium or northern France.

However, it was important to keep the USA 'on side' in the war, so Grey explained to the House of Commons that, while he did not believe Germany was sincere in seeking peace, the Entente did not wish to crush Germany completely. They were fighting, he declared, in the hope that by obtaining victory on the battlefield they might see Germany create a democratic, constitutional Government, free from the ongoing threat of Prussian militarism, one which would join with other nations in drawing up a mutual peace agreement and preventing war in the future – a hint at the development of the post-war League of Nations.

Colonel House duly toured the chancelleries of Europe in February and March 1915, and returned to Washington to tell Wilson that he saw no hope of a negotiated peace in the foreseeable future. By this time the Entente was drawing up further war aims under what became known as the 'Constantinople Agreement', in which the Russians made their aims known in the event of victory over Turkey, which had now entered the war on the side of the Central Powers. As with Germany, these post-war ambitions were . . . ambitious. Sazonov insisted that as her prize Russia should have control of Constantinople (the modern Istanbul), the western side of the Bosphorus, the Sea of Marmara, the Dardanelles, most of Thrace (the European part of Turkey) and the islands of Imbros and Tenedos. In short, Russia wanted total control of the vital waterway between the Black Sea and the Mediterranean, which would thereby give Russia year-round, warm-water ports.

All this assumed that the Turkish Empire could be defeated and then divided, which, in view of the developing Dardanelles fiasco, was by no means certain. Even so, in anticipation of this happy outcome, the other Entente nations quickly put forward their claims to parts of the Turkish Empire. France stated that she must have Syria, to which she had laid claim since the Middle Ages. Britain promptly put in a bid for Palestine and Sinai, which would give the British control of both banks of the Suez Canal. Then the Royal Navy came up with a plea for Mesopotamia and the Tigris delta, mainly because of the oil terminal and port at Abadan, while the British dominions, Australia and South Africa, pointed out that they had seized the German colonies in their areas of influence – New Guinea and South-West Africa (now Namibia) – and intended to retain them.

Possession of all this territorial loot depended on victory both over Turkey and in the more general war, and in the spring of 1915 neither victory seemed certain. It was no more certain after Italy entered the war on the side of the Entente on 24 May, declaring war on Austria-Hungary but not against Germany. This partial addition of strength also came with a list of post-war demands: as the price of her participation, Italy expected to receive much of the Austrian Tyrol, Dalmatia – which Russia hoped would go to Serbia – the offshore Dalmatian Islands, the port of Trieste and the Istrian Islands, territory that currently belonged to either Austria or Turkey. Italy also demanded that Britain should fund Italy's part in the war and provide the Italian Army with artillery.

The year of 1915 saw fading hopes in the chancelleries and on the battlefields. As the year wore on, a series of defeats and setbacks, however they were presented to the people at home, on either side of the front line, reduced hopes of rapid victory. This was true on the Western Front and at Gallipoli, and to Germany and Austria-Hungary as much as to France or Britain. Instead of a negotiated peace, the war escalated and the death toll rose with it.

At the end of May 1915, Asquith's Liberal Government collapsed and was replaced by a wartime Coalition – the National Ministry – of Liberals, Conservatives and Unionists. Although Asquith remained as Prime Minister, more power flowed into the hands of David Lloyd George, especially after the fall from office of Winston Churchill, the First Lord of the Admiralty, who was blamed for the Gallipoli débâcle. With hindsight, one might expect that the terrible battles in the summer of 1915, and the total lack of any territorial gain in the West, might have obliged the combatants to take a more flexible view of their war aims. In fact, the next move came from Washington, where there was a growing fear that if the war went on the USA might be dragged into it.

Once again the agent of peace was Colonel House. His proposal, as explained to President Wilson, was that the Entente Powers should be asked if they would welcome an American statement demanding an end to the war. If they agreed, the President would call a Peace Conference. If the Central Powers rejected this joint offer of talks, which the USA and the Entente were in favour of, then the USA would break off diplomatic relations with the Central Powers, with the threat of war thereby implied.

This was nudging the United States towards the war, but President Wilson agreed to back the scheme and, on 17 October 1915, Colonel House outlined the proposal in a letter to Sir Edward Grey. His letter went rather further than his discussion with the President and seems to have suggested that if the Central Powers refused this offer, the USA would enter the war on the side of the Entente. Grey declared himself grateful for the offer but added that the time for negotiation had not arrived – the Entente intended to carry on fighting, at least until next spring. The President's offer was therefore deemed untimely, but Wilson still agreed that House should go to Europe and press the proposal face to face with the various Cabinets, though he could not agree to House's extension of the original plan, that the USA would enter the war if Germany rejected these proposals.

Wilson added that his proposals were not only aimed at ending this war but also at preventing future wars: 'Peace negotiations have nothing to do with any local settlements – territorial questions, indemnities and the like – but are concerned only in the future peace of the world and the guarantees to be given for that . . . a league of nations to secure each nation against aggression and maintain the freedom of the seas.'

House arrived in Britain in January 1916 and quickly realized that the British were not currently interested in a negotiated peace, one involving a degree of compromise with the Central Powers. They placed their faith in the New Armies and a successful conclusion to the powerful offensives to be mounted in 1916 by all the Entente Powers – and especially the combined offensive, the Big Push, on the Somme. Germany was first to be defeated on the battlefield, after which a peace settlement would be imposed on her by the victors; until the end of the 1916 campaigns the British Government was simply not interested in President Wilson's proposals.

Colonel House went on to Paris and Berlin and got the same answer there. The French wanted the USA to stay on the sidelines and supply munitions. The Germans insisted that, while they wanted a peace, it would be a peace on their terms. Colonel House returned to Britain for another meeting with Grey and the two men drew up a memorandum on their discussions which was later amended by President Wilson into a somewhat ambiguous statement concerning America's attitude to negotiations at this stage of the war:

Colonel House expressed the opinion that if such a conference met it would secure peace on terms not unfavourable to the Allies; and if it failed to secure peace the United States would probably leave the conference as a belligerent on the side of the allies, if Germany was unreasonable.[4]

Lord Grey did not find this statement helpful but, writing to the British Ambassador in Paris in March 1916, he said:

> As long as the military and naval authorities of the Allies say they can beat the Germans, there need be no talk of mediation . . . but if the war goes to a stalemate the question to be asked will be . . . whether it will secure better terms for the Allies than can be assured without it. It would therefore be a great mistake not to treat Colonel House seriously, though if the Allies can dictate terms of peace in Berlin without the help of the United States, nothing will come of Colonel House's proposals.[5]

In November 1915, von Bethmann-Hollweg made another attempt to undermine the Pact of London by contacting peace groups within the various countries, urging them to call on their Governments to reach a negotiated peace. This attempt came to nothing, as did a German attempt to defuse the Belgian question by offering to discuss Belgian sovereignty with King Albert. At a series of meetings in Zurich during November 1915, the Germans offered the King terms that fell some way short of annexation but the King preferred to rely on Sir Edward Grey's commitment of August 1914, that the restoration of Belgian sovereignty was a non-negotiable British war aim. So, with negotiations at an end, the war would continue into another year . . . or longer.

The last two chapters have outlined two somewhat neglected areas in Great War studies: the ever-increasing power and deployment of modern weapons and the inability of the belligerent nations to reach even the outline of an agreement that would prevent these weapons being employed. Both these factors have to be seen against the background to a war that had already been going on for far longer than any of the combatants had anticipated and had cost an undreamed-of quantity of lives.

Yet somehow the lessons provided by the losses had not been learned. All attempts to end the war by negotiation had failed, largely because both sides were still convinced that victory in the field was possible. To obtain it they intended to employ those weapons in even greater quantities in the year ahead, for one lesson of the fighting so far had been fully grasped by all the combatants.

However little the war could deliver in terms of territorial gain, it could be relied on to kill a great quantity of soldiers. So 1916 opened, with peace as far away as ever and the nations mustering all their strength for a renewal of all-out fighting a few weeks ahead, at Verdun.

Notes

1 Cabinet Papers, 2 August 1914.

2 *Lloyd George* by John Grigg, quoted in *British Strategy and War Aims*.

3 *Germany's Aims in the First World War*, 1967.

4 Memorandum by President Wilson, quoted in *British Strategy and War Aims*, p. 193.

5 Ibid.

6

The Battle Begins
21–25 February 1916

'We shall hold every metre of ground although their
bombardment is infernal.'
Lt-Colonel Émile Driant,
56th/59th Chasseurs, Verdun, 21 February 1916

The ten-day pause in the opening of the Verdun battle came to an end
soon after dawn on 21 February, when a shell fired from a German 380
mm (15-inch) howitzer sited in a wood 20 miles from the city landed
in the courtyard of the Bishop's Palace. That first shell had been aimed
at the river bridges in the city centre but only succeeded in shattering
all the windows in the cathedral of Notre-Dame and knocking down
a wall. From then on the shellfire at Verdun continued relentlessly by
day and night until the fighting there petered out nine months later, a
driving rain of steel which provided one of the most terrible features
of the battle.

Seen on those flickering, monochrome, Great War newsreels, shellfire does not seem too terrible. Infantry are seen advancing, there is a sudden puff of smoke, the men scatter and one or two fall down. Then, after a brief pause, the rest pull themselves together and press on. That is the image; the reality is very different. An exploding shell fills the air with a terrible, lung-collapsing blast, and shards of red-hot metal, ranging in size from slivers of steel no larger than a pencil to a solid mass of jagged metal the size of a house brick, fly in all directions.

The damage this whirling metal does to human flesh and bone is truly awful. Heads are crushed, limbs are blown off, flesh disintegrates, ribs cave in. The blast collapses lungs and stops the heart, leaving men shattered, or dead without a mark upon them. In the aftermath of the explosion, the deaf and blind stumble about the battlefield, shocked by what has happened, knowing that shells rarely fall singly and more are already descending on them from the skies. Imagine that going on ceaselessly, for hours, days, weeks and months, and the mind begins, dimly, to grasp the horror and terror of Verdun.

The shell storm that swept Verdun and the French defences on that first day was one of the most intense bombardments of the Great War, which is itself a byword in history for the massive deployment of artillery. The main barrage came from batteries of heavy 210 mm guns and was concentrated on the French front line and its supporting defences, with a number of long-range guns tasked to shell communication targets further back, like the bridges in Verdun. Hundreds of guns pounded the French positions on the right bank between 0700 hrs and 1600 hrs that day, and they did so systematically, sweeping to and fro across the ground, destroying what cover existed, playing havoc with the trenches and dugouts of the defending infantry and field gunners.

Under this continuous shellfire the earth seemed to heave and bubble like some monstrous pot of porridge. Behind the support lines, the battery positions of the French artillery were drenched in gas and then picked off by carefully directed artillery fire, controlled by observers in German aircraft circling above the battlefield. This shellfire forced General Bapst of the 72nd Division to evacuate his headquarters at Bras on the French left flank, cutting him off from the units of his command for some vital hours. An equally heavy bombardment fell on the positions of General Boulange's 51st Division on the right, cutting the telephone wires and forcing the division to rely entirely on runners.

This fire was directed on to the French positions by German artillery observers, hanging over the lines in balloons. Any French aircraft which rose to attack these observation balloons were quickly driven off by the swarming squadrons of German Fokker aircraft which had already established air superiority over the line, or came under accurate anti-aircraft fire. As a result of the lethal combination of gas and high-explosive shells, very little counter-battery fire fell among the German guns. In the forward defences of Colonel Driant's Chasseurs in the Bois des Caures, the German fire fell unabated for hours, concentrating first on the forward outposts, gradually easing back towards the reserve positions and the command posts, slowly isolating the Chasseurs from any possibility of support.

One estimate has it that some 80,000 shells fell on the Bois des Caures that day, shattering the trees, turning the ground into a pitted mass of shell holes, transforming Driant's positions into a maze of tumbled earth and splintered treetrunks. By midday the French positions in the Bois des Caures or around the village of Consenvoye, at Crépon and Beaumont and elsewhere along the line, were being steadily battered to pieces. More than 80 years later the marks of this shelling can still be seen around Verdun. Anywhere the plough has not been used to smooth the fields, the landscape is still a moonscape, dimpled with countless shell craters, each one touching or overlapping its neighbour.

There was calculation at work in this shelling, first in changing the range constantly so that the entire French position was periodically drenched with fire, but also in stopping the bombardment from time to time, partly to let the crews rest and the guns cool, but mainly to encourage the French infantry to emerge from their trenches. When the barrage ceased the French *poilus* would come cautiously out, rifles in hand, wondering if the expected infantry attack was about to come in, anxious to see what damage had been done to their positions and to help their wounded comrades. This brief pause in the shelling was a trap; after 10 or 15 minutes, when the French soldiers had gained enough confidence to stand about in the open and move away from their trenches and dugouts, the bombardment started again, catching many of the *poilus* unawares. These pauses also enabled German observers to see which parts of the French line were still intact and subject those areas to yet more drenching fire.

The shelling did more than kill soldiers and destroy emplacements. It cut the telephone communications between the front-line trenches and dugouts and the company and battalion headquarters. Within an hour of the barrage starting there was no contact between the front and rear other than by runner. Signallers who went out to repair the telephone wire failed to return; signallers who went out as runners, taking messages to and fro, failed to arrive; men did not live long in the barrage now falling on the defenders of Verdun. Those who went forward could only move slowly. One account states that reserve companies sent up to Verdun could manage no more than one mile every four hours that day, and lost men all the time as they went forward.

This barrage went on all morning and then into the afternoon, and the French gunners were unable to do much about it. Their positions had been drenched with gas, which choked or disabled the crews. Individual guns and batteries were picked off by the accurate 150 mm German guns, which had the range to reach any of the French positions around Verdun. Even without the vast superiority in artillery the Germans possessed, counter-battery fire was impossible because of the morning haze which reduced the view of the French observers on the ground. This ground mist was thickened later by smoke and burning trees; the German observers, high above the haze in balloons, had better visibility and could bring fire to bear on French gun flashes.

Having no other option, the French guns fired blindly across the lines until they were knocked out. By noon, most of the French batteries still firing had been reduced to one gun and, as their fire diminished in the early afternoon, German fighting patrols and stormtroops prepared to move forward, spearheading the attack towards Verdun, XV Reserve Corps heading for the Bois d'Haumont, XVIII Corps aiming to eliminate Driant's forward positions in the Bois

des Caures, III Corps heading in towards the left flank of the French
51st Division in the Bois de Ville. Nine German divisions, supported
by a massive amount of artillery, were about to fall on the two French
divisions – the 51st and 72nd – in the front line and drive them back
into Verdun.

The tactics employed at Verdun in 1916, for both attack and
defence, were ahead of their time. The French front line at Verdun was
not a continuous trench, of the type then common on other parts of
the Western Front. This was mainly because the wooded ground and
hills around the city, and a chronic lack of manpower, made the
construction of a continuous trench line difficult. The French had
therefore adopted a system of forward pickets, or outposts, small,
section positions, often no more than deepened shell scrapes, manned
by half a dozen men equipped with a light machine-gun. These men
were to stand guard, engage the enemy when seen and alert the larger
forces waiting in platoon (30-man) strength in *grandes gardes*,
entrenched positions a little farther back, many of them laid out
around a concrete blockhouse. These platoon posts were arranged for
all-round defence and most of the battalion riflemen and machine-
gunners were deployed here. The reserve company and company HQ
were in a support line or in the concrete emplacements which formed
part of the pre-war defences; behind that again was the Battalion HQ
and the reserve company. Had it not been for the terrible effect of the
powerful German artillery fire, this system would have provided a
stout defence and taken a heavy toll of the attacking infantry. As it
was, most of these positions were quickly smashed by that heavy,
relentless shelling.

The French positions in the Bois des Caures, the central position in
the French front line at Verdun, were not unlike those prepared by the
Germans in the Hindenburg Line in 1917 and adopted by the British
of the Fifth Army before the March Offensive in 1918. This layout
recognized one of the lessons of 1915, that a linear trench system
could be penetrated if attacked in sufficient strength by infantry
supported by artillery, though exploiting that penetration was a
different matter. The new layout gave the defence flexibility and made
it difficult for the enemy to overwhelm a single battalion or brigade by

a rapid advance or even by heavy shelling; the dispersal of trenches and dugouts was too wide and all-round protection between these outposts was provided by interlocking fields of fire from machine-guns, trench mortars and rifles. But no system is the complete answer to every form of attack, and the way to attack one of these well-deployed positions was by a heavy barrage of shells to shatter them, followed by infantry infiltration.

Infiltration – picking a way around and through the enemy defences rather than overwhelming them by an all-out frontal assault – is a task that calls for well-trained and intelligent troops. At Verdun this was the prime task of the German fighting patrols and stormtroopers, who had been specially trained in fighting forward in close, forested country and were now waiting in their squelching concrete dugouts, anxious to get out and get on with the task before them. The order to advance finally came at 1600 hrs, when the French line had been under heavy artillery fire for more than eight hours.

The essence of infiltration is movement, not combat. An infiltration attack seeks out the enemy position but then avoids it; the initial forward movement is best imagined as that of a wave flowing up a beach, finding and sweeping round obstacles without overwhelming them, until a second wave comes forward to complete the task. The task of the first wave, composed of fighting patrols, was to locate the French positions but pass them by, to gain as much ground as possible, leaving the business of mopping-up to the following waves of stormtroops, who would tear larger gaps in the French line but still keep moving. This was another lesson the Germans had learned by watching the mistakes of their opponents in 1915 – that an attack must keep moving, must have momentum, or it would grind to a halt and the ground gained would be pinched out and eventually lost.

In time, the forward troops would probably bump into a position they could not get round. Then their serious fighting would begin but, with any luck, by that time other advancing infantry units would be farther forward on the flanks and levering the French rear lines loose . . . and at this point the guns would be brought forward to do their work again on another, deeper part of the defenders' position, and thus get the next phase of the attack moving. So, like some monstrous, shell-powered juggernaut, the German attack would roll inexorably forward over the defenders' positions.

Bearing in mind von Falkenhayn's original intention, it would be a mistake for the Crown Prince and his Chief-of-Staff, von Knobelsdorf, to let these advancing troops get too far forward, and a serious mistake if the advancing German infantry should take too many French positions and gain a rapid victory around Verdun. That was not the idea at all, at least as far as von Falkenhayn was concerned. The task of the stormtroopers was to provide a threat to Verdun and force the French to commit their men to a battle in which the German artillery could dispose of them in quantity.

The German attacks on 21 February were therefore supposed to be little more than strong fighting patrols. On two of the corps fronts that is what they were and what they remained for the rest of the day. Only one general, von Zwehl of VII Reserve Corps, which was tasked to attack General Bapst's 72nd Division on the western end of the line, around Brabant, Consenvoye and the Bois d'Haumont, ordered his men to push forward vigorously towards Verdun. On this part of the front the stormtroopers were swiftly followed up by strong detachments of infantry, which went forward in the late afternoon gloom. After several hours of heavy fighting in the woods, this infantry took the Bois d'Haumont, pushing on from there to outflank Driant's men in the Bois des Caures.

Von Zwehl's infantry had closed to within 100 yards of the French line before they were detected and, when fire was opened on them, it came too late to stem their advance. After such terrible shelling the defenders were too exhausted, too shocked by the bombardment, too depleted in numbers to offer much resistance, and the Germans rapidly overran many of the French positions. By late afternoon this was not too difficult, for in many places the French line had virtually disappeared. With their weapons clogged with mud and their dugouts unusable, French casualties were severe: up to 50 per cent of the French front-line infantry were killed or wounded in the first day, most of them by artillery fire, most of them without seeing a German soldier or firing a shot. Now the survivors were coming under attack by swarms of German infantry who came running in to the attack out of the growing dusk, or could be heard somewhere to the rear, engaging the French support lines with rifle fire and grenades.

However, those French soldiers who had survived that day-long bombardment – the *Trommelfeuer* – were more than willing to fight. As dusk fell, a hand-to-hand struggle flared up in the chaotic woodland of the Bois des Caures and the Bois d'Haumont. Here and there, the French mounted counterattacks and retook some of their positions at the point of the bayonet, only to be driven out yet again when the Germans brought up a yet more terrifying device, the flame-thrower, or *Flammenwerfer*, a weapon to which the *poilus* had no answer.

These early flame-throwers were fairly primitive weapons, basically a metal tube attached to a small oil tank, light enough to be carried by one man. Compressed air was used to power the jet and once the oil had been ignited, the *Flammenwerfer* could squirt flaming oil for a distance of some 30–35 yards. In open ground the *Flammenwerfer* was dangerous to the operator, who could be spotted and shot down, or turned into a fireball, before getting close enough to use his weapon, but in the dark, in the close country of the Bois des Caures, over ground pitted with shell holes and laced with fallen trees, the *Flammenwerfer* operators were able to infiltrate the French defences and sweep the trenches and dugouts with fire. Before long, a new tactic was invented by those using this weapon; German infantry would pin the French soldiers into a dugout or blockhouse and keep their heads down with rifle fire until the *Flammenwerfer* operator was able to move in and scald the position with fire. So, slowly, with the use of grenades, rifle fire, machine-gun fire and the *Flammenwerfer*, the German infantry clawed their way into the French position. The greatest gains were made by von Zwehl's VII Reserve Corps, for XVIII Corps, pressing their attack on the lines proposed by von Falkenhayn, were held up by the stout resistance offered in the Bois des Caures by Colonel Driant's Chasseurs. By the end of the day, and well after dark, the majority of XVIII Corps infantry was still waiting in the *Stollen* for the order to advance.

The infantry fighting petered out after dark, only to be replaced by more shelling which blew down French defences as fast as the exhausted soldiers repaired them. Nor was there any help from the rear. Communications were non-existent, the front line was cut off by a blanket of shellfire to its rear, and movement was virtually impossible through the tangled jungle of fallen trees. Lacking any orders to the contrary, the defenders did what they could; they hung on, they fought back, they held every yard of ground; here and there they even counterattacked, in the best Grandmaison tradition. These tactics were expensive, but up to a point they worked; the Germans had infiltrated the French line in many places and reduced it to a shambles almost everywhere but, in spite of their losses, the French soldiers held on. In the Bois des Caures, where Colonel Driant's Chasseurs had endured the heaviest German fire, they even managed to take a few Hessian prisoners from XVIII Corps, one of whom assured Colonel Driant that another, even more powerful infantry attack would come in next day, after yet another morning of bombardment.

This stubborn French resistance on the first day came as something of a surprise to the Germans, at every level. After such a bombardment it had been anticipated that the French positions would consist of nothing but pitted earth, cracked concrete and corpses – a conviction that the British generals would have about the first day on the Somme some months later. This indeed was the sight that confronted their advancing infantry in the early afternoon, but the shelling had not quelled all resistance. Here and there a machine-gun sprang to life, raking their advancing line, or a group of men came out to challenge their advance. The stormtroopers soon learned that the German bombardment, impressive though it was, had not been totally effective. The advancing stormtroopers had taken heavy losses and reported back that the French were still in position and still full of fight. They also reported that if more was to be done it should be done quickly, as the French could only recover and fight even harder on the morrow.

Here was a fundamental failure in the German tactics and one that can be traced directly to von Falkenhayn. If he wanted to get the infantry forward into Verdun, or even gain a commanding position inside the French defences outside the city, then the time to do so was in the immediate aftermath of the first artillery barrage, using the stunning effect of shellfire and the basic advantage of surprise. By the following day the advantage of surprise would have gone and the defenders might well be reinforced – and von Falkenhayn certainly hoped so, as these reinforcements were to be more fodder for his guns. Since von Falkenhayn did not intend to take Verdun at this time, whatever he may have said later, he could be fairly satisfied with the position at the end of the first day. Only later would the flaw in his plan become evident.

The Fifth Army commanders were far less satisfied with the first day's results. They had obtained a degree of surprise, thanks to that opening bombardment, but now they were throwing it away by waiting for a further day of artillery fire before sending in their infantry again. The Great War maxim that 'artillery conquers and infantry occupies' is a good one, but both parts have to be employed; it is no good leaving it all to the artillery in the hope that the infantry can then simply take over empty enemy positions. The attackers usually discovered that there would always be some troops willing to engage them, and these had to be rooted out as well. In short, an attack, once begun, must be pressed home rapidly and kept up until the enemy line is penetrated and all opposition quelled. Any failure to press on quickly will certainly be penalized later.

Von Falkenhayn had not endorsed General von Zwehl's tactic of pouring in his troops on the first day, because it did not fit in with his original strategy, but von Zwehl's tactics clearly paid off. VII Reserve Corps quickly took the Bois d'Haumont, sweeping over the French 165th Regiment, where captains were now commanding the remnants of battalions, and further east the *Flammenwerfer* crews were already clearing out the dugouts of the 351st Regiment. Von Falkenhayn's general strategy, of only attacking on one bank of the Meuse, a narrow advance supported by sudden and overwhelming artillery fire, seemed to be vindicated by the gains achieved so far, but only time would tell whether this move was entirely wise. If the advance on the right bank continued, it would expose the German troops to fire from French positions on the left bank – and that fire could be crippling – but, for the moment at least, von Falkenhayn could be pleased with his strategy.

In the centre, at the Bois des Caures, the German attack had gone well, though Driant's Chasseurs still held on. On other parts of the front, where the German infantry were kept back on the first day, their gains were limited, although the artillery bombardment had fallen

right along the French line, from Malancourt on the left bank to
Brabant and Consenvoye, two villages on the banks of the river, and
then round to Beaumont, Ornes and Maucourt. A study of the map on
page 136 will be helpful at this point, and particular attention should
be paid to the villages close to the Meuse, which were about to be
attacked in strength. French reinforcements were now coming forward,
but very few actually arrived in the front-line positions; those
searching, balloon-directed guns found them and shattered the
arriving battalions before they got well forward. Finally, to make
matters more difficult for all concerned, not least the wounded, that
night it began to snow again.

The second day of the fighting at Verdun was a mirror of the first, at
least for the Germans: artillery fire throughout the morning and
infantry attacks in the afternoon. The commander of XVIII Corps,
General von Schenck, had been ordered to 'get on with it' and take the
Bois des Caures, where Driant's men held on until their positions were
finally overrun late in the afternoon. Colonel Driant then ordered his
men to break out in small groups and make for the reserve line at
Beaumont-en-Verdunois, just over half a mile to the rear. Very few of
them got there, most of them falling under the shelling or machine-gun
fire – and Colonel Driant was killed as he left his headquarters. Driant
had lost 700 men – 60 per cent of his force – in two days of fighting.

Inevitably, under this incessant shelling and infantry pressure, the
French front line finally began to buckle. The Bois des Caures fell, the
Bois d'Haumont and Haumont village had gone, and casualties had
soared but still, just, the French line held throughout yet another day.
Then, on the third day, 24 February, their line crumbled on the bank
of the Meuse – a sudden collapse caused not by German artillery fire
but by confusion in the orders between General Chrétien, XXX Corps
Commander, and his beleaguered subordinate, General Bapst of the
72nd Division.

On the night of the 21st, the Germans had forced the French out of
the Bois de Consenvoye. This put von Zwehl's men in a good position
to outflank the village of Brabant, on the right bank of the Meuse.
Brabant was the key to the entire 72nd Division position and should
have been held – *tenir coute que coute* – whatever the cost, but for some

reason, perhaps fearing that this village would fall anyway and the loss expose his flank, General Bapst elected to abandon Brabant and pull the men there back to the village of Samogneux, which also lay on the river bank, closer to Verdun. No sooner had the French infantry left Brabant than an order arrived from General Chrétien, the Corps commander, ordering them to retake it. Order and counter-order always lead to disorder, especially when communications are poor, and so it was here. Chaos reigned along the river bank as the troops milled about, some pulling out of the village, others heading back. The Germans were quick to take advantage of the confusion and by nightfall on the 23rd Brabant had fallen and Samogneux was closely beset, but holding. The troops in Samogneux continued to hold out until well after midnight on the 24th, when a final barrage and a strong German infantry attack finally took the village. It was then discovered that the supporting artillery barrage falling on the defenders' lines had come from French batteries, wrongly informed that Samogneux was already in German hands.

During the first days of the Verdun battle, the French soldiers drew on their infantry tradition, and on the Grandmaison doctrine, and when driven out of a position promptly tried to retake it with a series of counterattacks. All of these failed; the advantages of the defence were shared by every nation, and these French attacks, rarely co-ordinated and all small scale, quickly withered away in the face of German machine-gun fire and that pounding artillery. The aerial observers also quickly spotted any movement behind the French line and brought down shellfire on any troops attempting to get forward to shore up the front line. This was worn down by heavy attacks, notably from von Zwehl's infantry, which was now pushing down the right bank of the Meuse, close to the river, and getting up on to the heights of the Côte de Falou ridge, round which the river swung to the west. With his flank resting on the river, von Zwehl was now preparing to prise the French line loose and roll it up, right across the right bank position.

It was the same story in the centre and on the left flank of the German advance. By the morning of the 23rd, XVIII Corps had taken the Bois des Caures and was pressing forward towards Beaumont; III Corps was moving towards Fort Douaumont; and, on the left flank,

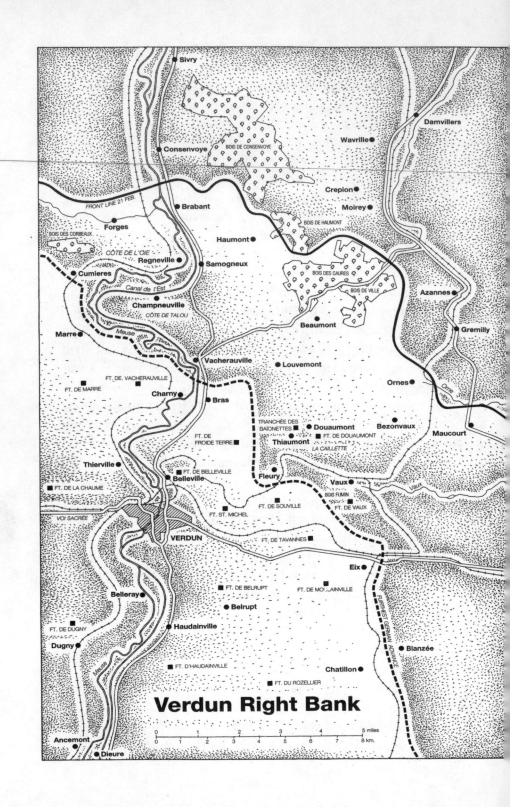

Sivry

Damvillers

Wavrille
BOIS DE CONSENVOYE

Consenvoye

Crepion

Moirey

FRONT LINE 21 FEB.

Brabant

BOIS DE HAUMONT

Forges

BOIS DES CORBEAUX

Haumont

CÔTE DE L'OIE

Regneville

Samogneux

BOIS DES CAURES

Cumieres

Canal de l'Est

BOIS DE VILLE

Azannes

Champneuville

CÔTE DE TALOU

Beaumont

Gremilly

Marre

Meuse

Vacherauville

Louvemont

FT. DE VACHERAUVILLE

Ornes

FT. DE MARRE

Charny

Bras

Orne

TRANCHÉE DES
BAÏONETTES

Douaumont

Bezonvaux

FT. DE DOUAUMONT

FT. DE
FROIDE TERRE

Thiaumont

LA CAILLETTE

Maucourt

Thierville

FT. DE BELLEVILLE

Fleury

Vaux

Belleville

BOIS FUMIN

FT. DE LA CHAUME

FT. DE SOUVILLE

FT. DE VAUX

Vaux

VOI SACRÉE

FT. ST. MICHEL

VERDUN

FT. DE TAVANNES

Eix

Belleray

FT. DE BELRUPT

FT. DE MOULAINVILLE

Haudainville

Belrupt

FURTHEST GERMAN ADVANCE

FT. DE DUGNY

Dugny

Blanzée

FT. D'HAUDAINVILLE

Chatillon

Meuse

FT. DU ROZELLIER

Verdun Right Bank

0   1   2   3   4   5 miles
0   1   2   3   4   5   6   7   8 km.

Ancemont

Dieure

XV Corps was pushing forward to the villages of Ornes and Bezonvaux, which were captured, recaptured and then taken again that day, the houses being totally destroyed in two days of fighting. One by one the positions on the French front began to give way under this relentless pressure; French counterattacks in the Bois des Caures and the Bois d'Haumont were repulsed, and the village of Haumont was in German hands by nightfall on the 22nd, with the loss of nearly 2,000 French soldiers.

By the end of the third day, in spite of a most gallant resistance, the original French front line had gone. The German tactic of heavy artillery fire followed by infantry attacks preceded by infiltration was steadily eroding the French position; there seemed to be little the *poilus* could do but hang on and await the fate that had befallen Colonel Driant and his troops. The French artillery, which had mustered fewer than 300 guns of various calibres when the battle began, was already much diminished and unable to give much help to the hard-pressed infantry. Nor was what fire they could deliver very effective. Without balloon or aircraft observers to spot their fall of shot, the French gunners were firing blind, and the German 150 mms were relentless in seeking out and picking off their batteries. And, while the 150 mms knocked out the French guns, German heavy guns, the 380 mms and 420 mms, were steadily shattering Verdun and pounding the surrounding forts. So the third day ended, with the full extent of the crisis as yet unrecognized at GQG.

With the fall of Samogneux, however, the French position at Verdun suddenly became desperate. The trench line constructed on de Castelnau's orders between the existing first and second line positions on the right bank – a barely completed series of trenches and outposts – had been occupied on the night of 21–2 February by troops withdrawing from the front line. But when the Germans came forward on the second day they swiftly overran this 'de Castelnau' line and, keeping hard on the heels of the retreating French, soon reached the second line as well. The French second line, already wrecked by shellfire and full of wounded men, fell within hours.

By now many French formations had either ceased to exist or been so whittled down as to be totally ineffective. The 72nd Division, which had opened the battle with 12,000 men, had lost nearly 10,000 men in three days; this is as many as all the Allied armies, navies and air forces lost on D-Day 1944 – and the French losses came from a single division. Other divisions were in no better case, fought out, exhausted or reduced to a remnant. The losses had been particularly high among the officers, and the policy of instant counterattacks to retake any lost position only tended to make these losses higher. The French had been caught on the back foot by this attack and, on 24 February, the entire French position outside Verdun suddenly came apart.

This collapse was signalled by the breaking of an elite French Colonial Division, the 37th African, composed of Zouaves and Tirailleurs, the reserve division of XXX Corps. These Algerian troops were noted in the French Army for their verve in the attack, a reputation earned the hard way in the ruthless Algerian colonial war. The fighting at Verdun, however, was nothing like colonial war, in which battles were fought with light weapons against tribesmen. This was a European war, fought with heavy guns and flame-throwers, where men were subjected to days and nights of artillery fire, under freezing skies and frequent snow storms. February in eastern France is a far cry from the North African *bled*, and it was the weather, rather than the enemy, that broke the heart of this fine division.

The 37th African Division had not been well handled. The Tirailleurs were herded up to the front, put into positions that did not exist in any meaningful way, and then left to get on with it, under a steady rain of shells. A night of this in sub-zero temperatures lowered morale to breaking point and, when the German infantry tide swept forward with the dawn on 24 February, the Tirailleurs collapsed; it took a little time for the panic to spread but eventually the entire division, Tirailleurs and Zouaves, officers and men, was in full retreat, followed by the exultant Germans up to the first French artillery positions, where several batteries of 75 mm guns fell into German hands.

These events – and this brief account of what happened to the 37th Division is only a microcosm of what was happening at other points along the Verdun front – were now having a deleterious effect on the morale of other French units. This is hardly to be wondered at, for the Germans had developed tactics to which the French currently had no answer and they were applying them with ruthless efficiency. The crux of the problem was the relentless artillery fire. As von Falkenhayn had intended, artillery was grinding men and terrain to a common clay; the French infantry who were enduring this torment did not even have the dubious satisfaction of knowing that the enemy were in a similar situation.

Quite the contrary; as the days passed the French guns gradually fell silent, until the forward infantry began to wonder if their gunners had pulled out and left them to their fate. Added to this were other factors inhibiting morale: a lack of food, rest and mail; the death of respected officers and valued friends; the terrible and obvious suffering of the wounded, who could not be evacuated; above all, the creeping, insidious feeling that nobody cared, that their commanders had lost control of this battle, that they were on their own and were going to be left out there until they died, alone and unsupported under the freezing skies.

By the night of 24 February, General Chrétien's XXX Corps was effectively finished as a fighting force. His divisions, even General Bapst's ragtag division, had done well, far better than could be expected in the circumstances, but they could do no more. They had nothing left to fight with; by nightfall on the 24th, III Corps had not as much as a company of soldiers left in reserve. Without adequate reserves, to fill in gaps, to replace the wounded, to retake positions and shore up the front line, a military unit cannot function – and General Chrétien was completely out of reserves.

Those brigades he had held in reserve on the 21st had been fed in piecemeal to help the various divisions and by the 23rd all had been committed. General Chrétien and XXX Corps could do no more and, on the night of 24 February, they were relieved by General Balfourier and XX Corps, which had been rushed up from the rear. It would take a day or two before all the XX Corps brigades were in the line and the depleted battalions of XXX Corps had gone out for long rest but, by the morning of 25 February, four days into a battle that would continue for ten months, the situation was grave indeed.

It is arguable that only the fact that von Falkenhayn did not wish to take Verdun prevented the city falling, for one strong push now would probably have carried the German infantry into the city. The defence now depended on the tattered remnants of XXX Corps and the rapid arrival of General Balfourier's XX Corps, the famous Iron Corps, the unit that Foch himself had commanded in 1914 in the defence of Nancy – but not even the Iron Corps could shore up the line at Verdun on its own. Only two XX Corps brigades had arrived by 24 February and, before they could take up their positions, a further disaster smote the French defenders of Verdun. On the morning of 25 February, Fort Douaumont, the most famous and formidable bastion in the Verdun defences, fell into German hands.

Douaumont was to Verdun what Verdun was to France; a linchpin of the defence and a symbol of resistance. Douaumont was also the key to the entire French position on the right bank; if Douaumont fell, the French position before Verdun might be fatally compromised. This fact was known to both sides, but there was another fact concerning this vital position of which the Germans were in ignorance. By February 1916, the fortress of Douaumont had been stripped of its garrison and most of its guns and when a small party of German soldiers forced their way up to the outer glacis on 25 February and clambered in through the gunports, they found this outwardly formidable fortress little more than an empty shell.

Joffre had concealed his removal of guns from the forts of Verdun from his Government masters, including the current Minister of War, General Galliéni, and had assured those generals who knew the guns had gone, and expressed doubts about the wisdom of this action, that as long as the Germans thought the Verdun forts retained their heavy guns they would never attack and the situation would remain a secret. The officers charged with defending Verdun, notably the hapless General Herr, had therefore been told to keep their mouths shut and devote their men and energy to turning Verdun into a 'fortified region'.

Fort Douaumont was, and still is, a massive, six-sided construction, a star-shaped fortress on the Vauban style, 440 yards in width. Crouching low on the ridge like some monstrous carbuncle, the superstructure stands at over 1,115ft, offering sweeping views over the surrounding countryside. The roof is constructed of solid concrete, many feet thick and topped with several yards of packed earth. The outer walls of Douaumont were surrounded by a ditch 26ft deep,

Left to right: Hindenberg, the Kaiser and Ludendorff. Courtesy of The Imperial War Museum

LEFT: (*left to right*) Albert Thomas, Haig, Joffre and Lloyd George (XIV Corps HQ, Méaulte, South of Albert). © Chrysalis Images

RIGHT: (*left to right*) Hindenberg, the Kaiser and Ludendorff. © Chrysalis Images

RIGHT: Presentation to Marshal Pétain of the Baton of a Marshal of France. *Left to right:* Petain, Joffre, Foch, Haig, Generals Pershing (USA), Gillain (Belgium), Albricci (Italy), and Haller (Poland).

Courtesy of The Imperial War Museum

LEFT: *(left to right)* Joffre, Haig and Foch. © Chrysal's Images

Fourth Army HQ. King George V with British and French generals and staff. © Chrysalis Images

LEFT: Battle of Somme. A Lewis gun in action in a front line trench near Ovillers, July 1916. Courtesy of The Imperial War Museum

RIGHT: Somme offensive, July 1916. The Vickers machine gun was the standard heavy machine gun. It was fed by means of a 250-round belt and cooled by water. Courtesy of The Imperial War Museum

RIGHT: Cavalry Hotchkiss gun team practising coming into action. Near Querrieu (4th Army HQ) 29 July 1916. Courtesy of The Imperial War Museum

LEFT: Excavating machine used for digging trenches.

Courtesy of The Imperial War Museum

RIGHT: The H Class in 1916. Length 171 feet; displacement on surface 440 tons, submerged 500 tons; four 21 inch bow torpedo tubes; eleven knots on surface; crew of three officers and twenty men. A torpedo is shown on the casting preparatory to being struck down into the submarine for loading. © Chrysalis Images

RIGHT: British submarine C3 underway.
Courtesy of The Imperial War Museum

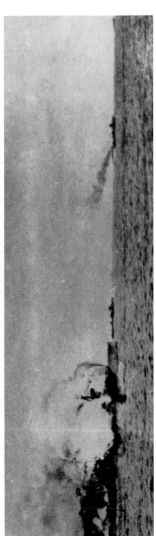

RIGHT: Destruction of *HMS Invincible* at Jutland in 1916. Courtesy of The Imperial War Museum

RIGHT: Siemens E II in 1916. 120 HP Argus engine.
Courtesy of The Imperial War Museum

LEFT: Sopwith 1½ Strutter in 1916. 100 HP Clerget engine. Two-seat fighter reconnaissance biplane.
Courtesy of The Imperial War Museum

RIGHT: Damage caused by a Zeppelin raid on King's Lynn.

Courtesy of The Imperial War Museum

RIGHT: Tank crossing a British trench on its way to attack Thiepval, 25 Sept 1916.

Courtesy of The Imperial War Museum

ABOVE: Somme battle, 15 September 1916. New Zealanders in a forward trench. © Chrysalis Images

LEFT: British infantry advancing in Somme battle, 25 September 1916. © Chrysalis Images

RIGHT: A communication trench showing a type of revetting. July 1916. Courtesy of The Imperial War Museum

LEFT: An old German trench is visible from the Albert–Pozières road over Ovillers, September 1916. This white chalk trench could be followed for miles. © Chrysalis Images

RIGHT: German prisoners captured by the British during the Somme offensive.

ABOVE: View of a devastated battlefield, Somme 1916. Courtesy of The Imperial War Museum

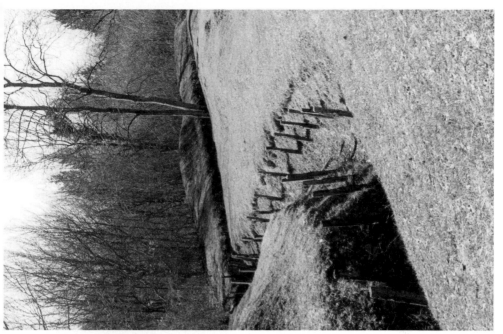

ABOVE: Retractable machine gun and cannon cupola, Fort Douaumont, Verdun.

© Robin Neillands

RIGHT: A French trench line in Verdun. © Robin Neillands

NEAR RIGHT: 'Here fell Colonel Driant'. Verdun. © Robin Neillands

MIDDLE RIGHT: The *Tranchée des Baïonettes*, Verdun. © Robin Neillands

FAR RIGHT: Road sign, *Voie Sacrée*, Verdun.

© Robin Neillands

RIGHT: Memorial and main cemetery, Verdun.

© Robin Neillands

which was protected by a belt of barbed wire 33ft wide. For local defence, every corner turret contained machine-guns and quick-firing cannon capable of raking the ground close to the fort and wiping out any attacker entering it while, for long-range defence, Douaumont had – or at least should have had – a number of heavy cannon and artillery pieces of 75 mm or 155 mm calibre, firing from well-camouflaged emplacements or retractable metal cupolas.

Fort Douaumont could accommodate a garrison of up to 1,000 troops, not counting those in the exterior trenches and this combination of men, guns and fortifications should have made it virtually impregnable. Unfortunately, between July and October 1915, no less than 43 heavy gun batteries and 11 75 mm field gun batteries had been removed from the forts of Verdun, together with a large amount of ammunition. This alone would have made the forts vulnerable but the final element in the loss of Douaumont, the main bastion, can be traced to those ongoing and now-familiar Great War problems, command and communications.

Although General Chrétien commanded the troops at Verdun, the fortresses came under the direct command of the area commander, General Herr . . . who had no troops to man them. Indeed, when General Chrétien attempted to enter Fort Douaumont some time before the battle, he was refused entry by an NCO on the grounds that he did not have an official pass. On the 23rd, with the Germans three miles inside the French front-line defences, and heading directly for Fort Douaumont, Herr sent a frantic message to Chrétien, ordering him to send troops into the fort and prepare to hold it.

General Chrétien had no men to send. He therefore sent the order on to General Deligny, the officer commanding one of the brigades of XX Corps, which was now coming up on to the right bank. Unfortunately, General Deligny did not receive it but when Chrétien left Verdun he firmly believed that XX Corps troops were already in Fort Douaumont – while the commander of XX Corps, General Balfourier, thought that Chrétien's troops were still in possession. In fact, the only troops in the fort were a few gunners and about 50 Territorial soldiers from Herr's scanty command.

The story of how Douaumont fell has been told in detail elsewhere

and need only be briefly summarized here.[1] The area between the fort
and the German front line should have been held by the Zouaves but
they had abandoned their trenches on the previous day. Therefore,
when the leading German unit, the 24th Brandenburg Regiment,
advanced on 25 February, there was little to stop them as they
advanced more than one mile over the outer French defences and
found themselves close to the fort. The sound of firing came from
other parts of the battlefield and the shelling continued, but the fort
itself was silent, brooding over the battlefield, an awesome sight, the
walls dented and scarred, the surrounding ground pitted with
blackened shell holes.

The reputation of Fort Douaumont as a defensive bastion had
reached the German Army and the Brandenburgers cautiously slowed
their advance, but a party of pioneers led by a Sergeant Kunze kept
going and eventually made their way through the barbed-wire belt
and up to the side of the moat, where a sudden shell blast blew
Sergeant Kunze over the edge without doing him any harm. His men
followed him down, crossed the dry moat and, by piling up some
planks, were able to reach a window and enter the fort. This was as far
as most of the men wanted to go. Most of them stayed in the moat,
but Sergeant Kunze pressed on into the fort, creeping up the dank,
dark tunnels on his own, gradually coming to realize that this famous
fort, this bastion of Verdun, was virtually unoccupied and his for the
taking. By now other Germans had arrived, including a detachment of
infantry and three officers, Captain von Brandis, Lieutenant Radtke
and Captain Haupt, all of the 24th Brandenburgers. They also entered
the fort without encountering opposition, and Radtke captured three
French soldiers who gave him the almost unbelievable news that the
garrison of mighty Fort Douaumont consisted of just two platoons –
about 60 men.

Eventually these three German officers met, compared notes and
sent runners back for more men. Inside a few hours, the Germans had
secured a position that might, had it been fully armed and properly
defended, have held up their advance for weeks or months. As it was,
the capture of Douaumont took less than four hours and cost the 24th
Brandenburg Regiment just 32 men killed and 40 wounded. It was later

estimated that French losses resulting from the fall of Douaumont, or incurred in its recapture many months later, amounted to around 100,000 men.

The loss of Fort Douaumont sent shock waves through France and a wave of jubilation through Germany. The credit for capturing Douaumont was given to Captain von Brandis, who had played a very minor role in the action, but was quick to report success. When he met the Crown Prince, who was in a state of exhilaration over the taking of Douaumont, nothing would do for this hero but the Pour le Merité, Germany's highest decoration for gallantry, which was also awarded to Haupt; Radtke and Sergeant Kunze got nothing.

On the French side of the line the reaction was little short of despair. That Douaumont should fall at all was a disaster; that it should fall like this, without taking a heavy toll of the enemy first, was a humiliation. Besides, what would follow? With Douaumont gone, it seemed that further retreats and disasters were sure to come. The thought being father to the deed, a retreat duly followed when General de Bonneval's 37th Division, which had already failed once, failed again and fell back towards Froidterre and the Belleville ridge. This ridge, east of the main road, was buttressed by two small forts, Fort Belleville and Fort St Michel. From the ridge between them it was possible to look down into the streets of Verdun.

The situation could not have been worse but at least the fall of Douaumont had done something that four days of disaster had so far failed to do: it persuaded General Joffre that the situation at Verdun was serious and that unless something was done the city would fall. The first step was to appoint a new commander and the choice fell on an officer that General Joffre and many of his officers cordially disliked, the current commander of the Second Army, General Henri Philippe Pétain.

Note

1 See *The Price of Glory, Verdun 1916*, by Alistair Horne, chapter 9.

7

Enter General Pétain
February–March 1916

By the evening of 25 February, four days into the battle, the French were hanging on to the Verdun position by their fingertips. On the right bank all was disaster; the French had been forced back for about four miles, Fort Douaumont had gone, the Germans were fighting in Douaumont village, Fort Vaux was threatened, casualties had been terrible and the rain of shells fell without ceasing. It seemed that nothing could stop the inexorable advance of the Fifth Army down the right bank of the Meuse and into the city. At the front all this was apparent but, at GQG in Chantilly, General Joffre maintained his habitual unruffled calm.

Although his staff were far less confident, poring anxiously over their maps and mustering reserves, Joffre's confidence had been bolstered on the evening of the 24th by a report sent in that afternoon from Verdun by a GQG observer, Colonel Claudel, who claimed that the German attack, whatever its initial gains, was now faltering. This view was not shared by the overall commander of the Verdun sector, General de Langle de Cary, commander of Army Group Centre. His telephone report on the evening of the 24th was deemed so serious that he was even allowed to interrupt the *generalissimo*'s dinner, normally a sacrosanct period in Joffre's day, in order to voice his concerns.

De Langle de Cary reported the full extent of both the German advance and the casualties in General Herr's command and requested permission to evacuate the Woevre valley to the east of the Verdun salient before the French position there was outflanked by the German advance at Verdun. Joffre heard this report out in silence but declined to comment or give orders for reinforcement or relief. He simply referred all decisions back to de Langle de Cary, telling him to do what he liked, and calmly returned to his dinner. This interruption of Joffre's set routine may have marked the first step towards the end of de Langle de Cary's career; bearers of bad tidings tend to be remembered, and when someone had to be sacrificed for the Verdun débâcle, de Langle de Cary's name would come to mind.

However, the *generalissimo*'s hopes of a quiet evening were dashed yet again by the arrival of his Chief-of-Staff, General de Castelnau, who was fully aware of what was happening at Verdun and had plans to remedy the situation. De Castelnau had visited the Verdun front the previous month and had urged General Herr to proceed at once in developing the defences, though without offering to provide either the men or the means to do so. De Castelnau knew that the German attack was serious and would not be stemmed with the replacement of a single worn-out corps or a steady trickle of divisional replacements. What Verdun needed now – and quickly – was a full Army and a fighting general.

Like a number of French generals, including Joffre, Noel Marie de Castelnau came from the Pyrénées. Although de Castelnau was an aristocrat and Joffre came from peasant stock, their common roots may have helped to cement their relations, for it is certain that their relationship was very close. De Castelnau was one of the few officers in the French Army who had access to Joffre at any time, day or night, even during meals. In 1914 de Castelnau was 65, old enough to have served as a young officer in the Franco-Prussian War, an experience that marked him for life, for after that defeat he had become a stout advocate of *attaque à outrance*, an apostle of the Grandmaison doctrine. Fortunately, de Castelnau also had brains; at the start of the war, when commanding the Second Army, he had masterminded the defence of eastern France and, with Foch, saved the city of Nancy. De Castelnau was also a front-line soldier, never happier than when leading troops in action or serving within earshot of the guns. This may have been a family trait; three of de Castelnau's sons had already been killed in the war.

De Castelnau was far from hopeful about the situation at Verdun but he had worked out a solution. His previous command, the Second Army, should be despatched to Verdun at once and the defence of the entire sector should be handed over forthwith to the current Second Army commander, General Pétain. This latter suggestion did not go down at all well with General Joffre, who had distinct reservations about Philippe Pétain.

The son of a farmer from Picardy, commissioned into an Alpine regiment and 58 before he reached the rank of general, Henri Philippe Omer Pétain was no longer a young man when his hour of destiny arrived in 1916. He was now 60, a tall, remote figure but apparently still full of vigour. When the call from GQG reached the Second Army headquarters at Noailles later that night, the General was not in his quarters. He was eventually tracked down by his aide, Captain de Serrigny, who found him in bed with a young lady in the Hotel Terminus by the Gare du Nord in Paris; one of the most curious sidelights of the Verdun campaign is the scene on the landing outside that bedroom, with Serrigny shouting the news of Pétain's new task – and the urgent request for his presence at GQG – through the door to the general and his girlfriend within.

This love of the ladies was one of the less well-known facets of Pétain's character – and would seem to clash with his equally well-earned reputation, first as a thinking soldier and later as a disastrous politician – but the Pétain of 1916, the Pétain of Verdun, was not the

Pétain of 1940, the Pétain of Vichy. His later infamy as a collaborator with Nazi Germany, founder of the Milice, persecutor of the Resistance and head of the Vichy Government of 1940–5, should not obscure the fact that in 1916 Pétain was the man of the hour and one widely seen in the post-Great War world as the saviour of France. This may have been the view of the public and the private soldier but, in the higher circles of French military and political life, Pétain was not at all popular.

Pétain was a complex character for a military man, and his personality is hard to sum up or put a precise finger on. Serrigny, who was Pétain's loyal aide and subordinate for much of the war and for years after it, including Pétain's time as Commander-in-Chief, eventually came to the reluctant conclusion that his much-admired chief was weak; that behind his professional military façade Pétain simply did not believe that the war was worth it or that the losses, the deaths, the endless suffering, were justified by either the causes or the results. Many will say that in holding this view Pétain was not weak but absolutely correct.

Perhaps it is more accurate to say that in uncertain times Pétain compounded the difficulties with his own uncertainties. Other generals – Nivelle and Haig spring to mind here – always seemed to know what they were doing and appear to have had complete faith both in themselves and their professional ability; doubt does not seem to have troubled them. Pétain knew what he was doing professionally – but beyond that, one wonders.

Even before the war, when he was an instructor at the École de la Guerre, Pétain was the odd man out among the French commanders. He was adamantly against the *attaque à outrance* doctrine, which marked him out from the rest, but the difference went beyond professional disagreements. Put simply, most of the other French generals simply did not know what to make of General Pétain. He did not fit into any group or clique. He was not flamboyant or thrusting, like Foch or Nivelle; on the other hand, he was clearly not incompetent, like most, but not all of that host of French general officers sent into premature retirement in Limoges, hence described as *limogé*, since the outbreak of war. He was an unknown quantity, and that in itself made his colleagues uneasy.

Pétain was not inarticulate and could put over his views with clarity and precision. While other generals and the staff at the École Supérieure de la Guerre argued for the doctrine of relentless attack and rapid counterattack, Pétain stubbornly maintained that, in the modern age, weapons of defence would dominate the battlefield and render all-out frontal attacks by unsupported infantry, however brave and well led, a recipe for disaster.

Pétain saw this fixation on *attaque à outrance* as one of the reasons French losses were so high, especially among the officer corps, and on taking over command of the French Armies in 1917, he dismissed the Grandmaison doctrine like this: 'Modern tactics are no longer Napoleonic tactics. They are dominated and controlled by the progress in armaments, by the extraordinary growth in fire power.' Even more extraordinary is the fact that this still needed pointing out to the French officer corps as late as 1917.

Pétain may have seen quite early on in this war that, if it continued, a battle of attrition was inevitable. In his book *The Two Marshals*, Philip Guedalla states: 'his [Pétain's] own preference at this time [May 1915] was for a sparing use of men, since he had arrived at the conviction that the appointed instrument of victory was attrition, and that the war would be won by the side which could bring up the last reserves.'[2] This does not mean that Pétain would welcome a campaign of attrition; indeed, given the disparity in population, attrition was a contest which the French could only lose but, unlike many other soldiers, he could see which way the war was going – in the direction of attrition.

Pétain's beliefs in the dangers of France's military doctrines proved to be all too accurate when war arrived in Western Europe in 1914, but the fact that Pétain's reservations proved well founded did not add to his personal popularity. He had advanced to command of the Second Army because he was a good soldier but the instructions from de Castelnau, to go to Verdun and hold it at all costs, cannot have pleased him. There is little doubt that, given the freedom to do so, Pétain would have evacuated the Verdun salient and fallen back behind the Meuse. This fact did not escape Joffre's notice and it was made clear to Pétain during the battle that any attempt at, or even the suggestion of, anything more than a short tactical withdrawal would result in his instant dismissal.

That de Castelnau should choose Pétain to defend Verdun flew in the face of GQG's wishes, but Pétain commanded the Second Army and it was the Army, rather than its general, that de Castelnau wanted at Verdun. Given the choice, Joffre and de Castelnau might well have chosen someone else for the post, some general who could wrest the lost territory back from the Germans, but for the soldiers around Verdun the choice of Pétain as their commander proved a godsend.

The private soldiers of France were not well treated during the Great War; compared with their lot, the soldiers of the other armies on the Western Front were blessed with good food, reliable mail, adequate pay, frequent reliefs and regular leave. For all the obloquy heaped upon them, the staff officers of the British armies saw to it that in these areas at least British troops had little to complain about. These benefits did not reduce the general misery of trench life but they demonstrated that the private soldier had value.

Not so the French *poilu*. His pay was meagre, his food disgusting – though his wine was drinkable – his leave infrequent, letters from home often failed to arrive, and his life was all too often thrown away in frontal attacks that usually achieved nothing but an extensive casualty list. Much of this was simply due to poor staff work, to incompetence rather than indifference, but if the ordinary French soldier gradually gained the impression that his officers – and especially the general officers – were, or appeared to be, indifferent to his welfare, that is hardly surprising; most of the French generals were, indeed, totally indifferent to the welfare of the men, provided the attacks went in.

No other army positioned machine-guns *behind* front-line trenches to mow down any men falling back under attack or failing to advance when ordered to do so. As for the company officers, while there were many exceptions, the British Army belief that the first duty of an officer was the welfare of his men was not a widespread concept among the French officer corps. The day-to-day welfare of the troops was left to the NCOs and 'adjutants', or warrant officers. The role of the officer was to command in battle and lead from the front – a role which they performed with great gallantry and at considerable cost.

Fortunately, there were exceptions to this bleak generalization and one of these was Philippe Pétain. Pétain cared about his men, the ordinary soldiers of France, and in some strange way they knew it. Although he rarely showed his feelings, Pétain was able to communicate this concern to his men and, even if he presided over some terrible battles, this fact kept the men at their posts and their confidence in his ability high.

Pétain certainly never went out of his way to be popular. As is frequently the case, a care for the men proved incompatible with tolerance for politicians and the more chairborne officers of the General Staff. Pétain had a knack for making enemies; even before the war he had made an enduring foe of President Poincaré by telling him to his face: 'Nobody is better placed than the President himself to be aware that France is neither led nor governed.'

General de Castelnau's report to Joffre reinforced de Langle de Cary's concerns about Verdun and obliged Joffre to pay attention to his unwelcome suggestion regarding Pétain. If retreat was not an option, said de Castelnau, then General Pétain's Second Army, which had just been replaced by a British Army on the line of the Somme, should be moved at once to Verdun and put into the line there. While Second Army was coming up, de Castelnau would go to Verdun, view the situation on the ground, and prepare orders for Pétain and his Army. Joffre, anxious to go to bed, promptly agreed, and de Castelnau departed into the night.

General de Castelnau arrived at Verdun sometime after dawn on 25 February and made his way to General Herr's headquarters. Pausing there to ginger up the general and his staff with a few well-chosen threats, he pressed on around the defences to see the situation on the ground for himself. The ability to sum up the difficulties and make a rapid 'appreciation of the situation' – on what is happening and what can be done about it – is the mark of a good general and, by mid-afternoon, de Castelnau had made his appreciation and come to a decision that would radically alter the situation at Verdun.

De Castelnau's first decision was that the Verdun position could be held. The fury of the initial and current German onslaughts could hardly be maintained, so the situation could be contained, even retrieved, if the left bank, which had not yet been attacked, was held at all costs and there was no further retreat on the right bank. In de Castelnau's rapidly formulated plan, these two banks were indivisible and must be defended as one. The Second Army must come up and occupy the remaining French positions on both banks – and there must be no retreat from these positions. De Castelnau did not yet know that the situation had been gravely impaired by the loss of Douaumont; that news came too late to affect his decision. Having decided what needed doing, he returned to Herr's HQ for a meeting with General Pétain.

De Castelnau's appreciation was sound on two counts. First, he had appreciated that any serious attack aimed at taking Verdun must eventually involve an attack on both banks. The fact that the Germans had not yet attacked on the left bank was not material; if their attack was serious, with a strategic objective, then it would, it must, soon develop on the left bank as well. Secondly, given this fact, it was essential to reinforce the left bank now, so that when the attack did come, the positions there, especially the crucial Mort Homme and Côte 304 hills, could be held.

As long as the French held these positions, the German attack down the right bank would, sooner or later, run into a blast of flanking artillery fire and grind to a halt. De Castelnau may not yet have realized what von Falkenhayn was trying to do – to induce a battle of attrition – but he fully realized what Pétain's army would be able to do, if they could hold the left bank. It is also noteworthy that de Castelnau did not intend to repeat the German mistake of concentrating their attack on the right bank by placing all his defenders there.

On the other hand, by electing to hold Verdun, de Castelnau was doing exactly what von Falkenhayn wanted. He was opting to hold a position that could only be defended at a great cost in lives. The fact that it was to cost Germany as many men as France would prove a poor consolation; Germany had more men to lose. Though the fact was not yet apparent, the cost of Verdun was not only counted in the dead. The Battle of Verdun took a heavy toll of the spirit, the morale of the French Army – and the bill for that would come in 1917 when units of the French Army mutinied. For the French nation and Philippe Pétain, the bill arrived in 1940. Verdun had been enough; they could not go through that again.

By his decision to hold at Verdun, de Castelnau handed the purpose of the battle back to von Falkenhayn, and he need not have done that. If the situation permits, it is usually better to absorb an attack by pulling back from the impact, rather than by meeting the attack head on. It would have been possible to take the steam out of the German attack by withdrawing behind Verdun, into the woods and hills of the Argonne which provided ideal defensive positions. This move would also have greatly reduced the shattering effect of the German artillery barrage and presented the German commanders with a serious problem. To keep up the pressure on the French, their guns and a great deal of ammunition would soon have to be moved forward, over ground already savaged by shellfire, in order to maintain the barrage. Ammunition is heavy and guns in the open or on the move are vulnerable; a counterattack by the French during that move would catch the Germans at a disadvantage.

This tactic, of pulling back before a counterattack, *reculer pour mieux sauter*, would, if correctly timed, also oblige the Germans to expend their strength in taking a position that, for all its emotional appeal, was militarily worthless. With the Somme offensive pending as *the* major Allied effort for 1916, a holding action, even a gradual fighting retreat to some rapidly prepared position behind Verdun, would have been a very shrewd move but, in the circumstances prevailing in 1916, it is hardly surprising that the French did not make it. The Germans were on French soil, and the French did not intend to let them occupy another foot of it; withdrawal, however sensible, was not an option.

Two other points are worth consideration. The first is that one of Joffre's demands in December 1915 called on the other Entente armies to make attacks on the German lines during the spring in order to wear down – *usure* – the German reserves before the Anglo-French armies opened their major offensive astride the Somme. Haig had, rightly, rejected this demand, on the grounds that such attacks would probably do more harm to his forces than to those of the enemy, since the attacker on the Western Front usually lost more men. The second point to recall is the prediction of General Murray, the British CIGS, that in the coming year, the Germans would probably attack somewhere, probably in France, probably against the French. This appreciation was accepted by the British War Cabinet and presumably passed to the High Command in France, especially to the French – but there is no indication that any attempts were made by the French to anticipate this probable attack or to plan to take advantage of it when it came.

The attack at Verdun, in spite of numerous warnings and many indications, seems to have come as a total surprise to the staff at GQG. The fault lies mainly with General Joffre and can probably be attributed to his almost total lack of imagination, but the cause of a failure to act on the generals' own appreciations can once again be traced to the lack of any strategic overview. Since one of the requirements for success in the Somme offensive was a writing-down of the German reserves before Z-Day, the attack at Verdun, had it been anticipated, could have been the ideal opportunity to do just that. Had there been any strategic overview or more imagination at GQG, the German attack at Verdun could have been a welcome opportunity, not an impending catastrophe.

And here the lack of an Allied Supreme Commander in France becomes obvious. Although he was the *generalissimo*, Joffre could not compel the British to obey his orders – although the absence of such compulsion was not the problem here. Because there was no overall commander even in France, no one was obliged to take an overall view of the 1916 campaign. The German attack on Verdun and the French defence of that position, and the Franco-British Somme offensive, were treated as separate battles when they should have been treated as part of the same campaign, with a similar objective, pursued in different locations.

The Allied commanders had agreed to begin a joint offensive in the summer months. They can hardly have expected that the Germans would do nothing for a full four months after the arrival of spring, while the Allies completed their preparations. Something like Verdun should have been anticipated, as indeed it was by General Murray, but the German offensive was allowed to drive the entire Allied plan off

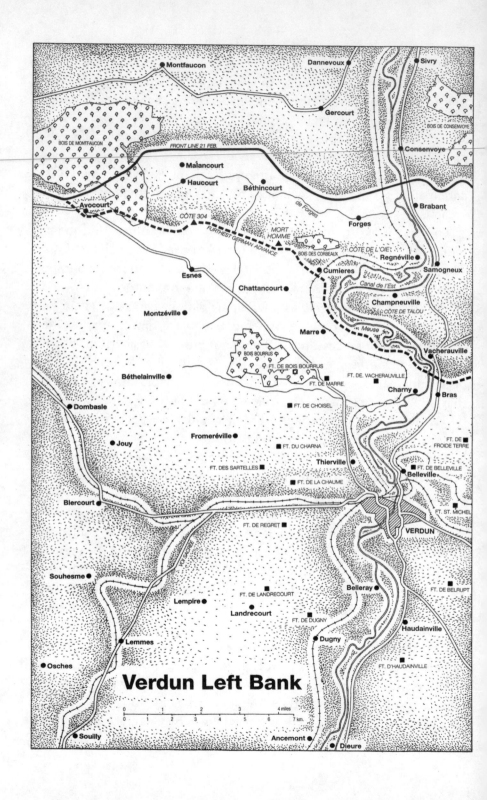

Montfaucon
Dannevoux
Sivry
Gercourt
BOIS DE CONSENVOYE
BOIS DE MONTFAUCON
FRONT LINE 21 FEB.
Consenvoye
Malancourt
Haucourt
Béthincourt
de Forges
Brabant
Avocourt
CÔTE 304
Forges
MORT
HOMME
FURTHEST GERMAN ADVANCE
BOIS DES CORBEAUX
CÔTE DE L'OIE
Regnéville
Esnes
Cumieres
Samogneux
Chattancourt
Canal de l'Est
Montzéville
Champneuville
CÔTE DE TALOU
Marre
Meuse
Vacherauville
BOIS BOURRUS
FT. DE BOIS BOURRUS
FT. DE. VACHERAUVILLE
Béthelainville
FT. DE MARRE
Charny
Bras
FT. DE CHOISEL
Dombasle
Fromeréville
FT. DE
FROIDE TERRE
Jouy
FT. DU CHARNA
FT. DES SARTELLES
Thierville
FT. DE BELLEVILLE
Belleville
FT. DE LA CHAUME
Blercourt
FT. ST. MICHEL
FT. DE REGRET
VERDUN
Souhesme
Belleray
FT. DE BELRUPT
Lempire
FT. DE LANDRECOURT
Landrecourt
FT. DE DUGNY
Haudainville
Lemmes
Dugny
Osches
FT. D'HAUDAINVILLE

Verdun Left Bank

0   1   2   3   4 miles
0 1 2 3 4 5 6 7 km.

Souilly
Ancemont
Dieure

course. Since the British were not ready to take part in any offensive in February 1916, on the Somme or anywhere else, not least because they had just taken over a large section of the French line and had new divisions to absorb and train, for the moment the French must fight it out alone. If that meant committing the entire French Army to the defence of Verdun, so be it.

Sometime after 0800 hrs on 25 February, General Pétain and Captain Serrigny arrived at Joffre's HQ, where the atmosphere was now close to panic and loud demands were being made for the court martial or prompt execution, *pour encourager les autres*, of General Herr. With lunchtime pending, Joffre gave Pétain a brief summary of the situation and sent him on his way to Verdun. The journey took most of the day, for snow was blocking the road and after they passed Bar-le-Duc the path of the General's car was constantly impeded by crowds of refugees, wounded men and deserters fleeing from the battlefield.

For Pétain this scene must have been a depressing introduction to the situation at Verdun, one far bleaker than that recently described to him by General Joffre. The French forces at Verdun were near to collapse and if the chaos now reigning between the battlefield and Bar-le-Duc was any indication, the French predicament at Verdun looked almost beyond redemption. The General's car crept through a mixture of shattered units heading to the rear, fresh units of XX Corps trying to make their way forward, and a great quantity of wagons, gun carriages, ambulances and ammunition limbers, horse-drawn or motorized, competing for a single narrow road and all in great confusion. When the General's party reached Herr's headquarters at Dugny, misery and despair were added to chaos.

It seemed impossible to get an accurate account of the current state of affairs at the front from any of the staff there present, though the steady rumble of German guns indicated that the situation was not good, a point confirmed when the desperate news arrived that Fort Douaumont had fallen, information which drove HQ morale down even further. To plunge into this maelstrom was pointless; Pétain needed to stop, to hear reports, to think and to plan. To that end, he retraced his steps to the village of Souilly, where accommodation for the General and his Staff was found in the house of the local *notaire*. De Castelnau, who heard the news of Fort Douaumont with an impassive face, arrived at Souilly after dark and wrote out the order confirming the GQG's decision to hold Verdun at all costs. It directed Pétain to take command of all the forces at Verdun at midnight – within 60 minutes of receiving the order.

Pétain was less than enthusiastic about this last point, pointing out to de Castelnau that he needed time to discover what was going on before he could be expected to exercise command and issue any useful orders. But de Castelnau was adamant, so at midnight, 2359 hrs on 25 February 1916, Pétain took up the reins of command at Verdun, a battle that was to make his reputation as the saviour of France – a reputation that would lead France to call on him again, 24 years later in 1940, a call that would lead to his total disgrace and ruin. On this first occasion at Souilly, he was faced with another problem: when he awoke on 26 February, Pétain was seriously ill with pneumonia.

His first order to the two corps commanders on either bank of the Meuse, to de Bazelaire commanding the forces on the left bank and Balfourier of XX Corps on the right bank, was that they must hold on while help was mustered and brought to their aid. As yet, the Germans had made no move against the left bank but if they were serious about taking Verdun they must soon do so; every military man in Europe knew that the way to take Verdun was by attacking on both banks of the Meuse. Certainly, with Fort Douaumont gone the French defence line on the right bank had cracked, but behind Fort Douaumont lay Fort Vaux and other forts . . . and, like the left bank, they must be held.

The very fact that Pétain was on the scene seems to have done wonders for morale. As soon as a staff officer arrived with maps, Pétain was able to study the ground in some detail and draw up a line somewhere behind the point where the present fighting was believed to be – the line that the French had to hold. This line – the Line of Resistance – ran around the north of the city, through Côte 304 on the left bank and through the remaining forts, which were to be immediately restocked with guns and ammunition and garrisoned with fresh troops.

Next, Pétain got a grip on the artillery and stopped the French batteries wasting precious ammunition by blazing away blindly into the hills and woods north-east of the Meuse. Instead, they were to concentrate their fire on the road and track junctions north of Douaumont or in the shallow valleys on the right bank, down which the Germans were surely advancing. This fast co-ordination of the French gunfire had an immediate effect on the German advance; casualties started to mount, the forward movement of troops and supplies was severely inhibited and accounts of the growing severity of French artillery fire began to appear in German diaries and reports.

Pétain's other, and major, problem was supply. Verdun lay in a salient and there were only four ways of getting men, ammunition and food up to the front line: three railway lines and a narrow road from Bar-le-Duc. The two main railway lines along the Meuse had already been cut by the German advance or were under shellfire; that left the single narrow road from Bar-le-Duc, and an inadequate narrow-gauge, single-track railway which ran beside the road. The road was the only viable way to supply Verdun, evacuate the wounded and withdraw exhausted units but, as Pétain had seen that afternoon, that vital road from Bar-le-Duc was in a state of chaos.

A general has to impose his will on the battle and the first steps to that end are to stamp out panic and ensure continuity of supply. Modern wars are mainly logistical wars. Without an assured supply of manpower, ammunition, petrol and food, a modern army cannot fight; if the supply line to Verdun broke, the position must fall, however gallant and tenacious to the defence. Pétain immediately sent out a sapper officer, Major Richard, to take charge of the road and the traffic upon it, giving him full authority to employ all and any means to keep the road open and the traffic flowing. Major Richard is one of the heroes of Verdun, an officer who instantly got a grip on the supply situation and took all and any necessary steps to keep the road open.

Richard brought in police to control the traffic, ordered refugees off the road, arrested deserters and returned them to their units, hustled troops forward and brought in hundreds of pioneers and tons of road material to keep the road intact and functioning. He did this on his own authority without bothering Pétain, pressing on with great determination, overcoming any opposition by sheer force of personality, and taking risks. Apart from staff cars, motor transport was not widely available in the French Army in 1916, so Richard simply requisitioned civilian trucks, bringing them to Verdun from all over France. Within days he had more than 3,000 assorted trucks at Bar-le-Duc, plus their drivers, and as soon as one arrived he had it loaded with supplies and sent up to Verdun. This was winter, and snow and icy conditions made the drivers' task even harder, but it was no easier after a sudden thaw, when deep mud lay in wait for any truck that dropped a wheel off the metalled surface.

Under the weight of this constant traffic, with up to 25 vehicles passing a given point on the road every minute, night and day, for months, the surface of the road soon gave way. There was no time to close and repair it, so Richard brought in 8,000 men from the Engineering Battalions and deployed them along the entire length of the road, hurling gravel under the wheels of the passing trucks, putting their shoulders to those that got stuck, keeping the road open day and night with muscle and sweat. During the battle more than one million tons of stores went up to the front and some 2,400,000 men from every unit of the French Army trudged up this road into the furnace of Verdun. The name given to this route later by Maurice Barrès, *La Voie Sacrée* ('The Sacred Way'), aptly describes this road into battle from Bar-le-Duc.

By ensuring a continuity of supply during the first hours of his command, Pétain did a great deal to guarantee the successful defence of the city. That done, the General went to sleep in an armchair . . . and awoke on the morning of 26 February seriously ill. Pneumonia rapidly turned into pleurisy and until he was able to get to his feet again a week later, Pétain fought the battle from his sick bed, using the information brought in by his staff officers to get a grip of the situation and command his forces.

Like de Castelnau, Pétain was a general with a feel for battle. It did not take him long to realize that, in spite of all that had happened, and was still happening, north of the beleaguered city, the situation at Verdun was far from irredeemable and could have been much worse. First of all, the city was still in French hands and, of the major forts, only Douaumont had so far fallen. Moreover, for some strange reason, the Germans had failed to attack on both banks; with every hour that passed the left bank could be made stronger for when they did attack there. The immediate task was to muster what forces remained at the front, get the artillery organized to break up the German attacks as they came in, and hang on grimly until fresh troops could arrive and be flung into the battle . . . if only they could be kept supplied. When he considered his options at Verdun, Pétain's thoughts came back constantly to the problems of supply.

The battle of supply was to last as long as the battle itself, but at the end of February the need was simply to hang on while the benefits of Pétain's determination and leadership began to take effect. The first bonus came early. On 27 February, six days into the offensive, the Germans made no gains whatsoever on the Verdun front: the Iron Corps brigades moved into position and the balance of the battle slowly began to tilt in the French direction, at least for the moment. A solid defence line was established on the right bank, between Bras and Hardaumont, and on the last day of the month the fighting began to coalesce around the village of Douaumont, which fell on 4 March after terrible and expensive fighting.

Any joy the Germans felt over their easy and rapid capture of Fort Douaumont was rapidly reduced by the cost of taking the nearby village. Street fighting eats up infantry, and in Douaumont village the French fought desperately, from street to street, house to house, cellar to cellar, engaging the enemy with rifle and machine-gun fire and bayonet charges, all under a steady rain of shells. The 24th Brandenburgers, who had taken Fort Douaumont with such élan, were reduced to a handful in the fighting for the village, and other German regiments and battalions suffered in proportion before Douaumont fell.

Pétain let it go; there were counterattacks, including one major attempt to retake Fort Douaumont on the day after it fell, but the losses in these attacks made it clear that immediate counterattacks to retake a lost position were counter-productive. Pétain was content with the cost the Germans had paid for Douaumont village; there would be no more counterattacks to retake the fort. The time to retake ground around Verdun had not yet arrived; the task now was to hold what could be held and make the attacker pay dearly for every foot of ground gained . . . in other words, to ensure that von Falkenhayn's battle took its toll of the German forces as much as of the French.

By the first week of March Pétain was back on his feet and able to take a close look at his dangerous inheritance. His impressions confirmed those he had formed on arrival; the initial German lunge at Verdun had failed and the battle would now continue on more equal terms, though it is doubtful if even Pétain realized at the time just how costly those terms would be. Of the two German plans for Verdun, that of von Falkenhayn and that of the Crown Prince and his overbearing Chief of Staff, General von Knobelsdorf, up to a point, von Falkenhayn could congratulate himself that *his* plan – to bleed the forces of France to death – was going very well. The Germans were killing a lot of French soldiers – and although they were losing many German soldiers in the process, there was always that proverb about omelettes and eggs. The problem was that the Fifth Army commanders were becoming frustrated by their inability to get forward on the narrow frontage offered by the right bank and were agitating for more reserves, and for spreading the offensive to the left bank.

By the end of February it was clear to all that the German attack at Verdun had stalled – and the fault for that rests entirely with von Falkenhayn. On 24 and 25 February, after three or four days of shattering shellfire, the way to Verdun lay wide open and everyone, French and German, knew it. In the previous days of fighting, however, the assault divisions of Fifth Army had used up their strength and energy, and urgently needed replacement by fresh troops. The Crown Prince, with Verdun almost in his grasp, telephoned von Falkenhayn and requested, begged for, the immediate despatch of two fresh divisions . . . and von Falkenhayn refused.

Von Falkenhayn had the troops; two fresh, full-strength infantry divisions, enough to take Verdun, were at Metz, just 30 miles away, and could have been brought to Verdun inside a day but he declined to send them. The simplest explanation can be found in his original intention, that taking Verdun was not on his agenda, but the effect on Fifth Army commander and his Chief-of-Staff was, to say the least, unfortunate, for the plans of the Crown Prince and von Knobelsdorf, to take Verdun and drive the French back in headlong retreat, were not going well.

Verdun had not fallen and the Crown Prince was well aware what the battle had cost his troops so far and, thanks to von Falkenhayn, apparently all for nothing. Fifth Army had suffered some 25,000 casualties since the start of the battle – about the same as the French – and the cost would clearly rise from now on, as the French got their breath back and began to dig in. The time to throw in the reserves and take the city was now – so where were they?

Von Falkenhayn was fully aware that a further advance needed reserves. On 28 February he called the Crown Prince and his staff to a conference at his headquarters, where he proposed to thrash out the situation. After a week of fighting the Verdun position had not fallen and, in spite of some well-publicized feats of arms in the first few days, the situation looked bleak. Clearly, said von Falkenhayn, for the attack to continue it must be broadened to include the left bank; the only other alternative was to call the offensive off. This sudden reversal of his 'narrow front' position may seem surprising, but it reflects another aspect of von Falkenhayn's character; behind his stern, Prussian façade, he always tended towards caution. As his proposals for this offensive indicated, he did not lack nerve when taking strategic decisions, but when matters went awry in the field his resolution faltered – and matters were going very awry indeed in the woods and hills around Verdun. Nothing more could be gained on the right bank until the left bank was taken; that was the classic way to take Verdun – and now was the time to take it and move on to the left bank.

The last thing von Falkenhayn can have wanted is either to break off the attack completely after so short a time, or to allow the Crown Prince and von Knobelsdorf to take complete charge of the battle . . . even now, he had not confided his prime intention to the men charged unwittingly with executing it. The conclusion has to be that he proposed extending the attack to the left bank, not to take the city but to renew the threat of doing so, and thereby suck more French troops towards his guns. This move would also pacify the Crown Prince and his divisional commanders – and if anyone mentioned that the last seven days had given the French ample time to bolster the left bank position so that the advantage of surprise had long since been lost, well, one could not have everything.

The Crown Prince believed that Verdun could still be taken if the attack was widened, if more reserves were brought forward and, above all, if the commanders committed themselves to halt the offensive should it ever become apparent that the attack was costing them more than it was costing the French. The word 'attrition' had yet to be mentioned, but the thought was there. Since the Crown Prince was resolute and was supported in this resolve by von Knobelsdorf, their plan was accepted. The decision was made to attack on the left bank on 6 March – in seven days' time – with a follow-up offensive on 7 March on the right bank, with the aim of capturing the next French bastion, Fort Vaux.

However, some severe tactical problems were now arising; many victories contain the seeds of their own defeat, and so it was before Verdun. The Germans had made rapid advances in the last few days – over four miles, a giant leap forward in Western Front terms – largely due to their immense superiority in artillery. That artillery had turned the ground to their front into a quagmire of mud and had created an almost impenetrable thicket of fallen trees. Now, as the Germans attempted to bring their guns forward to support a further advance, this combination of mud and timber created a barrier to the stormtroopers and a great obstacle to the forward movement of their supporting artillery . . . and then there were the ongoing problems of gun maintenance and ammunition supply.

The German guns on which so much depended were becoming worn, and the recent barrages had used up immense quantities of ammunition; the total expenditure of artillery ammunition at Verdun, French and German, was eventually estimated at more than 60 million shells . . . and after the opening bombardments, every one of those shells had to be brought up to the front, either over the *Voie Sacrée* or the shell-torn, German-occupied ground north of Verdun, and ammunition is heavy. Maintaining the *Trommelfeuer*, the great and continuous artillery barrages on the French forces around Verdun, was a Herculean task and one complicated by the fact that as the German guns came forward they moved into open, treeless ground where they could be spotted by the French artillery observers. These were soon bringing accurate fire down on the German lines and causing a steady loss of both guns and gunners. The long-range French 155 mm guns could pick off German batteries well north of Verdun, while remaining out of range of any German fire, and more French guns were arriving every day.

This increase in the French fire began to inhibit the German infantry attacks, whose success was predicated on heavy artillery support to destroy the French positions and, in particular, the many French machine-gun nests which enfiladed the ground around Verdun and created an interlocking field of fire that ravaged the attacking infantry. Try as they would, the German guns could never silence all the French machine-guns and the pattern of other Great War battles, of advances halted with great loss by machine-gun fire from the flank, became apparent yet again at Verdun. Finally, the German advance on the right bank had been checked with loss by the heavy and accurate artillery and machine-gun fire that descended upon the infantry from French guns situated across the river on the left bank, especially on Côte 304 and the twin-peaked hill called the Mort Homme.

So the steps that had to be climbed rose up before the German commanders. The obvious first position to take was the left bank but, before that could be taken, the Mort Homme must be seized . . . but then that was buttressed by Côte 304, so that must be taken before or at the same time as the Mort Homme. And when all that had been done, the right bank was still there with its forts and trenches – and behind that lay the immediate defences of Verdun itself. One can only wonder if any German commander, brooding over this prospect, ever attempted to estimate the cost in human lives of taking this interlocked defensive system.

When considering the dire prospect before Fifth Army, it is necessary to refer back to von Falkenhayn's plan. Battle is the ultimate arbiter of any plan and even the best plan can go wrong, but von Falkenhayn's plan, though shrewd in conception, contained a flaw he must have known about beforehand but chose to ignore. Bearing in mind the availability of reserves and the need to concentrate artillery, von Falkenhayn had opted to attack on a narrow front at Verdun. Verdun's capture had often featured in exercises carried out by the

German Army and in planning sessions at GHQ and the Imperial Staff College. From these widespread exercises and plans, one factor constantly emerged: the only way to take Verdun was by attacking on both banks of the Meuse *at once*.

Perhaps von Falkenhayn dismissed this knowledge as irrelevant, again possibly on the grounds that taking Verdun was not his prime intention. Even if that was his view, it was a bad tactical decision for, as related, the high ground on the left bank of the Meuse, notably Côte 304 and the Mort Homme, completely overlooks the ground on the right bank. Therefore, when the German advance reached up to and beyond Fort Douaumont, their forces would inevitably come under heavy and accurate fire from French artillery positions on the left bank, or fire controlled by artillery observers snugly ensconced on the hills beyond the river.

Losses had already been heavy in getting up to Douaumont. Now it became clear that before the Germans could move farther south along the right bank, the French positions on the left bank would have to be taken. This must cost many German lives, and that was not von Falkenhayn's intention. Perhaps his plan of bleeding the French to death at Verdun contained the most significant flaw of all. Because Verdun mattered to the French they had laid long-term plans to defend it and these plans, however flawed in execution, overrode the possibilities of von Falkenhayn's plan.

Von Falkenhayn was able to tell the Crown Prince that the other part of his proposal, the submarine offensive, had started and was going to plan. This was a hopeful statement, because on 21 February 1916, the Kriegsmarine only had one U-boat at sea. The first sinking came on 4 March when the U-32 opened the offensive by sinking the British tanker *Teutonian* in the Western Approaches, having given the crew time to get into their boats. More U-boats went to sea and there were eight boats on station in the Western Approaches by the end of March. Between the end of February and the end of April, 57 Allied ships were to be sunk in this area and 95 in other areas – in all, 152 ships with a total tonnage of 347,843 tons – a significant figure certainly, but only a small percentage of British shipping currently afloat.

A more telling and unfortunate effect of this offensive, at least from von Falkenhayn's point of view, came on 24 March, when a German submarine, the UB-29, sank without warning the French cross-Channel ferry *Sussex*, which was just about to enter Dieppe on her daily crossing from Folkestone. The captain of the UB-29, who had been observing the *Sussex* through the periscope, came to the conclusion that she was carrying troops and was therefore a legitimate target for an unannounced attack. A single torpedo sank the *Sussex* and 50 civilian passengers were drowned, among them the Spanish composer Granados . . . and 25 US citizens. The United States Government had only just got over the sinking of the *Lusitania* and the reaction in the USA to this fresh atrocity was volcanic. Press leaders blared that the sinking of the *Sussex* was an affront to decency and an outright challenge to the Government and people of the United States. President Wilson therefore sent a sharp warning to Germany:

> If it is the purpose of the Imperial Government to prosecute relentless and indiscriminate warfare against vessels of commerce by the use of U-boats, without regard to what the United States must consider the sacred and indisputable rules of international law and universally recognized dictates of humanity, the Government of the United States is at last forced to the con-clusion that there is but one course it can pursue. Unless the Imperial Government should now immediately declare and effect an abandonment of its present methods of U-boat warfare against passengers and freight carrying vessels, the Government of the United States can have no other choice but to sever diplomatic relations with the German Reich altogether.

The severing of diplomatic relations would be a long stride towards war on the side of the Entente, and the threat was enough. Chancellor von Bethmann-Hollweg instantly instructed the Kriegsmarine that the U-boats were only to act against commerce in accordance with the Prize Regulations, Article 112 again. The new head of the High Seas Fleet, Admiral Scheer, refused to accept this restriction and recalled all his U-boats to base by radio. Some boats failed to pick up his signal and a further eight vessels were sunk without warning before they returned, including the passenger liner *Cymric*, sunk on 8 May by the U-20, the same submarine that had sunk the *Lusitania*.

The Verdun battle was starting to make a mark on Allied strategy. Robertson, the CIGS, and Kitchener both regarded this attack as serious, and quickly realized von Falkenhayn's intentions, not least because, not knowing that the guns had been removed from the forts, they did not think the Germans could penetrate the French position. This being so, the German intention must be to bleed the French dry, but such a battle was likely to use up German troops at a similar or faster rate.

Even so, on 12 March, Haig and Robertson and representatives from the other Entente armies went to Chantilly to discuss the Verdun situation with General Joffre. Joffre urged all his colleagues to press on with their own offensives, which led the Italian representative to plead that they only had enough guns and ammunition for local offensives – a comment that inspired Robertson to the unhelpful remark that he would 'like to have kicked the Italian in the stomach'. No agreement was reached on when the supporting offensives could be launched, and when the report on this inconclusive meeting reached Whitehall, Lloyd George suggested to the War Committee that, with the Verdun battle raging, it might be an idea to consider abandoning all hope of an offensive in combination with the French. This suggestion did not go down well and Asquith had later to restate the French position, that if the Allies did not help – and soon – the French could not go on and France must 'put up the shutters'. War therefore continued, by land and sea.

The halting of 'unrestricted' submarine warfare did not end the sinkings of British ships. The Kriegsmarine continued to attack troopships and naval vessels and commissioned a number of smaller U-boats, craft displacing less than 200 tons, which were designed to lay mines in the Channel and attack coastal shipping. These smaller U-boats were based in the Belgian ports of Ostend and Zeebrugge, a fact that would provide Sir Douglas Haig with one of the reasons for his Passchendaele offensive in 1917. At the end of March, however, one month into the planned sea and land offensive for 1916, the naval element in von Falkenhayn's war-winning strategic offensive had been reduced considerably. Not so the battle at Verdun, which was now raging on both banks of the Meuse.

Note

1 *The Two Marshals* (Bazaine and Pétain), p. 289.

8

The Mort Homme, Côte 304, the Somme
March–May 1916

'This fighting without visible or – for the man at the front
– tangible result, afforded the sternest test imaginable of
the capabilities of our troops.'
General Erich von Falkenhayn,
General Headquarters 1914–1916 and Its Critical Decisions

While the Verdun battle grew in fury during March and April and on into May, the British armies in France had not been idle. They were as yet unable to launch any major attack, one that might divert German forces or reserves from Verdun, because the situation which had obliged General Haig to postpone the offensive proposed by Joffre until mid-summer had not substantially changed: he needed more men and those he had needed more training. Even so, fighting went on continually along the British front.

More British divisions, many of them New Army formations, were now coming out to the Western Front, but they needed further training and some time in the line before they could be fully effective. It was also necessary to increase the artillery element of Fourth Army considerably before even contemplating the details of an offensive. However, on 1 March, General Sir Henry Rawlinson took command of Fourth Army north of the Somme and, on 6 March, he called his Corps commanders together for a conference. He told them that, when fully formed, his Army would consist of four corps, and each corps would be twice the usual size and consist of four divisions.[1]

At that time Fourth Army contained XIII and X Corps, which were currently in the line, and VIII Corps, which was in reserve and as yet only had one division, the 38th. Only three of Rawlinson's corps commanders were present at Querrieu and not all of their corps were up to strength: the promised III Corps, which was now forming, still only had one division, the 8th. But, as the corps were formed, they were to move into line north of the River Somme and begin training for a major offensive to be launched sometime in June or July – unless it was necessary to attack sooner, to ease the growing pressure on the French Second Army at Verdun.

At Joffre's request, soon after the Verdun attack opened, Haig took over the entire front held by the French Tenth Army, a move completed by 27 February. On 25 February Haig discussed the Verdun situation with Kitchener and suggested three likely courses of action for his forces in the coming summer, all dependent on how the Verdun battle developed.[2] If Verdun became 'a kind of stalemate', Haig suggested the French should take over some of the British front in order to free British troops for an offensive between Ypres and Armentières – in Haig's favourite area.

On the other hand, if the French managed to defeat the Germans at Verdun, the British Third Army must attack at once, in expectation of a breakthrough, since the Germans would probably have thinned out their line in front of the British, in order to send more troops to Verdun. Finally, if the French were defeated and broken, the British must attack at once, as close to the German breakthrough as possible . . . though how this could be managed in such dire circumstances Haig was unable to say.

Joffre kept in regular touch with Haig and sent him information on the new infiltration and stormtroop tactics being adopted by the enemy at Verdun. On 28 February, Haig motored to Chantilly, where he was greeted warmly by Joffre, who was currently grateful for British assistance in replacing the Tenth Army and was able to assure Haig that he now had adequate reserves to stem the German attack. This view seems to have prevailed at the Allied Commanders-in-Chief's conference held at Chantilly on 12 March which was largely devoted to matters in other theatres of war but, by 26 March, some cracks in this common front were beginning to show. On that day a letter arrived from Joffre requesting that Haig, 'by way of compensation' for the heavy guns left behind by the Tenth Army, should supply the French Army with 2,000 labourers – and a further 1,000 labourers in payment for the ammunition.

Since Haig had just sent 150,000 men to take over the Tenth Army position, at Joffre's urgent request and in order to help the French at Verdun, he found this extra demand most irritating, writing in his diary that 'there are not many officers in the French Army with gentlemanly ideas. They are out to get as much from the British as they possibly can.'[3] Fortunately, Haig did not pass this blunt opinion on to Joffre for, on 4 April, Joffre not only withdrew the request for workers, he offered Haig another 68 heavy guns, if Haig could find the men to work them. Why these guns were not sent to Verdun remains a mystery – it is hard to believe that the French were short of gunners – but they came in very useful on the British front.

At Verdun, it is curious how soon it became apparent that all was not going as planned on the German side. One of the most significant developments of the Great War was that battles were no longer to last for a few hours, or at most a few days, as they had done in past European wars. Great War battles – perhaps campaigns would be a better word for them – took on the aspects of war first visible in the American Civil War or the Russo-Japanese War: a typical battle or campaign – the Somme, Passchendaele, Verdun – could last for weeks or months, while its component parts, the battle for Albert or the battle for the village of Douaumont, for example, could now last several days. Even so, the failure of the initial plan, or the dashing of early hopes, was often obvious at a very early stage . . . provided those in charge had the wit to see it.

At Verdun, this was especially so at the Crown Prince's headquarters, where the plan to take Verdun was clearly not going well and the Prince was rightly worried. At General Headquarters, on the other hand, von Falkenhayn's notion of 'writing down' the French Army appeared to be going very well indeed and might do even better as the French reserves came within range of the German guns.

On 28 February, von Falkenhayn, the Crown Prince and General von Knobelsdorf met to discuss the course of the battle, the present situation at the front, and where they might go from here. This was just seven days into a battle that would go on for ten months and, given that the Crown Prince's objections to von Falkenhayn's initial plan had now proved all too valid, and an initial success in capturing Verdun had been lost by von Falkenhayn's refusal to commit reserves, the atmosphere was hardly genial. Even so, the final and unanimous decision was to continue the battle and spread the attack on to the left bank, provided certain conditions were met.

According to his memoirs, von Falkenhayn reached this decision after considering other factors, including the possibility of halting the attack on the Meuse and switching the effort to some other part of the line. This idea was rejected, says von Falkenhayn, because 'it would have meant a complete departure from the views on which the attack north of Verdun had been based', and, he continued, 'we had hitherto achieved what we set out to achieve, and there was every reason to hope we should do so again in the future.' This last comment is highly debatable. What had been achieved so far fell far short of what either von Falkenhayn or the Fifth Army Commander had selected as their aims for this battle: the city had not fallen and the battle of attrition desired by von Falkenhayn was costing Germany as many men as France. The notion that German guns alone could 'bleed the French Army to death' at Verdun was already questionable.

This being so, it is reasonable to examine what the Germans had actually achieved in the first days of this offensive. They had certainly killed a lot of French soldiers and demonstrated yet again that, given sufficient artillery and a prodigious expenditure of ammunition, it was possible to make deep advances even over ground covered by machine-guns and pre-war defences – but that lesson had been learned in the 1915 offensives and hardly needed this bloodbath to underline it yet again. The German success had also been helped by their infiltration tactics and by the fact that the French had not acted to shore up their front and bring in more men before the battle started. But they had now done so, and were charging an ever-higher price in lives for every foot of ground lost.

The Fifth Army had certainly driven the French back for some miles and captured Fort Douaumont but the French line had not collapsed. If the intention was to take Verdun and breach the French line in a decisive fashion – and von Falkenhayn had not yet openly denied that intention to either the Crown Prince or von Knobelsdorf – that achievement lay as far away as ever. For the moment the German attack was stalled on the right bank, its centre blunted at the village of Douaumont.

Pounding away in that area only offered the likelihood of further losses, for in the process of getting that far the German Fifth Army had already expended a colossal amount of artillery ammunition and lost a considerable number of soldiers, as had the French. The estimated casualty figures for the first nine days were in excess of 30,000 men on either side; von Falkenhayn had anticipated that the main losses would be incurred by the French. Surprise had been lost, and since surprise had accounted for much of the success so far, one can only wonder – with von Falkenhayn – if there was any point in continuing the attack at Verdun or whether there was an advantage in switching it to some other part of the line, perhaps by launching a spoiling attack on the Somme, where the British preparations for a summer offensive were slowly getting under way.

The decision to continue attacking at Verdun was made subject to certain conditions, most of them imposed by the Crown Prince. First of all, he wanted the width of the attack extended to the left bank and, in lieu of more frontal assaults around Douaumont in the centre, he wanted more effort on the wings. Secondly, he wanted a guarantee that more reserves would be forthcoming, and in adequate quantity, and no repeat of what had happened on 24 and 25 February. Finally, if it seemed that the Germans were losing more men than the French, the battle for Verdun should be broken off at once.

The Crown Prince, in short, was willing to try again, but unwilling to enter into a battle of attrition. Nevertheless, by electing to continue the attack at all, a battle of attrition was what he got. It is surprising that even now, ten days into the battle, the commander of the Army chiefly concerned still seemed unaware that a battle of attrition was what his superior officer wanted and had been planning since the start.

Von Falkenhayn agreed to the Crown Prince's demands and preparations for an attack on the left bank in seven days' time, on 6 March, duly commenced, with the commitment of a fresh Army corps, VI (Reserve) Corps, to the left bank. This corps was tasked to attack and carry the Mort Homme feature. If successful, this attack would do something to quell that persistent French artillery that currently impeded all progress on the right bank. On the following day, 7 March, another attack would be launched on the right bank, this time aimed at Fort Vaux, which was now fully manned and in position to resist or inhibit any attacks by Fifth Army.

This met another of the Crown Prince's requirements, that the weight of the attack should be shifted to the wings – which clearly required the elimination of the garrison of Fort Vaux. This demand would have been a sensible move earlier in the battle, but now it simply extended the front and so, inevitably, thinned out the effect of the artillery fire on which all now depended. There was also a problem with the ground.

In many accounts of Verdun, much has been made of the cover provided to the German offensive by the woods north of Verdun. This is a strange claim, because the attack began in February, in deep winter, when the leafless trees in those woods provided scant cover to the infantry, even before the trees were shattered by artillery. Cover was a declining asset on the right bank as the battle continued but even less cover was available on the left bank, where the ground is much more open. Though rolling, and well supplied with 'dead ground' (terrain, usually in valleys or hidden behind trees or hills, where the movement of troops cannot be observed by the enemy or hindered by direct fire), the left bank terrain gave little help to the infiltration tactics that had stood the stormtroops so well in the first hours and days of the Verdun battle. The valleys offering dead ground could be raked with plunging howitzer or mortar fire and the dominant feature of the left bank was the Mort Homme, a ridge 975ft high and topped by two knolls, which overlooked most of the ground over which the Fifth Army divisions must advance.

Observation is the key to a successful artillery battle. The reverse slope of the Mort Homme feature gave protection to many of those French batteries which plagued the German troops on the right bank, and the two knolls provided a perfect, 360-degree view over the entire battlefield to the French artillery observers. The Germans hoped that taking the Mort Homme would, in effect, blind the French guns, but just taking the Mort Homme would not solve the artillery problem. West of the Mort Homme lay another, more isolated feature, Côte 304; this not only offered equally good observation, it also commanded the approaches to the Mort Homme.

Here, again, was the problem: to take the right bank it was necessary to take the left bank. The key to the left bank was the Mort Homme, but the key to the Mort Homme was Côte 304 . . . and all these positions were mutually supporting, with interlinked fields of fire from their machine-guns and supporting artillery. In an ideal battle they should have been attacked and taken at the same time, but this was not an ideal world. This was Verdun, and the only possible decision, given the man- and gun-power available, was to go for the left bank and take it a foot at a time . . . at whatever cost.

Clearly, any serious attack on the left bank must have as its prime aim the rapid capture of these two commanding features. With Côte 304 and the Mort Homme in their hands, the Germans could sweep south and east and, after taking the four smaller forts on the left bank – Forts Choisel, Sartelles, Chana and la Chaume – press on into Verdun, which might by then have fallen anyway to an attack down the right bank.

Capturing the Mort Homme and Côte 304 would offer more than just the elimination of the guns and observation points: it would give the Germans a jumping-off point for the next, and possibly final, phase of their advance, a bound south towards the Bois Bourrus ridge, from where they could hope to see down into Verdun. All they had to do in the first attack was shatter the defenders on the Mort Homme with artillery and then send in the infantry to occupy it. The guns began to execute that intention as soon as the morning mist cleared on 6 March and, as on 21 February, this was no long bombardment. Under cover of this fire, German infantry crossed the Meuse in two places, jumping off from around Brabant and taking the village of Regnéville on the left bank without opposition. As before, this initial phase went well and by nightfall the Germans were into the edges of the Bois des Corbeaux and edging up on to the Côte de l'Oie ridge, which ran west-south-west, away from the river, directly up towards the Mort Homme.

Pétain and his commanders were well aware of the importance of the Mort Homme, and Côte 304, to the defence of Verdun. It had been obvious to Pétain that when their right bank attack stalled, a German attack on the left bank would surely follow. This being so, a plentiful amount of artillery had been brought up, including a number of quick-firing 75s, and ranged on the No Man's Land between the Mort Homme and the German line. Four divisions of infantry had been moved into position on the left bank, three in the forward positions either in front of or on the Mort Homme, and one in reserve. Once there, they dug in, but this preparation did little to lessen the force and shock of the bombardment which fell on these defenders on 6 March.

The *Trommelfeuer* that smote the French positions on the left bank that day was equal in weight and duration to that which had blasted the Bois des Caures on the first day of the battle and had an equally devastating effect. Within 30 minutes all telephone lines connecting the forward troops and their artillery observers with the rear were cut, and a terrible weight of shellfire was sweeping to and fro over the French line, demolishing hastily dug trenches and dugouts, blasting the soil from the face of the earth, felling trees, churning the ground and slaughtering the infantry crouched to defend it.

Under cover of this drenching fire, grimly prepared to accept casualties from their own, short-falling shells in order to get forward, the German infantry swept in, not from the front, but from the right flank, from the river. A brigade of General von Zwehl's VII Reserve Corps had crossed the Meuse in small craft and, as the artillery fire lifted, they surged up the hill to take up positions before the Mort

Homme and well inside the French front line. This flanking attack was
supported by shellfire from an armoured train and by the rapid
advance along the left bank of the river by troops of General
Riemann's 22nd Reserve Division, who joined up with von Zwehl's
men to take two left bank villages, Forges and Regnéville, as well as
the Oie ridge which led up towards the Mort Homme and the Bois des
Corbeaux. As on 21 February, Fifth Army had begun its attack with
great skill and determination and had gained a significant amount of
ground, at least on the left flank, close to the river.

In the centre it was another story. The main thrust towards the
Mort Homme ridge was stopped almost as soon as it began by artillery
fire from batteries of French 75s that swept No Man's Land with
shrapnel from positions astride the Mort Homme. These guns had
been anticipating the attack for the past week and had the ground
before them ranged to the inch. The German infantry came forward
again and again, always with the same result: terrible casualties from
constant and heavy shellfire. Artillery ruled this battle as it was to rule
other battles on the Western Front and infantry that went against it,
British, French or German, pitting flesh and blood against iron and
steel, would simply incur unacceptable losses. Yet in spite of their
losses in the centre, the Germans coming in from the flank took the
Bois des Corbeaux, below the Côte de l'Oie ridge.

If the main German thrust had been held, the flanking movement to
the Bois des Corbeaux thoroughly alarmed the French commanders
and the sudden collapse of the 67th Division, from which over 3,000
men surrendered to the enemy, enraged Joffre and the officers at
GQG and those at General de Bazelaire's HQ on the left bank. Orders
were issued that ground was now to be held at all costs – *coûte que coûte*
– and that artillery and machine-gun fire would be brought down on
any French troops attempting to withdraw.

By midday on 7 March it was clear to the French that the next move
on the German side would probably be to 'reinforce success' by
renewing the attack on the flank of the Mort Homme from positions
in the Bois des Corbeaux. It was equally clear that the wood must be
retaken as soon as possible, to deny the Germans this useful forming-
up position. The wood was duly retaken at dawn on 8 March, and in

traditional style: a sweeping bayonet charge across the open ground and into the trees by three battalions of French infantry, led by their commanding officer, Lt-Colonel Macker, armed only with a cane.

This successful counterattack had the desired effect. The barrage planned to support a renewed attack on the Mort Homme was cancelled and the Germans dug in to beat off a series of violent French counterattacks which aimed to drive them off the left bank entirely. The Germans duly counterattacked in their turn and the pattern was set on the left bank which would endure for the next month; attack followed by counterattack, and men dying in their thousands for a few yards of bloody, shell-torn ground.

These counterattacks cost the French very many lives and were exactly the kind of attacks that von Falkenhayn wanted. But although costly, they bought the defenders time; time to consolidate their positions around the Mort Homme after the losses and upsets of the past few days. When the Germans renewed their attacks on 9 March, pushing again for the Côte de l'Oie ridge, they found French resistance as dogged as before and could make no progress. Artillery fire was to plough up the left bank by day and night for another month before the German infantry went forward again in force to renew the offensive.

Nor were the Germans enjoying any greater success on the right bank. The original intention, to mount a co-ordinated attack, moving down the right bank on the day after the opening of the left bank offensive, was defeated by the state of the ground, which was torn and pitted by weeks of shellfire. As a result, the attack on the right bank did not go in until 8 March, which enabled the right bank guns to flay the Germans on the far side of the river for a full day. When it did go in, the attack stalled yet again in the face of French shellfire and the dogged resistance of the infantry in and around Fort Vaux.

There was also another of those all-too-common Western Front communication disasters, this time on the German side, when the commander of this assault, General von Guretzky-Cornitz, came to believe that Fort Vaux had fallen and sent up a brigade of fresh troops to take over from the assaulting battalions. Elated with this supposed success, this brigade marched up in column-of-route – directly into the sights of the French machine-gunners still occupying Fort Vaux, who lost no time in cutting these marching columns to pieces.

The village of Vaux, which lay between Douaumont and Fort Vaux, had by now almost vanished, taken and retaken a dozen times in infantry attacks and obliterated by shelling, but the remaining ruins and cellars provided ideal defensive positions from which the chattering French machine-guns could slash at the advancing German infantry. The fighting went on for days but the fact that Fort Vaux continued to hold out – plus the stalling of the German attack on the left bank – led Joffre to the bizarre conclusion on 10 March that the German offensive at Verdun had reached its climax, and that the Germans could now be driven back by an all-out counterattack. This suggestion horrified Pétain and the two men were still arguing about it when the Germans returned to the attack on 14 March.

The Crown Prince had never anticipated an easy victory on the left bank. In spite of his youthful appearance and playboy reputation, Crown Prince Wilhelm of Prussia was a shrewd and intelligent officer – far shrewder than his supposed mentor and adviser, General Schmidt von Knobelsdorf – and his demand for a steady and adequate supply of reserves before opening the attack at all is one indication that he intended to continue the struggle until it was clear that the offensive had failed or that victory was his. The first attack on the left bank had failed. Therefore, there would be a second attack, stronger and more aggressive than before – the Crown Prince was a Prussian general, and aggression was bred into him, both personally and professionally.

The new assault went in on 14 March, an attack on the centre of the left bank line by six full divisions, preceded by the now familiar hurricane bombardment. This time there was no pulling back or halting after a few hours or a day. From 14 March, the fighting for the Mort Homme continued without ceasing for weeks, a constant repetition of artillery followed by infantry attacks.

Although these attacks were beaten off by French firepower, backed by courage and tenacity, none of the attacks returned precisely to its departure line. Slowly, painfully, almost imperceptibly, the German line crawled towards the Mort Homme. Each step of that advance exacted a heavy toll in lives. By the end of March, German losses in five weeks of fighting at Verdun had topped 80,000 men;

French losses were close to 90,000, and no significant strategic advantage to either side had accrued from this terrible sacrifice.

The process of a Western Front attack has certain similarities with a more common civilian experience, involving builders: the builders come in to do a particular job but, in the course of doing it, they discover something else that has to be done. Doing that reveals yet another problem and so the work and the disruption continues until it seems that the work will never end and the builders will never leave. The analogy with the fighting at Verdun may be crude but it is apt in this one respect. The Germans had found it necessary to attack the Mort Homme to free up their advance on the right bank. Now, as they moved closer to the Mort Homme, they found their attacks on that position increasingly inhibited by fire from that other main feature on the left bank, the ridge called Côte 304.

Côte 304 lies just to the west of the Mort Homme and, as its name indicates, reaches a height of about 1,000ft. This height provided the French with the usual assets of good observation, protection from direct fire and cover for their artillery, particularly those galling batteries of quick-firing 75 mms. By the last week of March the Crown Prince had decided that taking Côte 304 was the key to capturing the Mort Homme. The task of taking it was entrusted to the 11th Bavarian Division, which would attack Côte 304 from the west after capturing a forming-up position in the Bois de Montfauçon, a spur of which juts towards Côte 304 from the village of Malancourt, which lies north of Avocourt.

A study of the map on page 154 will help to explain this situation. It was clear to the French that the Bois de Montfauçon was the obvious jumping-off position for such an attack, and it had therefore been kept under observation and subjected to harassing fire over the past weeks, even when strong German attacks were proceeding elsewhere. Even so, on 20 March, the Bavarians swept into the wood and caught the defending French 29th Division totally unprepared. The French position fell inside a day, more than 3,000 French soldiers were taken prisoner, with a great quantity of kit . . . and the road to Côte 304 was wide open.

However, in spite of the shock occasioned by this sudden collapse, the French instantly subjected the wood to a drenching fire from 155 mm guns and brought up more machine-guns to enfilade any advance from the wood towards Côte 304. This advance was attempted on 22 March and caused the Germans as many casualties as the French had suffered two days before – between 2,000 and 3,000 men, most of them by shelling.

The answer to an attack is a counterattack and the French duly counterattacked the Bois de Montfauçon one week later, on 29 March. So the fighting continued into April, with no sign that this struggle would end. The battle at Verdun had now been joined on both banks of the Meuse, more men were coming forward to join in, and the losses, already severe, would continue to mount as the weeks and months went by, or until the British did something to relieve the pressure by attacking on the Somme.

Over on the Somme, the British were still building up their strength. On 31 March, Haig's diary records that he had just finished his third day with the 'three Corps' that now made up the British Third Army, units which were currently occupied in rebuilding or improving the positions taken over from the French, or were in training.

Haig's account does not impart any particular feeling of urgency. On 14 April he saw Kitchener at the War Office and sought confirmation from the CIGS, General Robertson, 'that H.M.'s Government approve of my combining in a joint offensive during the summer'. Having been assured that the Government did, Haig went on to see Colonel Swinton and some of the staff at the War Office, for he was now actively interested in obtaining a number of these new-fangled 'tanks'. Swinton and the Staff at the War Office told him that 150 tanks would be available, but not until 31 July, when Haig wanted at least 50 by 1 June.[4]

Haig appears to have forgotten his earlier estimates on what might result from Verdun. That battle had now effectively become a stalemate, but Haig made no attempt either to attack, or to hand some miles of front back to the French. He was clearly gripped by the forthcoming Big Push on the Somme, although it was becoming clear that the French share of this 'combined offensive' would be less than Joffre had proposed.

In his memoirs, Foch records that in April 1916 the French forces available for this combined offensive were already declining. 'The Northern Group of Armies [Foch's command] could only count on nine Army corps instead of fourteen; thirty divisions instead of thirty-nine; its front of attack reduced to twenty miles.'[5]

This was still more than the anticipated British contribution but, on 20 May, there was another reduction in Foch's forces for the Somme. 'Now only seven corps and a maximum of twenty-six divisions could be counted on for the initial attack,' Foch wrote, 'and the French front must be limited to that occupied by their Sixth Army, between Maricourt, just north of the Somme and the Amiens–Péronne road, with its main function that of supporting the British attack north of the river.' Thus Verdun began to erode the strength of the offensive on the Somme, effectively reducing the French to a supporting role.

On 28 March, in an attempt to resolve the current costly stalemate at Verdun, von Falkenhayn wrote to the Crown Prince, asking him what he proposed to do next. A reply was duly received, not from the Prince, but from von Knobelsdorf, whose optimistic estimate of the prospects irritated von Falkenhayn considerably. Von Knobelsdorf claimed that the action at Verdun had sucked in so many French divisions that it precluded the possibility of Allied action elsewhere, and that therefore more divisions could be committed at Verdun. Von Falkenhayn rejected this claim as fanciful, since it failed to take account of the British Armies mustered north of the Somme.

Von Knobelsdorf also claimed that the French were rapidly using up all their reserves at Verdun. Pétain's insistence on replacing French divisions at Verdun before they were totally depleted, as opposed to the German system, where a constant supply of drafts went up to divisions kept in the line, had caused von Knobelsdorf to reach this erroneous conclusion. The Fifth Army Chief-of-Staff finished his letter by proposing that pressure should be maintained on both banks, and that a major right bank attack should also be mounted on Fort Vaux . . . provided enough reserves could be provided. Von Falkenhayn noted tersely that meeting this last requirement was 'impossible'.

Battle has a way of stripping off the veneer that covers a man's character in more peaceful times. Under the stress of the Verdun fighting, a battle von Falkenhayn had requested, organized and created, a battle on which his entire career depended, von Falkenhayn's underlying character was starting to appear. His reply to Fifth Army shows a new von Falkenhayn, somewhat different to the one previously noted, a commander now suggesting caution and a limit to the attacks. He was getting the kind of battle he had wanted, and killing a lot of French, but the cost was proving far too high. Having already lost a great number of German soldiers, von Falkenhayn was now losing his nerve.

The Crown Prince and his Chief-of-Staff wanted to expand the fighting on the right bank, while keeping up the pressure on the Mort Homme until something gave. In this, von Falkenhayn replied, they were being wildly over-optimistic, failing to take account of the enemy, forgetting the broad picture, ignoring the evidence of a big build-up by the British north of the Somme – and making demands for reinforcements and *matériel* that were beyond his capacity to supply.

This assessment, which was entirely accurate, might have put an end to the matter and led to the breaking off of the Verdun offensive but, having gone that far, von Falkenhayn changed his tone yet again and said that, provided these points were borne in mind, he agreed to a renewal of the offensive on the right bank. Vacillating yet again, he then added that if no rapid results were achieved serious consideration should be given to breaking off the Verdun attack entirely, and switching their effort to another part of the front.

The conclusion has to be that von Falkenhayn was starting to see the errors in his own policy. He was realizing that the German Army was suffering as much as the French Army in this interminable battle, and he was starting to build up a set of protective memoranda against the recriminations to come. What he needed was a clear-cut victory, some definite territorial gain, one that would prove these recent sacrifices worthwhile, strengthen the German tactical position at Verdun, and offer hopes of final success in the not too distant future. It took more time and many more losses before von Falkenhayn got what he needed, with the fall of the French positions on the left bank. Before that could happen, at the end of May, the British had begun to show their hand in the trenches north of the Somme.

The British front had not been quiet since the Verdun offensive opened. On 14 and 15 February, the German Sixth Army commanded by Crown Prince Rupprecht of Bavaria, had attacked British Second Army positions north of the Ypres–Comines canal. Had all gone to plan this would have been two days after the start date for the Verdun offensive – 12 February. This attack was successful and it took two days of hard fighting before the British front line was stabilized. The Second Army counterattacked on 2 March and retook the ground lost; total British casualties in the fighting for the Bluff position exceeded 4,000 men; German losses were given as 908 men, killed, wounded and missing.

Further fighting, starting on 2 March and ending on 19 March, took place around the Hohenzollern Redoubt on the old Loos battlefield, a series of attacks and counterattacks proving yet again, in the words of the *Official History*: 'That it was always possible, by a carefully planned assault, to capture a portion of the enemy's front, but impossible to stay in it if he objected to its retention.'[6] The Germans did so object and, by the end of the month, had driven the British out again with a series of furious counterattacks. On 27 March, further fighting took place around the St Eloi craters south of Ypres, a sharp local engagement which continued until 16 April and cost the main unit engaged, the 2nd Canadian Division, 1,371 men killed, wounded and missing. So it would continue as spring gave way to summer; the British sector of the Western Front, if shorter than the French sector, was never quiet for long.

March had been a busy, if more peaceful month, for General Sir Henry Rawlinson and his newly formed Fourth Army. He had already determined that the success of his forthcoming attack would depend almost entirely on an abundance of artillery and was therefore seeking to ensure that his army should have the support of at least one heavy gun, a heavy howitzer, per 100 yards of front to be attacked. This only amounts to some 200 heavy guns and in the event Rawlinson was to have almost twice that number by 1 July, but assembling this amount of heavy artillery would not be easy.

Apart from heavy guns, 60-pounders and above, Rawlinson also needed a large quantity of medium artillery and mortars and a vast quantity of ammunition. While this was being sought and a further infantry corps added to his strength, Rawlinson told his corps commanders to study the ground before them carefully and draw up plans for his consideration on how they would attack the German positions east of the Ancre, and what forces they would require in order to break through them. He would consider their plans, add his own thoughts and proposals, and forward the finished document to General Haig at GHQ.

This process, of laying plans from the bottom up, rather than imposing them from the top down, was common to all the Western Front armies, and was based on the sensible notion that the man on the spot would have a better idea than someone at GHQ on what was and was not possible in the forthcoming battle. There was also the belief that since the local commander would have the responsibility for carrying out the attack, he should have the first say in what was planned.

This did not prevent the plans being altered, amended or even rejected entirely by the senior commanders but, as a general rule, any minor dispute was usually resolved in favour of the subordinate. As part of these plans for the Somme offensive, work was begun on some extensive preparations, laying telephone cable – up to eight feet deep in narrow trenches where possible, preparing gun positions for when the heavy artillery eventually arrived, and laying new roads and railway track for the supply trains.

On 26 March the opening of the Somme offensive grew closer, with the staff at Haig's HQ informing General Rawlinson what he might realistically expect in the way of troops, heavy guns and ammunition, for an offensive which might have to be opened on 1 May or 1 June, somewhat earlier than previously planned. On troops, by 1 May, Fourth Army might expect to have 15 divisions and, by 1 June, 17 divisions. In either event there would also be one cavalry division, while a further three infantry divisions and perhaps two cavalry divisions would be held in GHQ Reserve, from which they could only be released on a direct order from General Haig. Haig asked Rawlinson to draw up plans for either date, based on these troop numbers and submit them to GHQ as soon as possible.

Before Rawlinson could do so, General Joffre wrote to General Haig with some fresh proposals concerning their combined offensive. This letter arrived on 27 March. It stated that, in view of the now obvious fact that the Verdun offensive was going to be the main German effort for the year, Joffre proposed that the Franco-British combined offensive should aim at breaking the enemy's front on a line from Hébuterne in the north of the Fourth Army position, and come south of the Somme as far as Lassigny, a total distance of some 40 miles. Joffre also proposed that after achieving a breakthrough the Allied armies should push east towards the Bapaume–Péronne–Ham road. This suggested that the Allies attempt to advance some ten miles, on a front where a good gain to date was a few hundred yards – and Joffre's proposal included the rider that the French Sixth Army should attack 'some days' after the British. Apart from quickly rejecting this last proposal, Haig did not reply further until he had seen the plan proposed by General Rawlinson.

Rawlinson presented his plan on 3 April. This first draft presented two problems that were to affect the Somme battle from the opening shot – the problems of the width and depth of the attack. Following their experiences in 1915, the Allied commanders believed that an attack must be made on a wide front, since an attack on a narrow front could easily be sealed off, gave little room for the deployment of more troops and the passage of reserves, and resulted in a salient which would soon be under attack from three sides. This was the theory supporting the 'wide-front' attack, but there was, as ever, a problem – artillery support.

Rawlinson knew that his attack depended on artillery and that the currently proposed level of heavy guns, at one per 100 yards of front, was going to be quite inadequate. These problems were mutually contradictory. The wider the front, the thinner the gunfire support would be, unless a vast number of guns were made available, which was unlikely. Given the amount of support he was likely to get, Rawlinson estimated that he could attack on a front no wider than 20,000 yards and, in the event, when the Fourth Army and two divisions of the Third Army went over the top on 1 July, they attacked on a front of 25,000 yards, so Rawlinson's estimate was not far out.

Confronted with the choice he chose the 'more-guns-per-yard-of-front' over the wide-front option.

The problem of depth had been aired before. This was the great tactical argument of the Great War, between advocates of a series of small, limited attacks, usually known as 'bite and hold', and the rather fewer advocates of all-out attack aiming to break the enemy line and produce a 'breakthrough' to the open country beyond. Rawlinson was a stout defender of 'bite and hold', while his superior, General Haig, was always striving for a breakthrough. This difference was not profound; it owed as much to their relative positions and responsibilities as it did to their military expertise.

Rawlinson's concern was, quite correctly, with what his troops could reasonably be expected to achieve in any particular battle or offensive, and here he considered that a limited advance, supported by artillery all the way, was all he could expect. Douglas Haig, on the other hand, was concerned to proceed with his mission, which was to drive the German Army out of northern France and Belgium, and he wanted – needed – a breakthrough on the Somme front as a step towards achieving that end.

The two men were therefore at odds over what they hoped to achieve in this battle. Rawlinson felt that with an attack on a front of 20,000 yards (say 12 miles), an advance of between 2,000 and 5,000 yards (say between one and two miles), would be a real achievement and one that could only be achieved if he had an abundance of artillery and ammunition, far more than was currently being proposed.

This proposal, on the depth of attack, produced another tense discussion between Rawlinson and Haig. The German defences consisted of three main trench and dugout lines. The first, the 'Front Line', close to the British line, ran from Mametz in the south to Serre in the north and was about 2,000 yards in depth. Behind that came the 'Second Position', about 1,000 yards deep, running from Fricourt to Pozières, to Thiepval and along the Ancre, and then running back to Longueval and Delville Wood. It was some distance to the rear of the 'Front Line', but equally well built. Finally, there was the German 'Third Position', beyond the Pozières ridge, which was as yet little more than a marked-out line, with shallow trenches and a few belts of wire.

A Western Front 'trench-line position' should not be imagined as it is normally presented on television, in films, or shown in photographs, as a single trench filled with muddy troops, staring out towards the enemy trenches, but as a complex system of trenches – front line, support line and reserve line – linked by communication trenches, laced with wire and buttressed by machine-gun posts, mortar positions, snipers and field artillery.

A 'front-line position' was, in fact, a complex, painfully constructed and carefully integrated defensive zone, largely composed of trenches dug in a zigzag pattern. For example, although the Western Front only extended for something over 400 miles, from the coast to the Swiss frontier, the Germans dug some 1,400 miles of trenches to defend it, in the first front line alone. Thus, the construction of three defence lines, as on the Somme, meant the excavation of some 5,200 miles of front-line trenches; add in the communication trenches and the German defensive system, as a whole, probably amounted to some 10,000 miles of trench on the Western Front, all of it excavated with picks and shovels.[7]

The German position north of the Somme consisted of two such completed 'lines' and one in preparation and the task before Rawlinson's Army was to break through the German Front Line and Second Line positions, into the open country beyond. The argument was how to do this, in one attack or two? Rawlinson felt that a two-stage attack was more viable. Haig wanted both lines taken, or at least penetrated, in the first attack, and demanded great efforts to capture the Montauban ridge, on the right flank near Fricourt.

There were other discussions – the word 'argument' is too strong – before these matters were decided. Although the generals did not see eye-to-eye on what should be done, this was not an argument to establish one point of view over another; the generals' only aim was to arrive at a plan that would ensure the success of their attacking infantry on Z-day. Another discussion centred on the duration of the bombardment and the hour of attack. A short bombardment, as at Verdun, offered the possibility of surprise. A long bombardment would wear down the enemy's nerves and should, with any luck, do serious damage to his trenches, dugouts and wire.

A case could be made for both arguments but in the end, Rawlinson, the general charged with making this attack, was permitted to go his own way. He went for the long bombardment, mainly because of the German wire and well-prepared positions, which he wanted reduced before the infantry went in. There would be a prolonged bombardment of at least a week, concentrating on the wire, the trenches and the dugouts, rather than on the enemy artillery batteries. The initial attack must be in daylight, so that the artillery observers could see what the guns were doing and where the infantry were. It would therefore go in at 0730 hrs on Z-day and not in the half-light of dawn, which many of the infantry commanders would have preferred.

With hindsight, it is easy to pick holes in the plans for the Somme offensive but given the circumstances of the time the plan appears workable and even sound. During his first visit to the Somme front, Rawlinson had spotted that success or failure depended on artillery. This was quite correct; no one now disputes the fact that the success of the Somme attack depended on the work of the artillery before the infantry went in. 'If the artillery did its work well,' Rawlinson maintained, 'the rest would be easy.' The precious gift of hindsight should not blind us to the fact that Rawlinson's statement is perfectly correct . . . but note also that important 'if'.

Rawlinson's forecast was also somewhat optimistic. Many other factors, large and small, were to conspire against the British infantry on 1 July; the failure of the artillery to quell the German resistance, smash the deep dugouts and beat a path through the enemy wire was only one failure among many. For the moment, Rawlinson proceeded with his planning and the corps and divisional commanders got on with training their men, drawing up plans for carrying out their part in the offensive – and observing the steady growth of enemy fortifications and preparations on the higher ground to their front.

General Haig now had to discuss all this with Joffre and see how far Rawlinson's plan would mesh with that of General Foch, who would be attacking with his Sixth Army to the south of Rawlinson's Fourth. On 10 April, Haig replied to Joffre's letter of 27 March, stating that Fourth Army would attack from a point just south of Hébuterne, as Joffre wanted, but that Allenby's Third Army would extend this attack to the north as far as Gommecourt. This was necessary, because otherwise the German salient at Gommecourt would enfilade the attack of Fourth Army's VIII Corps, attacking just to the south. The southern limit of the British attack would be at Maricourt, on the north bank of the Somme, where Fourth Army trenches met those now occupied by XX Corps of the French Sixth Army, recently brought over from Verdun.

Regarding the aims of his attack, Haig stated that in the centre he proposed first taking the high ground east of the river Ancre, between Thiepval and Pozières. On his left, he hoped to take the Serre spur, and on the right push up north, towards Mametz and Fricourt, advancing in conjunction with the French. This done, he would then push on to the Montauban ridge, which offered access to the Pozières ridge, running to the east of the River Ancre, and then to the line between Ginchy and the Bazentin le Grand ridge, beyond the German second line. (See map on page 244.) It should also be noted that General Haig was proposing a breakthrough, not a battle of attrition.

These references to 'ridges' and 'high ground' in Haig's letter reveal that his immediate aim, in the early phases of the battle, was to break the enemy line and get on to some commanding ground which offered observation for the artillery – a need constantly revealed by Haig's extensive experience at Ypres. What he would do after that would depend on the circumstances. Here again, although our knowledge is coloured by our knowledge of what happened on 1 July, the First Day on the Somme, the plan appears sound, not least in the fact that if it succeeded it would put Haig in a good position for subsequent advances.

There was then an exchange of correspondence between GQG and GHQ, mostly concerning the proposal that the British should attack some time before the French. The idea behind this proposal was that it would pull German reserves off the French front to oppose the British and make the later French attack that much easier. Tactically it made some sense, but what if the French failed to attack, or decided that, for whatever reason, their attack must be delayed? This had happened in other joint battles, and Haig would have been very foolish indeed to take French assurances on trust. If there was a delay in the French attack, the full force of the German reserves would then come north and drive into the flank of any advance the British had made to the east. On balance, Haig preferred that the two armies should attack at the same time, so the idea of a delayed attack, which originated with General Foch, was eventually abandoned.

Joffre was also in favour of a phased attack, with the Bapaume–Péronne–Ham road as the ultimate objective. The second phase, after breaking the German front line, would consist of an attack by the British towards Longueval (High Wood and Delville Wood) before pressing on down the easterly axis of advance – the Albert–Bapaume road – towards Warlencourt, while the French farther south pushed on to Péronne and Bouchavesnes. This differed from Haig's proposal, to wait and see how the battle for the German second line went before drawing up further plans, but Haig accepted these proposals, at least in principle.

Although even a month later, in May, General Joffre had still not finally fixed the date for commencing this operation, Haig was not concerned. Every day that passed saw the British divisions in France a little stronger and a little better trained, and more guns in the line. If the Somme attack was delayed beyond mid-June, Haig and Rawlinson could hope to have at least 20 divisions, perhaps as many as 25 divisions. This might have been an argument for further delay, perhaps even until the tanks Haig wanted were ready for the fray, but there was that other overriding factor to consider – Verdun, where the fighting went on and reached a new pitch of intensity during April and the first weeks of May. As this fighting continued, the problems of Verdun began to impinge on the problems of the Somme offensive.

Notes

1 As stated in the *Official History, 1916*, vol. 5, p. 246. But Fourth Army began to form at Tilques, near Calais, on 5 February 1916. Fourth Army HQ moved to Querrieu on 24 February.

2 *The Private Papers of Douglas Haig*, p. 133.

3 Ibid., p. 136.
4 Ibid.
5 *The Memoirs of Marshal Foch*, pp. 245–6.
6 *Official History, 1916*, vol. 5, p. 174.
7 Estimates from *The First World War, Germany and Austria-Hungary, 1914–1918*, Holgar Herwig, pp. 244–5.

9

Enter Nivelle
April–May 1916

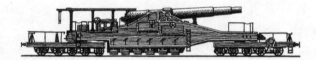

'Our precise problem is how to inflict heavy damage on
the enemy at critical points at relatively small cost to
ourselves. But we must not overlook the fact that previous
experience of mass attacks in this war offers little
inducement to imitate them.'
General Erich von Falkenhayn,
General Headquarters 1914–1916 and Its Critical Decisions

By the end of April 1916 it was becoming apparent, even to populations now inured to tragedy, that something unusual in the scale of slaughter, something of an entirely different order of magnitude, was taking place around the beleaguered city of Verdun. Moreover, the relentless shelling, the mounting casualty lists, the massive expenditure of shells and blood which arose from that conflict did not appear to be paying either side any kind of dividend in territory gained or assaults repulsed. As the weeks lengthened into months, the fighting went on with unabated fury, without apparent advantage to either side.

Battles on the Western Front were invariably subject to the law of diminishing returns. Given sufficient artillery and manpower and a degree of surprise, an attack might succeed in taking some or all of its immediate objectives. Then the attack would falter; command and control would weaken, largely because of poor communications; the enemy, though initially stunned, would bring up reserves and any successes gained would either be hotly and expensively contested, or rapidly contained. So it had been throughout 1915; so it was now at Verdun.

There were often good reasons for this seemingly inevitable process. Since little could be done about the problems of artillery, mobility, communications and supply, a wise general might conclude that his greatest talent lay in an accurate estimate of when to call off his battle, dig in for the inevitable counterattack, and husband his gains. This was the thinking behind 'bite and hold' assaults, which might often succeed and offered some limited gain.

The problem with 'bite and hold' was that it did little to prosecute the eventual outcome of the war. Grabbing a few hundred yards of enemy trench at the cost of a few thousand lives might make for good headlines, or demonstrate some tactical competence in the command, but it did little to drive the German Army out of France and Belgium. On the other hand, 'bite and hold' did offer some gains – it was a series of 'bite and hold' attacks that ended with the capture of the Passchendaele ridge in 1917. These gains seemed to justify the tactic – though the gains were always accompanied by terrible losses.

Even assuming that the initial assault achieved some measure of success, the second problem would then arise. Should the battle be continued, in the hope that the attackers, by skilful use of their artillery and reserves, could overwhelm the enemy reserves now being committed to their containment – a decision that might lead to a battle of attrition – or should the attacking commander break the battle off and, if so, when and how?

The argument over these complementary processes will be aired more fully when we come to the battle of the Somme but these problems were equally applicable at Verdun where, although the aims of the battle were different – and indeed differed between the Fifth Army HQ and the German High Command – the problem of whether to continue the attack or break it off and dig in began to exercise von

Falkenhayn and the Crown Prince as the battle wore on towards the summer – a problem given stark relevance by negligible territorial gains and ever-rising casualty figures.

By the end of March the German Army at Verdun had lost 81,607 men, the French 89,000, both totals up by over 50,000 in the last four weeks. Both sides fudged these figures, claiming in their intelligence reports that enemy losses were far higher than their own; at the end of March the French estimated German casualties at over 200,000 to their own estimated 65,000. Von Falkenhayn also chose 200,000 Frenchmen as his estimate of enemy casualties to date. But even with that claim von Falkenhayn's basic plan, to bleed the French Army to death with artillery fire while sparing the German infantry, was clearly not working.

Although the communiqués attempted to ignore this fact, there can be no doubt that von Falkenhayn was well aware that the margin of loss between his forces and those of France was now slim indeed. The difficulty with von Falkenhayn's original concept was that since the city had to be defended, the French had made it defensible. Once the Germans had lost the advantage of surprise and failed to take Verdun in the first few days, the French were fully alert to the threat and responded to it with increasing force, more weaponry, and not a little skill. Therefore, neither German commander was achieving his aim at Verdun; the Crown Prince had not taken the city and von Falkenhayn was bleeding his own army to death as well as that of France.

Added to this were two further problems, one of them chronic. It is axiomatic that an attacking force must commit more men than the defence can muster; the usual ratio is three attackers to one defender, so a company would be sent in against a platoon, a brigade against a battalion, and so on. This 'rule' is simply a working average and subject to all kinds of modifications, but it is the accepted yardstick, not least because it allows for the harsh fact that men advancing in the open are more exposed to fire than men under cover.

On the Western Front, with its unique defensive combination of wire, artillery, dugouts, machine-guns and open ground, the attacking force invariably lost more men than the defending force but if von Falkenhayn really wanted to suck the French into a major commitment on 'the anvil of Verdun', where his artillery could hammer them, he had no option but to commit his troops to a continuous series of expensive assaults. Simply demonstrating in front of the French lines would not do it, or not do it for long, after Pétain got a grip on the situation and began to organize an effective defence. Von Falkenhayn had hoped to slaughter the French with shellfire, not with superior manpower; now it appeared that his battle was descending into 'pure' attrition and that the Germans would win, not because they had killed a lot of French soldiers at little cost to themselves but because, however similar and terrible the losses were, Germany could afford them and France could not.

The second point, however, is that there was a limit to the application of this crude statistic. Troops do not like being committed to a battle where their lives are expendable and, by the end of March, problems of morale began to manifest themselves among the soldiery. There is particular evidence of growing weariness and carelessness among the German troops and a small but increasing number of German deserters began coming over to the French lines. This was largely due to the physical and mental exhaustion which resulted from the German custom of keeping units in the line and topping them up with a stream of new soldiers recently arrived from the depots. Quite apart from the fact that this gave no relief to those who were still alive and unwounded at the front, these young soldiers, flung into battle without even a modicum of front-line experience, were frequently shocked by the exposure and were of little use to their comrades. It also broke up or diminished that intangible but vital military asset, unit morale; the men now being thrust into the front-line units were strangers to each other, and the regiments they joined, and the spirit of comradeship on which men depend in battle suffered accordingly.

The French divisions, on the other hand, while equally exhausted in the combat, were relieved regularly under Pétain's relief system, now known as the 'Noria system' (a 'noria' is a chain of buckets used for lifting water to irrigate ground) and taken out of the line before they were totally shattered, for a period of recuperation in a rear area, far from the sound of shellfire. Under Noria, French divisions were sent into the line for the shortest possible length of time – a week at the most – before being replaced by a fresh or at least a well-rested unit. Pétain had to push the introduction of this system on Joffre, who was reluctant to commit more divisions at Verdun because he was attempting to build up his forces for the Somme, but Pétain was ada-mant and for the moment his view carried the day. The Noria system enabled the units to replace their losses and integrate the fresh men into the companies and platoons before returning to the battle; the drawbacks only appeared later, when the battle continued for month after month and division after division of the French Army went back up the *Voie Sacrée* to take yet another turn in the furnace at Verdun.

In the course of time Noria may have contributed to an overall deterioration in the French Army, as more and more units had to be committed at Verdun and were duly worn down by the shelling. For the moment, Noria certainly helped and further help was provided by Pétain's sensible handling of the troops in battle, ordering them to hold their ground, but forbidding all but the most necessary counter-attacks. Indeed, on taking command at Verdun one of Pétain's first orders was that the practice of instant counterattacks to retake some lost position should be abandoned forthwith. This order did not go down at all well at GQG, where the staff were still thoroughly imbued with the Grandmaison doctrine and could not understand why Pétain was yielding any ground at all. In fact, the Verdun front was virtually static. German gains on the left bank amounted to a few hundred yards, and that at terrible cost, but Pétain's abandonment of Grandmaison tactics was poorly regarded at Joffre's HQ and was soon to have repercussions.

In the German Army the effect of Verdun was deep but limited. The number of divisions committed was fewer in comparison with the French divisional commitment, although the 'trickle-drafting' of reinforcements to the divisions in the line meant that almost as many German soldiers fought there and suffered in the same proportion. By the end of April, some 40 French divisions had already been rotated through Verdun compared with 26 German divisions but in neither army did any of these divisions march away as strong and confident as they arrived.

In the French Army, the Verdun experience sapped many men of those vital reserves of courage and willpower they would need later on in the war, laying the grounds for the widespread mutinies of 1917. German resolve and morale suffered in much the same way, although the effects took longer to emerge. Years after the war the Crown Prince summed up the effect on his army accurately when he wrote: 'Verdun was the mill on the Meuse that ground to powder the hearts as well as the bodies of our soldiers.'

Equally apt is the comment of the German historian Michael Geyer: 'Verdun showed the military impasse of World War I, the complete disjuncture between strategy, battle design and tactics and the inability to use the modern means of war. But most of all it showed, at horrendous cost, the impasse of professional strategies.'[1]

In spite of this concentration on Verdun and the developing offensive on the Somme, it should not be forgotten that the war continued in other theatres with varying fortunes for the contesting parties. There was some good news for the Entente from the east, where the Russians were again playing their part in the series of offensives planned for 1916, having made a remarkable recovery from the reverses suffered in 1915. After the Verdun offensive began, Russia made an immediate effort to help the French by launching an attack at Lake Naroc in March, in an attempt to divert German reserve divisions to the east. This offensive soon petered out but another Russian offensive was launched in May, fuelled by a desire to help another ally, in this case Italy, which was now under great pressure following the Austrian spring offensive on the Trentino. This second Russian offensive also achieved very little, but before long the Russians attacked again. That apart, the British also had problems to contend with, in Ireland and at sea; the Great War was not confined to the Western Front.

The British suffered a major political alarm in April 1916 when a rebellion, the Easter Rising, broke out in Dublin. The Easter Rising of 1916 can be traced to the passing of the pre-war Irish Home Rule Bill, which recognized Irish statehood and should have led to immediate independence in the summer of 1914. This bill went through the Westminster Parliament but then came the war, and the implementation of the bill was suspended until the end of hostilities. Tens of thousands of young Irishmen duly flocked to the colours forming, among many other units, three full divisions, two of which, the 36th (Ulster) and the 16th (Irish) Division, would be committed to the Somme offensive and were already moving to the Fourth Army when the Rising broke out.

Frustrated by the delay in granting Home Rule, a group of armed Irishmen seized the Post Office and other public buildings in Dublin and declared Ireland free of British domination. Troops were called in and, within two days, field artillery was being used in the streets of Dublin. The Easter Rising did not last long but its effects have been far-reaching, partly because its aftermath was badly handled by the British authorities. The Easter Rising was extremely unpopular with the Irish people, who saw it as a betrayal of their young men now fighting on the Western Front. Those who took part were at first regarded as traitors by their countrymen, and, when the rebels were subdued and marched into captivity through the streets of Dublin, the population lined the pavement to shout abuse at them.

Then the British Government made the fatal error of trying the insurgents and shooting 16 of them – an action that instantly turned the traitors into martyrs. The British Government was fully entitled to do this: there was a war on and the Rising had been made in hopes of German assistance, some of it realized in the form of an arms shipment brought to Ireland by a German submarine. This submarine also put ashore Sir Roger Casement, the Anglo-Irish patriot, who was later hanged for his part in this affair. Even so, however justified the executions, such actions were unwise. The Rising and the subsequent shootings seem to have had little effect on the men at the Front, on either side of the religious divide, but they had repercussions after the war which extend to the present day.

Nor were the British doing too well at sea. The activities of German submarines had gravely curtailed the actions of the Grand Fleet which, apart from short periodic sweeps, had largely remained at anchor at Scapa Flow in the Orkneys, safe behind a screen of anti-submarine nets. From Scapa, the Grand Fleet was in position to block any move by the German High Seas Fleet, should it venture either towards the North Sea or the North Atlantic. Units of the High Seas Fleet made sorties to shell the English coast, but it was not until Admiral Scheer took command in 1916 that some definite action was decided on. Then, at 0948 hrs on 30 May 1916, the High Seas Fleet finally sailed, initiating what Correlli Barnett has accurately described as 'the last general action fought by a British Fleet.'[2] It was also the first British Fleet action since the Battle of Navarino in 1827 in the age of sail. Here at sea, as elsewhere on land, it revealed that war had changed.

This action, known to the British as the Battle of Jutland and the Germans as the Skagerrak, was at best a draw, although the Germans later claimed it as an overwhelming victory. Certainly, between 30 May and 1 June, the German Navy sank more ships – 14 British ships sunk and 6,945 sailors killed, to the Germans' 11 ships and 2,921 sailors killed – but the Royal Navy could and did claim that they had forced the German Fleet back into port, from which it never again emerged. In spite of the losses sustained at Jutland, the Royal Navy could muster 48 battleships and battlecruisers in all respects ready for sea, refuelled and rearmed, within 48 hours; Admiral Scheer could muster just ten.

Even so, this 'victory', if victory it was, would hardly have satisfied Nelson; British gunnery was poor and the armour on the ships proved inadequate. After this fleet action, matters returned to their previous condition, a contest between the German submarine and the Merchant Navy, the latter supported by light units of the British Fleet. These British actions and alarms, at sea and in Ireland, are part of the 1916 tapestry, but they had little effect on the fighting on the Western Front. The same cannot be said of the Russian Brusilov offensive, the last major Russian attack of the war and one rewarded with an outstanding but short-lived success.

At the Chantilly Conference in December 1915, the Allied commanders had agreed that they would launch 'simultaneous' assaults on their respective fronts during the coming year, hoping thereby to spread the Central Powers' armies, and especially the German Army, far beyond their operational limits and thereby exhaust their strength in men and *matériel* in a series of campaigns. Plans for the Russian summer offensive had been drawn up in April, when it was decided that the Southern Army Group, four armies under General Brusilov, should hold their positions while the other Russian armies engaged the enemy, probably in July, a major attack timed to coincide with the Anglo-French Somme offensive.

Brusilov opposed this plan for a holding action, arguing that if he attacked, he would at least prevent the Germans moving divisions off his front to oppose his colleagues. Brusilov's Army Group occupied a 200-mile front in the south-west, around Lemberg (Lvov) and along the River Bug, where he was opposed by the Army Group of General von Linsingen, who had two Austrian armies and two German corps under command, and was supported by the Army Group of the Austrian Archduke Joseph, with one German and two Austrian armies.

Brusilov made his preparations in great secrecy and his attack on this formidable array of foes, on 4 June, came as a complete surprise. Between 4 June and 9 July, Brusilov struck the Austrian Fourth Army near Lutsk and the Austrian Seventh Army at Bukovina; both armies promptly collapsed. Brusilov then drove the Austrian and German forces back all along the front for a distance of up to 30 miles, taking 450,000 prisoners and more than 400 guns. The Brusilov offensive rumbled on into the autumn, when the scale of loss gradually swung against the Russian armies and, according to Liddell Hart, contributed substantially to the eventual collapse of the Russian Armies and the Tsarist State in 1917.[3]

Brusilov had obtained a great victory but at terrible cost; more than 1,000,000 Russian soldiers were killed, wounded or went missing before his offensive ended. His attack represents the last major assault mounted by the Russian armies before they began their long slide down to defeat, disintegration and the revolution of 1917. On the other hand, Brusilov's success also contributed to the downfall of von Falkenhayn, and obliged the Austrians to call off their summer offensive on the Trentino. Although von Hindenburg and Ludendorff, the German commanders on the Eastern Front, attempted to make light of this defeat, the Brusilov offensive was widely seen as one of the great Entente victories of the war to date. It did not, however, do much to ease the relentless German pressure on the French at Verdun.

Brusilov's offensive forced von Falkenhayn to withdraw seven divisions from the west, but these divisions came from the Somme front, where they were being readied to resist the coming attack from the British, whose preparations were becoming obvious by the first weeks of June. Another effect of Brusilov's successes was to encourage

Romania to enter the war on the side of the Entente but this too proved a short-term gain. Romania declared war on the Central Powers on 27 August and was immediately attacked by strong German forces under General von Mackensen. These forces made good headway against the totally unprepared and ill-equipped Romanian army and entered Bucharest in triumph on 6 December. So the war continued, by sea and land, with no sign of peace on the horizon, and yet another Western Front offensive looming on the Somme.

At Verdun the battle rumbled on, with losses mounting steeply on either side. April opened with the Germans battering their way forward on the left bank, carpeting the ground with dead, as they moved painfully through the ruins of Malancourt, Haucourt and Bethincourt, and preparing to support this attack with yet another assault on the right bank in early May, aimed at Fort Souville. The current exclusive concentration of effort on the left bank cut both ways, as usual, for it enabled the French to concentrate their guns on the ground before the Mort Homme and raise the cost of progress there significantly. Once more the grey infantry advanced into the guns; once more the infantry in *horizon-bleu* held them off or drove them back; once more the death toll mounted, all under the pitiless torment of the guns.

Then, on 9 April, the Crown Prince tried a new tactic, the one dictated by all those pre-war exercises. This time he would try attacking towards Verdun simultaneously – on both banks of the river. Better late than never, perhaps, and for this attack the Crown Prince first divided the Fifth Army into two area commands, one for each bank. General von Mudra took command on the right bank, and General von Gallwitz, an artillery officer who had been soldiering with the Eleventh Army supporting Austro-Hungarian forces against Serbia, was brought back from the Balkans to take over on the left bank. Under von Gallwitz's command was another general, Eugène von Falkenhayn, the elder brother of the Commander-in-Chief, sometime tutor to the Crown Prince and currently commander of XXII Reserve Corps, which von Gallwitz charged specifically with the capture of the Mort Homme.

Thus reorganized, and with a plan that, had it been adopted earlier,

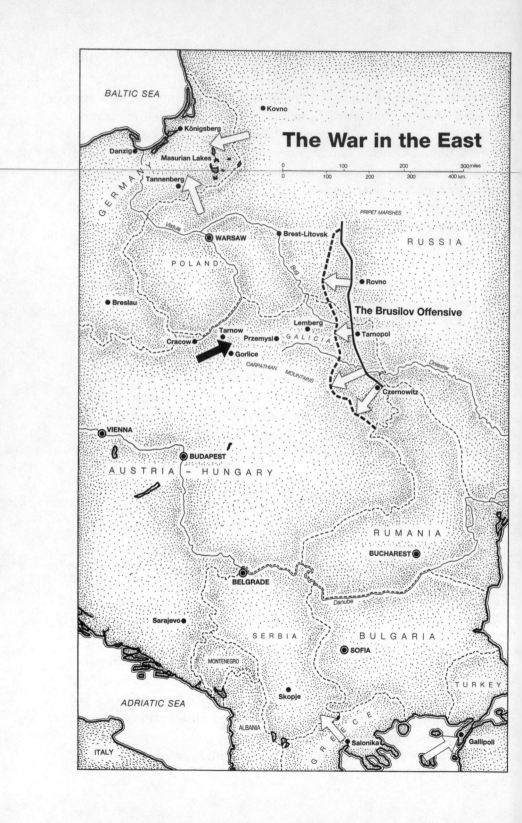

BALTIC SEA

● Kovno

● Königsberg

Danzig ●

Masurian Lakes

Tannenberg ●

The War in the East

0   100   200   300 miles
0   100   200   300   400 km.

PRIPET MARSHES

Vistula

● WARSAW

● Brest-Litovsk

R U S S I A

POLAND

Bug

● Rovno

● Breslau

Lemberg ●

The Brusilov Offensive

Tarnow ●

G A L I C I A

● Tarnopol

Cracow ●   Przemysl ●

Gorlice ●

CARPATHIAN   MOUNTAINS

Dniester

● Czernowitz

● VIENNA

● BUDAPEST

A U S T R I A – H U N G A R Y

R U M A N I A

● BUCHAREST ◉

● BELGRADE

Danube

● Sarajevo ●

S E R B I A

B U L G A R I A

MONTENEGRO

◉ SOFIA

ADRIATIC SEA

● Skopje

G R E E C E

T U R K E Y

ALBANIA

Salonika ●

● Gallipoli

ITALY

might have guaranteed at least partial success – the capture of Verdun – the new German offensive began . . . and at once ran into difficulties. This attack on 9 April succeeded in its first aim of stretching the French line thin on both banks, but that line did not break. Spearheading the advance on the left bank, Eugène von Falkenhayn's troops managed to force their way on to the northern edge of the Mort Homme and, at the usual terrible cost, take one of its two summits, the one topping at 870ft. Jubilation over this success was short-lived. When the smoke and dust cleared, the other, higher 970ft summit was seen spitting fire from farther along the ridge. Once again, as so often in this Western Front fighting, the attackers realized that a partial success was no success at all.

Pétain broke his normal silence on 10 April with an Order of the Day that was to ring out over the battlefield: 'April 9 was a glorious day for our army. The attacks of the Crown Prince have been broken everywhere. The infantry, artillery, sappers and flyers of the 2nd Army competed with each other in deeds of valour. Honour to you all! No doubt the enemy will attack again. So let us all strive to see that the success of yesterday continues. Courage. We shall beat them (*On les aura!*)!'

This advance had cost the Germans a few more thousand men and a great quantity of ammunition and had taught them, yet again, that the key to the Mort Homme was Côte 304, which had the new occupants of the slender German bridgehead on the Mort Homme under heavy and accurate fire. This defeat also concentrated minds at the Crown Prince's Headquarters at Stenay-sur-Meuse, where the Crown Prince and von Knobelsdorf, who were never close colleagues, were now beginning to drift apart. Meanwhile the battle on the left bank continued.

The next phase of the left bank fighting was the struggle on the Mort Homme itself, for the possession of the final 970ft feature. The distance between the two summits of this hill can be measured in yards but, even with the usual expensive combination of bombardment, attack, more bombardment, counterattack and again attack, until the ridgetop was bare of trees and increasingly denuded of soil, that short distance seemed impossible to cross. After three-quarters of a century, the effect of those weeks of bombardment can still be clearly seen at Verdun; the top of the Mort Homme is pitted with shell craters and without a square yard of level ground. What it must have been like in April 1916, when the shells continued to fall by night and day and wounded men drowned in craters filled by heavy rain, is beyond imagining.

By now there was no cover of any kind on the Mort Homme and precious little cover anywhere else on the Verdun battlefield. Trenches were little more than shell scrapes in the ground; dugouts, painfully excavated in the dark, were rapidly obliterated in the daytime. Over this pitted desolation hung the heavy smell of rotting flesh. Dead and dismembered bodies lay everywhere; they could not be removed and, when they were hastily buried, the shellfire promptly exhumed them again. As for the wounded, their case was pitiful. French medical services, never up to the standards of the British Army, broke down completely at Verdun, where the wounded could not be extracted from the battlefield without great difficulty. The unwholesome state of the area and of the cattle trucks used to evacuate the wounded to Bar-le-Duc and beyond added the horrors of gas gangrene and tetanus to the usual traumas of open wounds.

This failure to take adequate care of the wounded and remove them quickly to the casualty clearing stations put another burden on the front-line *poilu* who, apart from being distressed by his inability to help his comrades, saw from their state what his own fate was likely to be if one of those whirling shell fragments added him to their number. A total of 895,000 French soldiers died in battle during the Great War, but a further 420,000 died of wounds in the casualty clearing stations, from gangrene or septicaemia or some other sickness, much of it preventable.

The soldiers lay out in the open, under a rain of shells, finding what shelter they could in the craters, often hungry and usually thirsty – unless they were driven to drink from puddles contaminated with corpses – while the companies lost as many men in moving in and out of the front line as they did while in occupation. This depiction of the horrors of the Verdun battlefield is necessary, not simply to describe the battlefield itself, but to show that the conditions under which the men fought were as horrendous as the fighting itself.

A few days of this fighting convinced von Gallwitz that the Mort Homme could not be taken unless the Côte 304 feature was taken first. One way of achieving this end was the construction of tunnels in the chalk to bring troops safely into position for a sudden assault on this feature but, while these were being dug, the French, aided by the guns of Côte 304, retook all the ground taken on the Mort Homme. By 22 April, the French were again in full possession of this feature and their attackers must do it all again.

At least the Germans now knew that the way to take the Mort Homme was to take Côte 304 first. Careful preparations were made for this attack, not least the forward movement of more heavy guns; if necessary, the Crown Prince intended to take Côte 304 and the Mort Homme by removing everything on those features, the men, the guns, the remaining trees, the very earth itself, blasting away down to the underlying strata until there was nothing left. A frenzy was now gripping the contestants at Verdun; had the guns not been there to do the job, the impression grows that the men would have clawed the hill apart with their bare hands.

So the artillery boomed out without ceasing and the German attacks continued but this was not the only blow to fall on the French soldiers at the end of April. As a further, unwitting step towards the maintenance of von Falkenhayn's design, on 1 May, Pétain was replaced at Verdun by a new commander, General Robert Nivelle.

Although the French were stemming the German tide and charging a heavy price for every yard of ground lost, by the end of March Joffre had grown discontented with Pétain. Joffre had never wanted Pétain at Verdun in the first place. He wanted counterattacks and he could not understand why, if the Germans were now being held on both banks, Pétain was not immediately going over to a more aggressive style of warfare and rapidly driving them back. Joffre brought pressure to bear on Pétain, urging this course of action, and became steadily more infuriated by Pétain's refusal to comply. He was also alarmed by the steady consumption of his reserve divisions at Verdun, divisions Joffre had been hoarding for his main offensive on the Somme, which was scheduled to begin in a matter of weeks. The Somme offensive remained the major French priority for 1916; the Verdun issue must therefore be settled soon. If Pétain was not able to end it by retaking the lost ground and claiming a victory, some other general must be found.

Commanding generals have a habit of seeing what they want to see and Joffre felt that, since no less than 40 French divisions had now been committed to the Verdun battle, more should have been achieved. Granted, most of these divisions had replaced units shattered in the fighting and were only in the line for a few days before they too had to be withdrawn but, from Joffre's viewpoint, he was supplying Pétain with everything Pétain asked for; in return, he expected a decisive German defeat, not an expensive stalemate.

This conflict of opinion over the conduct of the Verdun battle put Joffre on a collision course with General Pétain. Joffre was totally determined on the Somme offensive, while Pétain considered that Verdun was – and would remain – the major French battle for 1916. Pétain also believed that the French position at Verdun could only be held if all available assets were devoted to it. Therefore, moving on logically from this belief, Pétain suggested that if Joffre was adamant about the offensive on the Somme, then that offensive should be left to the British. If their attack on the Somme resulted in a lessening of German pressure at Verdun, so much the better but, as far as Pétain was concerned, the major French battle was the one he was fighting now, here, at Verdun; if the British could not handle the Somme offensive alone, then that attack should be abandoned.

Pétain was also becoming increasingly disillusioned, even angry, about the British failure to help France in this, her greatest hour of need since 1914. This may have been the start of his deep-rooted Anglophobia, which surfaced in 1918 and appeared even more strongly in 1940. On the face of it, Pétain had a point: the Russians had mounted a massive attack, the Romanians had entered the war – even the Italians had attempted to draw off German reserves – but what had the British done? As far as Pétain could tell, nothing!

The situation facing Haig and Rawlinson on the Somme, and the mighty efforts they were making to prepare their troops for a breakthrough offensive, did not weigh heavily with Pétain. He saw only that his men were bearing the entire weight of the Western Front battle and getting precious little help from their British allies. Until he got such help, Pétain was doing his best for the French Army and for France . . . and as far as he was concerned, mounting counterattacks to take back some worthless acres of shell-torn ground at Verdun was a waste of precious French lives.

This attitude was not likely to commend itself to Joffre, who was not the man to maintain a general in post if that general failed to deliver what he wanted. By early April, if not before, Joffre was already regretting the appointment of Pétain but he could see no easy way to get rid of him. Pétain was now regarded as 'the saviour of Verdun' and as a result was extremely popular with the French Army, the French press and the French public. Joffre, on the other hand, was in bad odour with both the public and the politicians, not least because the fall of Douaumont and the rapid German advances at the end of February, and the losses since, were now being laid at his door. The fact that he had ordered the dismantling of Verdun's defences, and so contributed to the problems of French Army charged with defending that city, had not been forgotten either.

However, there was a solution to this delicate dilemma. Joffre could not remove Pétain, so he decided to promote him and to present this promotion to the French public as a just reward for Pétain's splendid services at Verdun; the fact that Pétain did not want this promotion was beside the point. This move also enabled Joffre to get rid of General de Langle de Cary, a perfectly competent officer who, as Commander of Army Group Centre, had first brought news of the Verdun offensive to Joffre's ears. Bearers of bad tidings are never welcome and so de Langle de Cary was *limogé* – dismissed and retired to a provincial command – at the end of April. On 1 May, Pétain, still protesting strongly, was appointed to the command of Army Group Centre, which had the Second Army among its components. Therefore, said de Castelnau blandly, General Pétain would still exercise overall control at Verdun but the command of Second Army and the decision on day-to-day operations there now lay in the hands of a new and rising star, General Robert Nivelle, currently commanding III Corps.

Robert Nivelle is a tragic example of an officer promoted beyond his ability. Because the French Army under his overall command mutinied in 1917, he has been adjudged one of the most incompetent generals to exercise command in the Great War – the general who presided over a series of disasters in 1917, in the fighting on the Chemin des Dames, defeats which finally drove the French Armies to mutiny. And yet, before 1917, few generals showed more promise or were more popular with their superiors or with the politicians than Robert Nivelle. They were captivated by his charm, admired his ability and found his optimism a refreshing change from the caution of General Pétain or the taciturnity of General Joffre.

By early 1917 he was so popular with David Lloyd George, the British Prime Minister, a politician who usually had little time for generals of any kind, that the Prime Minister tried to give Nivelle overall command of the British Army in France, thereby reducing Haig to the role of a subordinate army group commander. This move was only thwarted when Lloyd George faced an outcry in Parliament and because someone pointed out that not even the Prime Minister could give the armies of Great Britain and the Dominions into the control of another power. Lloyd George's action was taken largely because Robert Nivelle had achieved a certain level of success in the later stages of the battle at Verdun and claimed to have discovered the way to victory – 'the formula', as he called it.

Perhaps the root of the problem was that Nivelle was promoted not simply too high but too quickly. A regimental colonel in 1914, he rose in just over one year to the rank of general in command of III Corps. This was followed six months later, in May 1916, by promotion to the command of Second Army at Verdun. Six months after that he would replace Joffre as Commander-in-Chief, over the heads of Foch, Pétain and de Castelnau, a truly remarkable success story. And then came tragedy.

On the face of it, Robert Nivelle possessed certain fundamental assets that supported his rapid promotion to high command. In 1916 he was 58 and therefore one of the younger and more energetic French generals. He was an artillery officer, always a useful asset on the artillery-dominated Western Front and, although he had limitations, he was not without ability in the field. He was also a fighting general and he spoke fluent English (he had an English mother) – another useful asset in an alliance. General Nivelle was otherwise the archetypal French officer, charming, eloquent and supremely confident in his own military abilities.

The process of French military training, from the cadet academy at St Cyr to the staff course at the École Supérieure de la Guerre, seems to have had the inculcating of confidence as one of its prime tasks. Up to a point this is all to the good; a general needs to believe in himself. Problems arise when confidence, based on intelligence, competence and experience, becomes over-confidence, or is based on the belief that a French general is automatically superior to all other generals.

There is also the point that an officer is charged with responsibility from the first day of his commission and this responsibility grows at every level of command he reaches. Only the very best officers can, or should, rise to the extreme responsibility of high command and happy is the general who reaches the limit of his ability at a suitably high level and is not promoted above that level, where disaster for his men and his previous reputation usually lie in wait. At the lower levels of command, Nivelle had done well – he would not have been promoted otherwise – but his talents were not sufficient for the levels he was now attaining. Verdun needed an officer with brains but Robert Nivelle was rather short of brains. His principal asset was charm; as a result, he rose like a rocket . . . and came down like the stick.

Nivelle did have two other assets. The first was his Chief-of-Staff, Major d'Alenson, who was generally regarded as one of the most competent staff officers in the French Army. The French staff were not noted for their competence, so this may not mean much, but if Nivelle had the best the French staff had to offer, again he was lucky. His second asset was a mixed blessing, General Charles Mangin, the most famous fighting general in the French Army, a throwback to an earlier age.

Charles Mangin was a Napoleonic figure, a twentieth-century Ney, a man seemingly without fear, an officer who led from the front and sent his men forward into the fire regardless of loss. This dire doctrine had already cost France dear but such is the blanket provided by courage that its execution and its cost had only enhanced Mangin's reputation as a man who got results. In many respects, Mangin was simply immature. Physical bravery is essential in second lieutenants but dangerous in general officers. They should learn caution and judgement as they rise through the ranks; a general needs moral courage, not least the courage to make a hard decision and stick to it under pressure from his superiors and events. This return to the Grandmaison doctrine was to prove fatal to the French Army at Verdun but, for the moment, it was firmly back in place and the prospects for Nivelle looked good. With d'Alenson to do his thinking and Mangin to do his fighting – and both of them fiercely loyal to their commander – Robert Nivelle could anticipate success.

Pétain duly departed to his new appointment and Nivelle took up his command on 1 May 1916. On arriving at Second Army HQ at Souilly, he informed the assembled throng of officers and newspapermen that he knew exactly what he was going to do – 'We have the formula,' he declared – and passed inside to start applying his methods to the defence of Verdun. From now on there would be no more reliance on tenacious defence, no more dogged struggles to retain small patches of ground. Small-scale actions were not Nivelle's style; he intended to go over to the offensive, to attack and attack and go on attacking, right along the front and regardless of cost, until the enemy were driven back, defeated, destroyed. Two days after he took over, on 3 May 1916, the Germans struck again at the Mort Homme and Côte 304.

The attack on Côte 304 began with a massive bombardment by more than 500 heavy guns, one for every 10 yards of front. It is worth recalling at this point that for the 15-mile wide Somme front General Rawlinson hoped for one heavy gun every hundred yards, a total of 200 heavy guns. The bombardment of Côte 304 went on for the next two days and the shells fell on a front less than 2,200 yards wide. Eventually, under that shellfire, nothing remained; trees, grass, earth, guns, men, equipment of every kind, any trench system or dugout, everything was flung into the air by high explosive or simply disappeared in the blast. The existing shell craters were replaced by new craters, the dimpled ground changing shape, hour by hour, as the rain of shells continued.

This barrage was followed by three days of hand-to-hand infantry fighting with rifle, bayonet and grenade, as the Germans fought their way on to Côte 304; some 10,000 French soldiers died in that single battle and, when the Germans finally stood on that fatal hill, they came into possession of a charnel house. But with Côte 304 taken, the Germans were now able to advance on the Mort Homme from the east and west and end that three-month running sore that was eating into their flank.

A further recitation of the horrors attendant on that advance to the Mort Homme simply dulls the senses. By the end of May the Germans had taken Mort Homme and the village of Cumières on the south side of the Côte de l'Oie. This last success completed the German offensive on the left bank and cleared the way at last for a massive assault on the right bank. Now that the French positions on the Mort Homme and Côte 304 had been eliminated, those guns that had previously swept the right bank with fire would no longer impede the German advance. This offered the opportunity for a further assault on Fort Vaux; it also offered wider possibilities. By taking Côte 304 the Germans had also made the first breach in Pétain's Line of Resistance, that interlinked series of positions around Verdun that he had marked out on his first day in command as places that had to be held.

This concentration on the left bank fighting in April and May did not mean that the right bank was quiet. Although any significant advance there depended on the crushing of the left bank positions, it was necessary to keep up the pressure on the right bank, if only to disperse the fire from the French artillery and prevent troops being diverted to the defence of the Mort Homme. The fighting had now moved past Fort Douaumont and the village and was moving, literally yard by yard, towards Fort Vaux.

In the three months of March, April and May, the German line on the right bank advanced less than one mile. The month of April was almost entirely devoted to the capture of the stone quarry at Haudremont. As the fighting continued, the advance remained painfully slow and the casualties mounted, the German commanders began to change their opinions on the eventual outcome of this battle.

Up to this point, von Falkenhayn had been the one urging a battle of attrition, while the Crown Prince insisted on a calculated attack to take Verdun. Now these views began to diverge. At the end of March, von Falkenhayn reminded the Crown Prince that the promised reserves had been provided but no noticeable gains had been achieved; what did the Crown Prince propose to do next? On 21 April, after more weeks of bitter fighting, the Crown Prince finally came to realize that the Verdun offensive was simply too costly in lives and should be called off: 'A decisive success at Verdun could only be assured at the price of heavy sacrifices, out of all proportion to the desired gains,' he wrote, a sensible assessment by a man sadly underrated by his contemporaries and subsequently by many historians.

The Crown Prince Wilhelm of Prussia, the Kaiser's heir – a man generally known to the British soldiers as 'Little Willie' – had been given command of Fifth Army at the start of the war. Given his position, such an appointment was understandable and the Crown Prince had been provided by his father with an *éminence grise* in the shape of a professional Prussian officer, General Schmidt von Knobelsdorf, who, said the Kaiser, was to serve as his son's Chief-of-Staff . . . and make all the major decisions. Problems soon arose because the Crown Prince, for all his youth and playboy reputation, was far more intelligent than von Knobelsdorf and was a better-than-average military commander.

Perhaps part of the problem was that the young, foppish Prince did not look much like a soldier, while von Knobelsdorf, the archetype of the cropped-haired, bull-necked, pop-eyed Prussian officer, complete with bristling moustache, could not have been mistaken for anything else. Perhaps it was simply that the young Crown Prince failed to exert himself, ignore his father, and put von Knobelsdorf firmly in his place. It is notable that in Sixth Army, which was commanded by Crown Prince Rupprecht of Bavaria, the staff knew their place and Prince Rupprecht signed all the orders, while in Fifth Army that task was commandeered by von Knobelsdorf.

Though signing operational orders was frequently done by an Army Chief-of-Staff, von Knobelsdorf was not above issuing orders and paying little attention to the views of his commander. The problem for Prince Wilhelm was that the Kaiser had appointed von Knobelsdorf to tutor the Prince in the profession of arms and would not welcome any criticism of his appointee – and Fifth Army Chief-of-Staff had another small but useful advantage over von Falkenhayn: he was von Falkenhayn's senior on the Army List. All this meant that von Knobelsdorf had considerable influence at court and at Supreme Headquarters and was usually able to go his own way, without deferring to either the Crown Prince or von Falkenhayn.

It is significant that in reaching his decision about the Verdun offensive on 21 April, the Crown Prince was supported by his entire staff . . . with the single exception of von Knobelsdorf, who continued to urge attacks which the Crown Prince knew would lead inexorably to further losses. The Crown Prince now realized what von Falkenhayn was really attempting to do at Verdun. He also realized that, this being the case, the necessary reserves to complete the offensive and take the city would never be provided. He also realized that von Falkenhayn's plan was impracticable and that his Fifth Army was to be 'bled white' in an attempt to impose that same condition on the French.

On 13 May, a Fifth Army conference was held at the Crown Prince's Headquarters at Stenay to discuss the prospects for a continuation of the attacks on the right bank now that the left bank was in German hands. The capture of the left bank positions was a victory for von Falkenhayn and a clear defeat for the French . . . but at what a cost. German losses had soared again in the past few weeks and now stood at 120,000 men; French losses were higher, at just over 130,000 men, but there was no sign of an end to this battle. In another month, if the fighting went on like this, each side would have lost something in excess of 200,000 men.

The consensus among those present on 13 May – the Crown Prince, his staff and the corps commanders – was that further attacks on the right bank could not be made unless further reserves were made available. Since this was unlikely, the Crown Prince expressed the view that a major offensive should be postponed. In reaching this decision the Crown Prince was supported by von Knobelsdorf, and after the conference – somewhat to the Crown Prince's surprise – von Knobelsdorf even offered to take this opinion to von Falkenhayn and urge him to call off the entire Verdun offensive.

This offer may have been a ploy by von Knobelsdorf, a move to prevent the Crown Prince and von Falkenhayn from meeting in private and agreeing to end the offensive. Whatever the reason behind the offer, the Crown Prince's pleasure at von Knobelsdorf's proposal did not last. By the time von Knobelsdorf met von Falkenhayn at Charleville-Mézières he had apparently changed his mind completely and, abandoning his mission, presented his own views to von Falkenhayn. Having laid out the advantages accruing from the capture of Côte 304 and the Mort Homme, he urged von Falkenhayn to press on with further attacks on the right bank and storm on into Verdun. Von Falkenhayn duly agreed to this proposal – and the Crown Prince was in despair. Somehow the command of his battle had slipped into the hands of General von Knobelsdorf and further slaughter was inevitable.

Notes

1 'German Strategy in the Age of Machine Warfare', by Michael Geyer, in *Makers of Modern Strategy*, ed. Peter Paret, Princeton University Press, 1986.
2 *The Swordbearers*, p. 131.
3 *History of the First World War*, p. 208.

10

Attacks and Counterattacks
June 1916

'Verdun is threatened and Verdun must not fall. The
capture of the city would constitute for the Germans a
success which would greatly raise their morale and lower
our own.'
General Philippe Pétain, Verdun, 11 June 1916

And so, at last, we approach the first day of the Somme. On the British
front, and that of the French Sixth Army to the south of the river, the
preparations were almost complete, the plans laid, the guns and
ammunition moving into position, the training of the infantry
reaching its conclusion. These efforts would increase as the days and
weeks ticked away towards 1 July but the battle at Verdun was now
reaching a new pitch of fury, as Nivelle and his cohorts strove to drive
the Germans back from the ground they had gained in recent months.

When Nivelle took over at Verdun, General Mangin decided that
the first task was to recapture Fort Douaumont. To do this was his own
decision, one reached without any pressure from on high but, if
Mangin thought he could recapture Douaumont, Nivelle was not the
man to stand in his way. If Mangin could storm Fort Douaumont, the

prestige of both officers could only soar and, besides, it was surely possible to retake Fort Douaumont? The glacis of the fort lay less than three miles from Mangin's headquarters at Fort Souville and Mangin was well aware that until Douaumont was retaken the progress of any advance north along the right bank would be both difficult and costly.

Mangin's 5th Division had already attempted to take Douaumont by a *coup de main* on 22 April, soon after III Corps arrived at Verdun. On that occasion some of his men had even got on to the glacis before they were driven off. Mangin did not care to be repulsed and now that he had a free hand and the support of the Army commander, he decided to try his luck again. On 8 May, he even had a little extra luck, for a gigantic explosion ripped through the bowels of Fort Douaumont. This came after a stack of shells caught fire and blew up, killing more than 600 of the German defenders, destroying much of their kit and ammunition, and spreading alarm and confusion among the survivors.

News of this disaster rapidly reached Mangin's HQ and he quickly made arrangements to take advantage of it, issuing plans for an attack by six battalions on a narrow, 1,100-yard front astride the fort, an attack supported by more than 300 guns of various calibre, which amounted to all the French artillery available on the right bank. This plan went to Nivelle, who naturally gave it his approval, and then to Pétain who, sandwiched between Nivelle and Joffre, gave it a reluctant go-ahead. The bombardment of Fort Douaumont began on 17 May and went on for five days before the French infantry went into the attack, on the morning of 22 May.

By this time the Germans had restored Fort Douaumont to its original fortress state. Not all the guns had been replaced, but the trenches and dugouts surrounding the fort had been re-established and the fort itself filled with a garrison and a number of reserve troops kept there as a first-line reinforcement, ready to sally out against any French incursion. Therefore, when the French attacked, the Germans were ready and well aware of what was coming. Security was never a French strongpoint and the Germans had already broken off preparations for their right bank offensive to concentrate on improving and extending their defences around Fort Douaumont. Apart from the leak of information, they knew that five days of constant shelling must mean something – and the appointment of Nivelle and Mangin, two officers famous for their *élan*, had not gone unnoticed in Germany. Some spectacular exploit was only to be expected from these officers, and what could be more spectacular than the recapture of Fort Douaumont?

The French shelling destroyed many of the outworks but did no real damage to the fort itself. Mangin only had four 320 mm guns, the minimum calibre necessary to reduce the fort, and these proved totally inadequate, both in number and weight of shot. So the time came, the infantry attack went in and, incredibly, in spite of the German barrage that instantly fell on No Man's Land and the curtain of machine-gun fire drawn across the front of the fort, Mangin's infantry actually succeeded in reaching Fort Douaumont and swarming on to the ramparts.

The losses were dreadful, reaching more than 50 per cent in many of the assault companies. Whole battalions disappeared, pounded to pieces under the shellfire, but the survivors pressed home their attack and within minutes observers saw tiny figures in *horizon-bleu* running about on the glacis of the fort. Watching their advance, standing on the roof of Fort Souville and ignoring the incessant shellfire, General Mangin must have felt proud of his division.

Once at the fort, the French infantry not only occupied most of the glacis; some men even succeeded in entering the fort and began moving up the tunnels, bombing their way forward, using sackfuls of grenades. A battalion of the 129th Regiment even managed to establish a machine-gun post on the roof of the fort, from where it could provide covering fire across the surrounding area and beat off a series of unco-ordinated German counterattacks, launched from the exterior trenches.

By the evening of 22 May, therefore, reports came back to General Mangin claiming that the fort had fallen. Reserves were promptly sent forward but the reports were either over-optimistic or totally wrong; the fresh troops were met with artillery and machine-gun fire and very few of them lived to join the survivors of the first attack, who were still hanging on at the fort. By nightfall the Germans had already retaken much of the ground occupied by the French and, when more French reserves went up on the 23rd, most went to their deaths. One report notes that the advancing French reserves were piled up in a chest-high wall of corpses.

Much of the fighting around the fort was hand-to-hand, fought out with grenades, rifle fire, bayonets and shovels. On the afternoon of 23 May, a battalion of French troops close to the fort was cut off and forced to surrender, having lost more than two-thirds of its men. Ammunition was now running out among the forward companies and no support could get forward. A German counterattack on the morning of the 24th drove the last remnants of the French attackers out of the fort, across the open ground and back to their former positions. For all the *élan* of his infantry, Mangin's attack had been a total failure.

The harsh fact was that *élan* and *cran* would not do it, at Verdun or at any other point on the Western Front. Men cannot go against concrete, wire and steel with any hope of success and, by the evening of 24 May, Mangin's men, or what was left of them, were back in their trenches. Very few actually came back. More than 1,000 French soldiers had been taken prisoner and thousands more, the dead and wounded, lay in heaps on or around the fort. Mangin's 5th Division was so much reduced that it could not put 200 men into its trenches that night and 550 yards of French front lay wide open and undefended for hours until fresh troops could be brought up to plug the gap. Mangin's action was exactly the sort of attack that Pétain had feared and von Knobelsdorf and von Falkenhayn had wanted – pure attrition.

Mangin, quite unrepentant, was abruptly withdrawn from the sector with the remains of his division – General Lebrun, his corps commander, being less tolerant than Nivelle of attacks that destroyed entire divisions. More heads might have rolled after this débâcle but Nivelle and Mangin were saved by Pétain, who stepped forward to say that, as the Army Group commander, he had authorized the attack and he must therefore be responsible for its conduct and failure. This pacified GQG and the French Government, even the French public, but the news of this fresh disaster spread swiftly among the soldiery at Verdun. Their reserves of courage and temper were now being stretched dangerously thin and, by the end of May, some reports of ill-discipline were reaching Pétain's ears. And so the weeks crawled into June and there was still no sign of the long-promised British offensive on the Somme. *Eh bien*, then France would fight on alone.

By now we are more than three months into the Verdun battle, which had already gone on longer than any other battle in the war. The territorial gains had been negligible on the German side, while attempts to regain ground on the French side had only led to costly débâcles like the Mangin attack on Fort Douaumont. The regular lesson of the Western Front, one the generals seemed unable to learn, was that – using the currently conventional methods – most attacks simply did not come off, whoever carried them out – French, British or German; Pétain, Haig or the Crown Prince; Nivelle, Rawlinson or von Marwitz. The battle had become a bloody stalemate . . . surely the time had come to call it off?

But who would call it off? Who would be the first to cry halt? In some curious way the battle at Verdun had become a paradigm for the entire war. Verdun now exerted its own dynamic and needed no reason to continue. By the middle of 1916 it was, or should have been, clear to all that there was no reason in it; reason had ceased to play any part in this struggle. It was simply another battle in this war, and this war had developed its own momentum, rather like a tornado.

So, too, had the fighting at Verdun, and this fighting would continue to destroy everything in its path. In the end, it came down to a contest of national wills. The French fought, and would go on fighting, until they had expelled every German soldier from the soil of France but, at this rate, it would take the life of every French soldier to do it.

Now and again, the history of war throws up a battle that transcends reason. The soldiers fight because they cannot stop fighting, because too much has been committed to give up now. Too much blood has been shed, so much courage and will has been committed, that to admit defeat would be unthinkable. And so the battle grows, consuming the soldiers, the armies and the nations, like some monstrous hurricane, one that surges forward, feeding on the very air it passes, destroying everything in its path until, in its own good time, it blows itself out.

The battle that becomes a symbol develops an intensity all its own. Thermopylae, Senlac Hill, Agincourt, the battles at Tobruk, Cassino,

Kohima or Stalingrad in the Second World War, are battles that became symbols. In the Great War, only Verdun can match those encounters for symbolism and Verdun outmatches them all for duration and slaughter. Essentially, as Alistair Horne points out, this was not simply a battle between two armies but the ancient conflict of Teuton and Gaul, two ethnic groups letting one thousand years of envy and hatred out in one long pent-up explosion of violence ... 'like two stags battling to the death, antlers locked, neither would nor could give up until the virility of one or the other finally triumphed.'[1]

This at least partly accounts for the fact that, again and again in the battle for Verdun, the French generals made the fatal mistake of doing what the enemy wanted them to do. Part of this was the result of the Grandmaison doctrine, but it went beyond doctrine; to keep on attacking or defending a position far beyond the point of reason, to retain or recapture some feature that they found significant, whatever its tactical advantage, was simply madness. A general must be able to weigh the advantages and costs of his attacks or he is no general at all, but the deadly triumvirates of Joffre, Nivelle and Mangin – and across the wire von Falkenhayn, the Crown Prince and von Knobelsdorf – were now well beyond that point; they had something to prove at Verdun and were intent on driving the enemy back, whatever the cost, which as far as the French were concerned, was exactly what von Falkenhayn wanted. The British generals have been widely castigated for their actions in this war and their prodigality with lives; it is hard to find evidence that the French or German generals were any better.

That the French were worried about the present situation on the Western Front is evident from a short account in Haig's diaries. On 4 May he met Georges Clemenceau, President of the Military Committee of the Senate, a body with roughly the same function as the British War Cabinet. Haig recounts how Clemenceau asked him to 'exercise a restraining hand on General Joffre and prevent any offensive being made on a large scale until we are ready. "If we attack and fail," said Clemenceau, "Then there will be a number of people in France who will say that the time has come to make terms." ' Haig adds that he assured Clemenceau he had no intention of attacking until he was ready 'but he was ready to support the French if anything in the nature of a catastrophe were to happen at Verdun.' This conversation sounds strange; the French were not usually reluctant to see the British pushed into action and if the Verdun situation was not already catastrophic, it was very close to it.

In fact, Haig was now thinking of delaying the Somme attack until mid-August. He discussed this matter with the CIGS, General Robertson, on 25 May, for the longer they waited the stronger the British forces would be. On balance though, Haig decided to comply with Joffre's wishes and attack in early July. This was a fortunate decision, for on the following day General Joffre arrived at Haig's headquarters, accompanied by General de Castelnau. Joffre explained the overall situation: how the Russians had promised to attack in June – the Brusilov offensive – while the Italians were reeling back under an attack on the Trentino. He then pointed out to Haig that the French had now been fighting at Verdun for three months and had suffered heavy losses which, Joffre claimed, were around 200,000 men – a conservative estimate – and if this went on the French Army would be destroyed as a fighting force within weeks.

Joffre therefore declared that 1 July was the very last date for the start of the combined offensive. Haig demurred slightly at this, showing Joffre his estimates of British strength on various dates throughout the summer, 1 and 15 July, 1 and 15 August. At this point Joffre grew seriously alarmed, stating, according to Haig, that 'The French Army will cease to exist if we did nothing until then' but, Haig continued, in view of the unfavourable situation of the French Army, that he was prepared to commence operations on 1 July. De Castelnau assisted Haig in calming Joffre's fears and the meeting concluded with lunch, after which, Haig added, 'An 1840 brandy had a surprisingly soothing effect on him [Joffre] and Castelnau.'[2]

Joffre, Pétain and their colleagues were not correct in believing that the British had done nothing since the turn of the year. The *Official History* records that, in minor operations on their front between 19 December 1915 and 31 May 1916, the British lost a total of 5,845 officers and 119,296 men in various actions on the Western Front – a drop in the ocean of loss that would follow perhaps, but a significant number of men nevertheless.[3]

At Verdun, it is fair to say that von Falkenhayn was delighted with the results of the Mangin attack. For the moment, following the fresh débâcle at Fort Douaumont, the advantage lay with the Germans, and this was the time for von Knobelsdorf and von Falkenhayn to complete their design. Von Knobelsdorf was no fool; he must have realized by now that von Falkenhayn was interested in a battle of attrition and not in the capture of Verdun. Taking the city was still von Knobelsdorf's intention, but this hardly mattered; the capture of Verdun or further attrition of the French Army would be equally acceptable to the overall design.

As a result, Fifth Army response to Mangin's thrust at Fort Douaumont was another stab at Verdun, Operation May Cup, a major assault on the right bank using three corps, the 1st Bavarian, X Reserve and XV Corps, which together mustered a total of five divisions. This would be the largest assault since 21 February and be yet another dagger thrust into the French line, on a narrow front just three miles wide. The advancing infantry would be marching practically shoulder to shoulder and would be supported by a massive amount of artillery, some 2,200 guns, about 25 per cent more than the French could muster for the entire Verdun front.

Quite apart from these artillery assets, the attackers enjoyed some advantages that had not existed on 21 February and that far outweighed the absence of surprise. The French positions on the left bank, on Côte 304 and the Mort Homme, were now in German hands. In addition, the Germans had recognized the fact that men fight better for some clear objective. The focus of this attack would be Fort Vaux, the Thiaumont position, the village of Fleury and Fort Souville. If all these could be taken, Verdun would be within their grasp. This attack was scheduled to go in on 1 June and the usual bombardment began as soon as Mangin's men had been driven away from Fort Douaumont on 25 May; it continued relentlessly up to the moment of assault.

The assault on 1 June was a complete success, a rare event in this battle. The bombardment lifted, the infantry swept forward and, within the hour, the Germans were on the ridge supporting Fort Vaux, having advanced more than 800 yards, sweeping all French opposition out of the way. This included the French flanking forces on the Caillette and

Fumin slopes, which had been reduced to fragments by the shellfire. Once the Germans were on the Vaux ridge though, it was a different matter. The fighting there went on all day, as the tenacious French infantry were slowly prised out of their positions. It took every hour of daylight and considerable losses but, by nightfall, the French commander in the Vaux sector had to inform Nivelle that his position was in German hands, with the enemy now poised to assault the fort itself.

Nivelle naturally ordered an immediate counterattack. General Lebrun, III Corps commander, who had already lost one division under Mangin, was in no position to deliver an attack that was strong enough to drive the enemy back, not least because the enemy position was now protected by the fire from the guns on the Mort Homme. Lebrun needed time to bring up more men but, even as the French mustered their forces, the Germans struck again. Encouraged by their successes on the first day, at 0300 hrs on 2 June the German XV Corps moved against Fort Vaux. During the hours of darkness their bombardment battered the fort and at the first streak of dawn the German infantry rushed forward.

Fort Vaux was much smaller than Douaumont, lightly armed and thinly garrisoned. The main defence was just one 75 mm gun but this had been destroyed after the Germans took Douaumont. Nor had Vaux stood up well to the five days of artillery bombardment. Part of the superstructure had been damaged, and a number of the entrances had been blown in and were now sealed by sandbagged revetments.

The commander of Vaux, Major Sylvain-Eugene Raynal, was recovering from earlier wounds and should long ago have been discharged from further service. Raynal had some 600 men under his command in the fort on 2 June but very few of these were part of the official garrison. They came from an assortment of units; many were wounded or were soldiers who had taken shelter in the fort from the surrounding trenches. This number, far in excess of the 250 men the fort was designed for, was to prove less than a blessing when the fort was attacked. Raynal had watched the Germans sweep towards his position on 1 June; he had prepared his men as best he could during the shelling and had them standing-to long before the attack came in at dawn next day.

The initial German assault was made by two battalions – some 1,500 men – who made their way forward under cover of dark and formed up less than 220 yards from the fort. Dashing forward, they were over the remaining trenches, into the moat and swarming up the glacis of the fort within a couple of minutes; and the heavy machine-gun fire that the defenders poured into them was not sufficient to halt the attack. By 0500 hrs the Germans were inside the fort and fighting their way through the network of corridors, using grenades and flame-throwers. The troops occupying the outworks were soon crushed and, by dawn on 3 June, Fort Vaux was completely surrounded, with French and German troops fighting it out along the interior corridors.

The fighting inside Fort Vaux went on for another four days. Most of the combat took place in the bowels of the fort, in total darkness lit only by gun flashes and the explosions of grenades. Raynal's men put up a tenacious defence, building sandbagged barricades at intervals down the corridors and passageways, fighting to hold each one until they were forced back to the one behind. This was the way it had been at Fort Douaumont and the way it would continue at other underground positions on the Western Front, places like the Caverne du Dragon on the Chemin des Dames, where the opposing sides held either end of the tunnels dug under the ridge and fought each other in the Stygian underground darkness for more than two years.

Nothing the Western Front can offer, however, matches the intensity of the five days of fighting inside Fort Vaux. Major Raynal and his composite battalion were completely isolated and far beyond the reach of reinforcement, though Nivelle certainly tried to send troops forward. At dawn on 4 June, he sent an entire French division, the 124th, to retake the fort. The attack was led by the divisional commander, but got no farther than the western edge of the fort, where those who survived the advance over open ground were driven back by a German bayonet charge.

The fighting always cut both ways at Verdun; the Germans were as determined to take and hold Fort Vaux as the French were to hang on to it. More French reinforcements were sent up by day and night, but all to no avail; though a steady trickle of men arrived, any platoon or company that reached the fort had been cut to pieces getting there and they brought no supplies, little ammunition, no food and – vitally – no water. The Germans, on the other hand, could feed in fresh troops constantly and thus keep up the pressure on the shrinking band of defenders, though they also lost many men to French shelling as they made their way forward. Raynal's sole means of communication with General Lebrun and the outside world was by carrier pigeon, and the flight of one of these birds has been immortalized by a plaque on the face of the fort.

Raynal and his men held out for five days against constant attacks, shelling, flame-throwers, grenades and gas. All took their toll, but what finally drove the garrison to surrender was thirst. By the fourth day of the siege the men were reduced to drinking their own urine and, at 0500 hrs on 7 June, Fort Vaux surrendered; so bad was their thirst that as the survivors emerged they crawled to puddles and shell holes to lap up muddy water. It was another German victory but a Pyrrhic one; taking Fort Vaux and its garrison of 600 men had cost the Germans more than 2,700 soldiers.

French losses in their various attempts to retake or reinforce the fort had been even greater but, even after the garrison surrendered on 7 June and the fort was entirely in German hands, Nivelle continued to attack. The next day, Nivelle sent in a special composite formation – a Brigade de Marche – composed of North African troops, Zouaves and Moroccans. When Nivelle announced this further attack, even his divisional generals protested that it was pure folly, but Nivelle was adamant. The attack went in soon after dawn, in pouring rain . . . and ran straight into the arms of a full German division which was moving up towards Fort Tavannes.

The result was a massacre, a confused, scrambling battle, fought in the open under heavy skies, with shells falling indiscriminately on friend and foe alike. The Brigade de Marche blundered forward through the mud and up to the fort, where those who reached the glacis were promptly mown down by machine-guns. Even then Nivelle was prepared to go on, until Pétain came up to Souilly and ordered him bluntly to break off these pointless assaults. Vaux had gone and there was no point in losing more men in futile attempts to retake it. Besides, having taken Fort Vaux, the Germans would soon be coming on again, towards Thiaumont, Fleury and Fort Souville.

Pétain was well aware that the loss of Fort Vaux was serious. Vaux was one of the major points in that Line of Resistance he had drawn up back in February. With Vaux gone and the positions around Fleury now under attack, the entire Verdun position was threatened. Orders went out to prepare the city itself for defence, evacuate civilians and dig trenches around the suburbs on either side of the river. Pétain even considered the evacuation of the entire right bank in order to concentrate the troops around Verdun, though knowing that Joffre and de Castelnau would never agree.

Fortunately on the day Fort Vaux fell, the rains came and fell continuously for the next week, turning the battlefield into a swamp and impeding the work of the German artillery observers. Even so, the German advance on the right bank continued inexorably. The Thiaumont position – which is now occupied by a great grey *ossuaire* and a vast military cemetery – fell on 8 June, but was immediately retaken in yet another costly counterattack. The fighting for Thiaumont was to continue for most of the summer and has provided Verdun with one of its most terrible legends, the *Tranchée des Baïonnettes*. This tells of a company of French infantry – the 3rd Company of the 137th Infantry Regiment – which was waiting to go over the top when a salvo of shells landed on the parapet of their trench, blasting in the walls and burying them alive, leaving only the tips of their bayonets showing above the ground.

Whether this story is entirely true remains controversial; certainly the trench is there, protected now by a concrete roof, and one or two bayonets do indeed show above the surface of the ground, but even the grim shelling at Verdun was unlikely to bury an entire company of infantry. It is rather more likely that a number of men were killed and buried in the trench by their comrades, who then marked the spot with bayonets. Whatever the true story – and the legend has not been disproved – the story of the *Tranchée des Baionnettes* caught the imagination of the world . . . and it is some indication of the appalling situation at Verdun that such a story could be believed.

Summer now smote the soldiers at Verdun, adding thirst to their other privations. Since the first days of the battle the men at the front had been short of food; they were frequently very hungry indeed, for the men bringing up the rations were often killed by shellfire or had their dixies shot to pieces by bullets or shell fragments. As long as the wine came through, that rough red *pinard* that the *poilus* drank with every meal, the soldiers could endure hunger, but thirst was another matter. Earlier in the year a man could drink from a shell hole if he did not mind water polluted by dead bodies or fragments of rotting flesh but now the shell holes were drying up and the morale of the parched men finally began to crack.

Morale is a fragile thing. Its creation and maintenance are among the most important duties that can fall to a commander and neither Joffre nor Nivelle devoted as much thought to this issue as it deserved. Morale is maintained by a wide range of means: by discipline and training, by good leadership, by organization, by caring for the wounded, by regular reliefs, by the supply of letters from home, by tobacco and food – and by evidence that those in command know what they are doing and care about their soldiers' lives.

It also helps if the soldiers have a cause. The defence of Verdun and the French Republic was a splendid cause but that alone was not enough; it needed to be a two-way commitment – and what did the Republic care for them, the infantry soldiers of France, alone and dying in their shell holes, sent in again and again in attacks that withered away under the shelling and machine-gun fire, achieving nothing? By mid-June the murmurs heard among the troops in May were growing louder. No soldier knows how much he can take in battle before his morale cracks but, by June 1916, the French soldiers at Verdun had taken – and given – more than any nation could reasonably ask, and there was still no end to their sufferings.

The answer, such as it was, was the one provided by Pétain in February, regular reliefs under the noria system and a holding battle, letting the enemy wear themselves out against stubborn French resistance. Indeed, General Robert Nivelle, urged on by Joffre, who had abandoned the noria system shortly after removing Pétain, continued to attack, sending in exhausted, understrength divisions, regardless of loss. When evidence reached Joffre's ears that the men were complaining, that untenable positions were being given up or that attacks were not being pressed home with their former *élan*, his answer was not to question Nivelle or his own methods, but to call for courts martial and firing squads.

In the second week of June, two second-lieutenants were shot by firing squads drawn from their own companies, for allegedly failing to press home their attacks. Orders also went out that battalions abandoning positions or retiring during an attack were to be fired on by their own machine-guns or bombarded by French artillery. Some of these orders were actually obeyed but the resentment they caused far outweighed the influence they had on the front-line soldier.

Even without this simmering problem, by the middle of June the morale of Second Army was at an all-time low. That the situation at Verdun was desperate was beyond dispute – the problem now was that while Nivelle recognized that his Army could do no more, and might even have to abandon the right bank, he continued to press on with attacks and to demand more men. Joffre, on the other hand, was hanging on in anticipation of the Somme attack and refusing to send more units to Verdun, while Pétain, caught in the middle, knew, or felt in his soul, that the time to abandon Verdun was past. If Verdun fell after all that had been done to retain it, the effect on French morale, civilian as well as military, might well be catastrophic. In this Pétain was right. He was also right in expressing his impatience with the British who, six months after agreeing to an offensive, had still not opened it.

Pétain did not consider the fact that General Haig had agreed to open his attack in July, knowing that he would need every day of that time to get his men ready, or that the constant reduction in the French share of this offensive, because of the drain of forces to Verdun, was causing Haig and Rawlinson to re-evaluate their plans. All Pétain knew was that his men had been beaten into the ground every day for months at Verdun, while their British allies had done nothing to help them. In fact, the British attack was about to begin and, on 14 June, Rawlinson issued a formal Operation Order to the troops of Fourth Army.

This stated: 'The Fourth Army was to take part in a general offensive with a view to breaking up the enemy's defensive system and exploiting to the full all opportunities opened up for defeating his forces within reach' and ten days later the bombardment of the German wire along the Somme began.[4] That came as a great relief to General Joffre, who needed some optimistic news to put before his increasingly discontented political masters in Paris.

Continuous problems on the battlefield do not remain on the battlefield. By mid-June the French Government was becoming increasingly restive about Verdun and ever less willing to accept Joffre's assurances that the battle was going well and costing the Germans many lives. Even if this were true and, as far as it went, it was, it was also causing a great loss of French lives . . . and for no apparent gain. The political view, and one to which politicians were particularly prone, was that therefore something else must be done, to mitigate the losses and achieve more positive results. Exactly what this 'something else' was, the politicians did not say – that was left to the generals – but the political dissatisfaction with the conduct of the battle began to concentrate on accusations of incompetence. These led to the introduction, on 16 June, of a vote of censure against the High Command – essentially General Joffre.

This vote was instigated by M. Maginot, a Deputy who had recently been invalided out of the Army, in which he had served as a sergeant in the infantry. Maginot therefore had first-hand experience of the incompetence of the French High Command and staff and of the effect of this incompetence on the front-line soldiers. Although he was persuaded to withdraw his vote of censure, the debate was extremely heated and left Joffre in no doubt that some changes had to be made and some results achieved.

Joffre's reaction, inevitably, was to declare that all was going well, there was nothing to worry about, that Pétain, though under great strain, was understandably but unnecessarily concerned and that, anyway, the British would soon attack and take the pressure off Verdun. Towards this latter end Joffre redoubled the pressure he was already bringing to bear on General Haig and sent another appeal to the soldiers at Verdun, urging them to hang on. This they were doing when, on the night of 22 June, the Germans attacked again, moving against the Line of Resistance with an attack on Fort Souville and employing another new weapon, phosgene gas.

Fort Souville was the penultimate line of resistance before Verdun. Beyond Souville lay a couple of small forts on the Belleville ridge, Fort Belleville and Fort St Michel, but from there the ground fell away into the valley of the Meuse and Verdun. Granted, getting to Souville would not be easy, not least because the prior task of taking Thiaumont had still not been accomplished, but with the aid of gas it might be possible. Von Knobelsdorf certainly thought so, for he had assembled 30,000 infantry for the purpose and proposed to make yet another surprise, dagger-like thrust, again on a front of just three miles, aiming to push his infantry up to Souville, via Thiaumont and the ruins of Fleury, with a cloud of 'Green Cross' shells filled with phosgene gas to clear the way.

The assault on Souville began on the evening of 22 June and since it came without the usual prelude provided by days of artillery bombardment, it came as a complete surprise to the defenders. The shelling was normally at such a pitch of intensity that the infantry attack would not have unduly alarmed the defenders but the phosgene gas came as a total shock. Gas had been used constantly at Verdun, often a mixture of chlorine and tear gas, and was now employed regularly at all the Great War battles, but this was a new gas and the French soldiers had no defence against it. Phosgene had been used against the British at Ypres earlier in the year, but it was new to the French at Verdun and their gas masks could not keep it out.

Phosgene was a powerful asphyxiating gas, far more effective than chlorine. Men choked and died on it and many more men, unable to fight when unable to breathe, simply ran away, abandoning their positions. A great quantity of phosgene shells fell on the French artillery and, within a few minutes, the French bombardment, which had now gone on ceaselessly for months, started to decline. Phosgene gas drenched the French positions for ten hours until 0500 on 23 June, when the German infantry rose from their trenches and advanced across the ground. Only then did the rain of shells stop, for fear the German infantry would fall victims to the gas but by then it was too late for the French artillery to catch them in the open.

As a result, the initial attack paid good dividends. The Thiaumont position, one that had held out for weeks, fell within the hour and the German Alpine Corps, spearheading this advance, took the ruins of the village of Fleury in three hours. Then, as so often before, matters began to go awry. The advance of the infantry required a curtailment in the artillery barrage, and the French artillery, though briefly silenced by the gas, now came back into action and began plastering Fleury with a barrage of 75 mm shells. This came too late to save Fleury from falling into German hands but it took Alpine Corps the rest of the day to secure it and its losses mounted. While Alpine Corps was battling for Fleury, other German units were easing forward and, by noon on 23 June, a report reached Pétain's headquarters that advanced elements of the German Army were within two and a half miles of Verdun and indirect German machine-gun fire was raking the streets of the city.

The French now had their backs to the wall. This was the crisis of the battle, for the French had nowhere to go, no more room for manoeuvre. If they abandoned the right bank, then not only would Verdun fall – *and Verdun must not fall* – but also any withdrawal must mean the loss of most of their artillery, which could not be moved with the Germans so near. Certainly Pétain was worried – he had every reason to be worried – and begged Joffre yet again to order the start of the Somme offensive, but there is little evidence that Pétain intended to evacuate the right bank, even had it been possible. Four fresh divisions were sent forward and, thus reinforced, Second Army hung on . . . and as they did so, the scales began to turn in their favour.

It is a military axiom that a general whose army has been hurt cannot fully appreciate how much the enemy army had been hurt in the process. On 23 June, although the French had been driven back and their artillery silenced for a while by gas, this situation did not last long. The French guns were back in action by the early afternoon and took a terrible toll of the German troops moving forward in the open towards Verdun. Nor did the French artillery have any trouble deciding where to concentrate its fire; the German axis of advance from Fleury to Souville was obvious and the French gunners had the range to a yard; their shells began to plaster the ground on and ahead of the German infantry and soon brought their advance to a halt . . . while at the same time the German troops, after hours in the blazing summer sun, began to run out of water.

The outcome of an attack can hinge on small things. It might seem that in an assault involving gas, artillery and 30,000 infantry, the contents of a man's water bottle are of small account. That overlooks the fact that, in battle, nervous men get thirsty; this thirst is not the kind of thirst that arises on a summer's day but a parching, desperate thirst, partly caused by fear – the 'dry mouth' so beloved of novelists is no fiction – and if men do not have water they soon come to think of nothing else. Curious or not, the fact is that a shortage of water did as much as the French shelling to halt the German attack on 24 June.

By that evening, von Knobelsdorf knew that this latest attempt to take Verdun had failed. His men were exhausted and could do no more. The phosgene shells were almost gone, French resistance was stiffening, and with Nivelle and Mangin in front, a counterattack could be expected at any time against the narrow German salient now running from Thiaumont to Fleury. This attack was inevitably entrusted to Mangin and as usual he flung his men in regardless of loss, rapidly driving the enemy back . . . but not far. Mangin continued attacking, day after day, but after eight attacks in a week and a hideous loss of men, he had still not managed to retake Thiaumont and the battle swung back to attrition.

This was small comfort to von Falkenhayn; the British guns were now thundering along a 15-mile front north of the Somme and, as a final blow following the success of the Brusilov offensive, he had been forced to send three precious divisions east to help the Austrians. He had also ordered the Crown Prince to suspend all operations, pending the outcome of the British assault. As for the British, keyed up for the Big Push, one piece of bad news had briefly depressed the nation, not least the men in those New Army divisions moving through Arras towards Albert and the front line.

On 5 June, news reached them that Lord Kitchener had died, drowned when HMS *Hampshire*, the cruiser taking him to Russia, struck a mine and sank off the Orkneys. While the Army and the nation mourned, Kitchener was replaced as Secretary of State for War by the former Minister of Munitions, David Lloyd George, who thereby moved a step closer to the seat of power he was soon to occupy.

None of that mattered for the moment . . . all eyes were on the battlefields. Nivelle summed up what the French had achieved at Verdun since February when his Order of the Day on 24 June concluded with the immortal line *Ils ne passeront pas* – a phrase which history has largely attributed to Pétain but one which sums up the entire battle for Verdun.

The Germans had not got past. Though the cost had been awesome, Verdun had been held and at last the British guns were firing in the north, heralding the start of the 1916 combined offensive. Lord Kitchener had done his best work for Britain in 1914 and 1915, by realizing that this would be a long war and raising and training those new divisions, who proudly made up the 'Kitchener Armies', to fight it. Now these divisions must complete his work, by winning a victory on the Somme.

Notes

1 *The Price of Glory, Verdun 1916*, p. 242.
2 *The Private Papers of Douglas Haig*, p. 145.
3 *Official History, 1916*, vol. 5, pp. 242–3.
4 Ibid., p. 311.

11

The Road to the Somme
March–July 1916

'The principle of an offensive campaign during the
summer of 1916 had already been decided on by all the
Allies . . . but as the date on which the attacks should
begin was dependent on many factors a decision on that
point was deferred until the situation became clearer.'
Sir Douglas Haig's Despatch, 29 December 1916

As Sir Douglas Haig's despatch makes clear, the series of engagements
collectively known to history as the Battle of the Somme did not begin
as a battle of attrition. The Somme battle was designed from the first
as an offensive but major battles and offensives do not happen
overnight. They have to be planned and prepared for in the previous
weeks or months, and the amount of planning and preparation and
how well they are judged will have a profound effect on the conduct
and outcome of the subsequent battle.

This would be the case even if the planning for the battle went according to the original concept and intention but the planning and preparation for the combined offensive on the Somme were radically changed by the revolving needs of the battle of Verdun.

The concept for the Somme offensive had called for a combined Franco-British offensive astride the Somme on the widest possible front . . . up to 60 miles in one early declaration of intent. This width of front was gradually reduced throughout the planning phase, partly because, post-Verdun, the French were no longer able to provide the necessary divisions to fill such a front, but mainly because of a shortage of artillery.

The fact that the success or failure of the Somme offensive would largely depend on artillery is the first point to bear in mind but a sufficiency of artillery depended not only on the number of guns provided but on the width of the front attacked. The guns-per-yards-of-front ratio was crucial; to expand the latter, it was necessary to increase the former, or the infantry would go over the top without adequate support. General Sir Henry Rawlinson had come to that conclusion as soon as he saw the ground over which his Army had to fight back in February; he had seen no reason to change that opinion in the four months that had elapsed since. However, he had still not been able to find an adequate number of guns.

Rawlinson had taken over command of Fourth Army on 1 March, four months to the day before the opening of the Somme offensive.[1] This gave him exactly 16 weeks to turn his new Army into a battle-worthy fighting force and he would need every minute of that time in order to do so. By the time it went 'over the top' on 1 July, Fourth Army consisted of five Corps; from the north, these were VIII Corps, commanded by a Gallipoli veteran, Lt-General Hunter-Weston, whose front extended from Hébuterne to Beaucourt; X Corps, commanded by Lt-General Morland, responsible for the sector from Hamel to Authuille; III Corps, commanded by Lt-General Pulteney, responsible for the sector from Ovillers to la Boisselle; XV Corps, commanded by Lt-General Horne, an artillery officer who would later rise to the command of First Army and was currently responsible for the sector from Bécourt to Mametz; and finally XIII Corps, commanded by Lt-General Congreve, VC, in charge of the line from Carnoy to

Maricourt, where Fourth Army met up with XX Corps of French Sixth Army.

This army contained 16 divisions, three per corps, but with a fourth division in VIII Corps. Each division could muster around 15,000 men, so the total, with corps troops and the Army reserve, came to some 400,000 men. To this can be added, for the initial onslaught on the German line, two divisions from VII Corps of Third Army, the 46th and the 56th, who would attack the salient at Gommecourt, north of Fourth Army line. More than half the soldiers in this force had never been in action before.

Matters had improved on the staff side since the Loos débâcle of the previous September. In February 1916, GHQ issued a 57-page document detailing the preparations needed before a major attack. It covered all the necessary arrangements in a seven-week period leading up to the battle, everything from accommodation and food, to the construction of new railways and communication trenches and the laying of telephone cables. To supply Fourth Army's basic needs it was estimated that 31 trains must reach the front every day, bringing the day-to-day supplies as well as massive amounts of ammunition, food, water and trench stores that must be gathered for the main offensive. More than 3,000,000 shells were stockpiled close to the artillery batteries, ready to open the bombardment on 24 June. Existing railway lines were extended to forward unloading points, from which fresh tracks and wooden tramways were laid to move stores forward. More than 100,000 horses had to be taken care of, some of them cavalry mounts, most of them transport animals. Water was seen as a major problem – half a million men to supply and not a single tap – so more than 100 pumping stations were set up, to supply 1,000 water points via 120 miles of piping. This time, whatever else went awry, the British Army would be well prepared and, with the exception of artillery, superbly equipped.

By February 1916 the original scheme discussed in December for an offensive between the Somme and Arras had been scaled down somewhat. Joffre now wanted the British contribution to the combined offensive to be an assault on a 14-mile (25,000 yard) front north of the Somme, between Maricourt and Hébuterne and General

Haig had turned the detailed planning for this offensive over to Rawlinson. A careful study of the map on page 244 would again be helpful at this point.

None of the engagements in the Battle of the Somme actually took place along or across that river. They took place in the *département* of the Somme, between the towns of Albert and Bapaume, either in the narrow valley of the River Ancre, which flows south through Albert and into the Somme, or on the rolling, open downland east of that town, before or beyond the Pozières ridge. Across that ridge an old Roman road, now a modern highway, runs between Albert and Bapaume. This road was to provide the direction, the 'axis of advance', for Fourth Army during the offensive, and most of the battles took place either side of that road.

In July 1916, the German line across that front lay where it had been established in the autumn of 1914, after the 'Race to the Sea'. Crossing the River Somme, the front line ran north, up to Maricourt, and then swung west, past Mametz, which lay just inside the German line as far as Fricourt, a distance of about three miles. This change in the direction of the front line should be noted now, for it will have a bearing on what happened later. At Fricourt the line swung north again, up to la Boisselle, then across the Albert–Bapaume road to Thiepval, around the edge of the Pozières ridge and across the steep-sided Ancre valley to Beaumont-Hamel and so north to Hébuterne, where Third Army sector began. Third Army's task during the first day of the battle was to pinch out the German salient at Gommecourt; two divisions of Lt-General Snow's VII Corps in Allenby's Third Army – the 56th and 46th Divisions – were delegated for this task.

To understand any battle it is necessary to understand the ground. The ground over which the Somme offensive took place is fairly neutral, offering some advantage to both sides – offence and defence – in an open battle but, after two years of preparation, the German front line offered a strong preponderance of advantage to the static defence. First of all, the Germans occupied the higher ground and ridges, with all the advantages that provided in terms of observation and concealment in the 'dead ground' behind the ridges. They had also been able to tunnel out deep, shell-proof dugouts in the underlying chalk strata and had turned the many villages, farmhouses, woods and copses into defensive bastions, equipped with plenty of trenches, strongpoints and machine-guns, festooned with wire.

By any standards the German position on the Somme was a tough one and it was well defended by General Fritz von Bülow and his troops of Second Army. This was part of the Army Group commanded by Crown Prince Rupprecht of Bavaria, a very competent soldier and, on 1 July, General von Bülow would have ten divisions astride the Somme, a total of some 120,000 men, of which six divisions from the XIV Reserve Corps were facing British Fourth Army and French XX Corps north of the Somme. The four and a half German divisions actually manning the German front and support trenches and dugouts would be attacked by 13 British divisions. The five corps of Fourth Army, plus the two from Third Army, could muster a total of 192 infantry battalions, of which 138 battalions would be in the first assault on 1 July, leaving 54 battalions in reserve.

The German front line described above lay at varying distances from that of their British opponents, from less than 55 yards at la Boisselle to upwards of 800 yards in other places. A second defence line spanned the Pozières ridge, running north from Maurepas through Longueval and Bazentin Wood to the road and then north to Grandcourt and Puisieux. This second line lay between one and two miles behind the front line. Finally, there was a third line running from Combles to Flers, Le Sars and Achiet-le-Petit but this was still under construction.

The problem for Rawlinson and his Army lay in the first and second lines which were an interlinked system of dugouts, front-line, reserve and support trenches, communication trenches and barbed-wire entanglements. Many of them were in belts more than 40 yards wide – all covered by machine-guns, snipers and field guns already targeted to bring down defensive fire on these positions, and on the No Man's Land between the two front lines. Rawlinson's task was to break through those two lines into open country. To estimate whether that was possible, it is now necessary to look at the plan of attack, bearing in mind that what might be blindingly obvious to us, decades after the battle, might not have been so clear to the generals and commanding officers in the weeks immediately before it.

The dead ground south of Mametz offered concealment to the attackers and there was room to manoeuvre in the open country east of Pozières if the German front lines could be penetrated. There was also a geographical advantage created by the layout of the front line. Seen from the British side, this generally faced east or slightly north-east towards Bapaume, but between Carnoy and Fricourt a western kink in the line had the British trenches facing north and – if it could be penetrated – offered a route towards the second German line via the Montauban spur. Although this part of the line was overlooked by the higher ground of the Pozières ridge at Montauban and Bernafay, if the British troops on the right flank could get on to this end of the Pozières ridge, they could move along it, above the Ancre valley, and so outflank the German positions at Thiepval and Beaucourt . . . and if they could do that, the whole German line would come apart. Haig had spotted this opportunity and insisted on the early capture of the Montauban spur *if* possible – but so the terrible *ifs* accumulate.

Therefore, the two points of tactical advantage on this sector of the front were the Montauban spur and the Ancre valley. Push up either of those, get out on to the open ground beyond, and General Haig might have his breakthrough – and at this point it is necessary to stress yet again that Haig was searching for a breakthrough, a return to open warfare.

This being so, it is hard to understand why General Rawlinson did not deploy more of his forces in the attack on these two positions. Although he realized the importance of artillery to the outcome of his battle, which was absolutely correct, General Rawlinson does not seem to have appreciated that the German front-line position was not the same in every sector. Different parts of the line offered a variety of advantages and disadvantages but, instead of exploiting the former and avoiding the latter, Rawlinson chose to deploy the same force right along the line, in terms of both artillery and infantry.

Granted, the sectors vary in width, so that the concentration also varied, but the general point remains valid: the Somme offensive was a Big Push but the weight of that push was fairly equal all along the line. Much more might have been achieved if a greater weight, especially of artillery, had been employed at particular points. Given the odium that has descended on Haig's reputation over the Somme offensive, it is worth recording that this view, that the attack should vary in strength along the line, was also Haig's view, but Rawlinson wanted an even-handed attack and, as was customary, the local commander got his way.

Following the initial survey of the ground, Rawlinson and Haig had to agree on the extent of the offensive, on how wide a front should be attacked and on how deep a penetration should be aimed for in the first phase of the battle. A battle will have both long-term and intermediate objectives but none of these can be attempted, let alone achieved, if the battle falls apart on the first day. It is therefore essential to open the offensive by reaching some clear and achievable objectives . . . at which point the generals disagreed. Haig wanted Fourth Army to achieve a breakthrough of the first and second lines in the first phase; Rawlinson thought that if his men took the German first line in the first phase they would be doing well. This is the by-now-familiar 'breakthrough' or 'bite and hold' argument and, since Rawlinson's view prevailed, his proposals are the ones to examine.

Starting from his basic premise that it all depended on artillery, Rawlinson felt that taking the German front-line positions on a front of 20,000 yards (11 miles) and penetrating that line for 2,000 yards would be an achievement. This still represented a bombardment area of around 12 square miles, every yard of which needed shelling, but it kept the advancing troops within the covering fire of the guns. The British artillery had the range to cover an advance of perhaps 5,000 yards but Rawlinson had been in France since 1914, starting as a divisional commander, and knew that infantry advances start to waver after a mile or so, as a number of the battalion and company officers and NCOs get killed or wounded. Far better, then, to restrict the advance to a point at which control could still be maintained and where the artillery fire could be observed and kept accurate. If the infantry could advance just over one mile on 1 July, this would take them through the German front line and up on to the vital Pozières ridge. As far as Rawlinson was concerned, that would be a very good start – and up to a point he was right.

Then there was the question of the initial bombardment. Haig felt that a short but overwhelming artillery bombardment, as at Verdun, offered the attackers the benefits of heavy drenching fire, plus surprise. Rawlinson, viewing the dense thickets of German barbed wire and the white chalk marks created by excavating dugouts, believed that only a long bombardment, by as many heavy guns as he could muster, would give the artillery any chance of breaching the wire, stunning the defenders in their dugouts and getting the infantry through into the enemy positions. As for the weight-of-fire argument, Rawlinson did not have the guns to drench the enemy positions, as at Verdun, since his front of attack was much wider. Rawlinson felt that the artillery bombardment was crucial and that if it did its work properly the infantry's task would be easy. One of the most erroneous assumptions in the days before the assault was that the artillery had indeed done enough to make the infantry advance a virtual walkover.

Another area for debate was the matter of timing for the initial assault. Haig wanted a dawn attack, when his infantry would have darkness at their back and the enemy positions outlined against the eastern sky. Rawlinson wanted a few hours of daylight for the final bombardment and a long day to help the artillery observers control the guns in the assault phase. Rawlinson wanted the first attack kept under tight control, halted at certain times until the guns could be brought forward and re-registered on fresh targets to cover a further advance; Haig felt that any success should be immediately exploited and had the Reserve Army, under Sir Hubert Gough, ready for this task once a breakthrough had been achieved.

Neither man was wrong here and criticism based on hindsight is not helpful; no one knew what would happen on the day and both commanders, equally experienced in Western Front warfare, were trying to give their men the best possible chance. Rawlinson never wavered from his belief in the power and use of artillery. Haig, who had seen too many attacks falter with disastrous results after some initial success, wanted the attack to press on and take advantage of any situation. These arguments went on for some time but the outcome was embodied on 12 April in a formal letter of instruction from Haig to Rawlinson.

   The burden of this instruction was that Fourth Army was to advance
on a front of 14 miles and aim for an average penetration of one and a
half miles; averaging this out, if Fourth Army aimed to take the second
line on a 14-mile front, the task for the British guns in the week of
bombardment before the infantry attack was to dominate an area of
some 30 square miles and destroy all the opposition therein. By any
standards, this would be a formidable task.

   Whether this was to be achieved in one push or two was not
covered but it appears that Haig was happy to accept Rawlinson's view
on a two-phase attack, up to the German second line, provided the
second phase was not unduly delayed. Since the distance between the
German first and second lines varied, this meant an advance of just
over one mile at the Thiepval position in the centre, well over two
miles on the right and even more on the extreme left. To facilitate this
advance, the infantry assault would be preceded by seven days of
bombardment, to cut the enemy wire and destroy his first-line
trenches, dugouts, machine-gun posts and artillery batteries.

   These tasks called for different kinds of ammunition and guns of
varying calibre. The task of cutting the wire was entrusted, in the
main, to the 18-pounder field guns, firing shrapnel. Heavier guns, the
60-pounders and high-angle howitzers firing high-explosive shells,
would be used against the German trenches and dugouts, and all these
would be backed up with heavy mortars and field artillery. During that
week of bombardment, the German positions would be hit by millions
of shells, destroying the trenches and dugouts, demoralizing and
exhausting the defending troops. As plans go it sounded plausible but
there were a number of disadvantages.

   First of all, Rawlinson did not have nearly enough guns. Certainly
he had twice as many as the entire BEF had had at Loos in 1915, and
all that could be found before June 1916, but this quantity was simply
not enough for the task they had before them. Of the 1,400 guns
available, 808 were 18-pounders, suitable only for wire cutting. There
were 182 heavy guns, either the obsolete 4.7 inch or 60-pounders,
plus an assortment of other guns, and 245 howitzers of 6-inch calibre
and above; only these heavy guns stood any chance of shattering a
German dugout. Expressed in yards, this gave Rawlinson one field gun

for every 21 yards of trench and one heavy gun to every 57 yards of trench, which does not even sound adequate – and there were further problems. The guns-per-yard-of-front ratio is war by slide-rule; it assumes that every gun will be accurately laid, every gunner can hit his target and every shell fired will go off.

There was a problem with the artillery ammunition: a large number of the millions of shells fired at the German lines from 24 June until zero hour on 1 July simply failed to go off. This fact was plain for all to see in the days preceding the infantry assault, when the ground to their front became littered with unexploded shells; even today, 85 years after the battle, an average year of scavenging on the Somme battlefield provides the disposal squads of the French Army with 90 tons of dangerous ordnance.

Some preparations did go to plan. Seventeen mines had been dug under the German front line and most of them went up at 0728 hrs and did great damage to the German positions. However, a major tactical error was committed in the vital minutes before the assault. The mine under the Hawthorn Redoubt near Beaumont-Hamel had been set to explode at 0720, ten minutes before the attack. This gave the Germans – at least those who survived the blast – ample time to prepare for the British infantry onslaught, which they duly stopped in its tracks.

This crucial part of the plan, the artillery bombardment, was a failure along much of the front – the one exception being on the 30th Division front at Montauban in XIII Corps sector on the right flank, where the wire had been well cut and the German defences much reduced. The bombardment on this part of the front had been aided by fire from the heavy guns of French XX Corps, firing from south of the Somme. As a result, the 30th Division, the French on their right and the 18th Division on their left, all made good progress – in the case of the 30th Division through Montauban village to the ridge beyond.

Elsewhere it was a different story, of uncut wire and unquelled defenders. As a result, when the attack went in on 1 July, the German wire was usually found to be tangled but uncut and, if the German trenches had been levelled, the deep dugouts in the chalk had provided plenty of protection from which the German machine-gunners were quick to

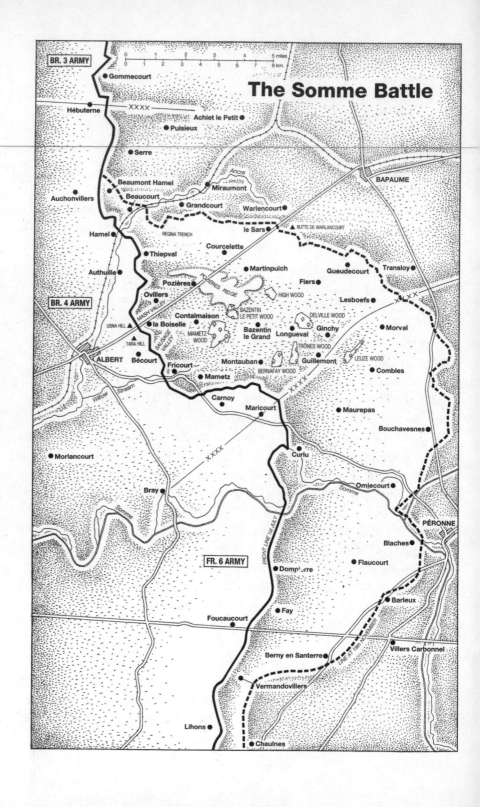

The Somme Battle

BR. 3 ARMY

Gommecourt

5 miles
8 km.

Hébuterne ● ——— XXXX ———
Achiet le Petit ●
● Puisieux

● Serre

Beaumont Hamel ●
Auchonvillers ●
Beaucourt ●
● Miraumont
BAPAUME

Hamel ● Grandcourt ●
● Warlencourt

REGINA TRENCH
le Sars ● ▲ BUTTE DE WARLANCOURT

● Courcelette
● Thiepval
Transloy ●

Authuille ● Pozières ● POZIÈRES RIDGE
● Martinpuich
Gueudecourt ●

BR. 4 ARMY Ovillers ●
● Flers
HIGH WOOD
Lesboefs ●

MASH VALLEY Contalmaison ●
BAZENTIN LE PETIT WOOD
DELVILLE WOOD

USNA HILL ▲ ● la Boiselle
Bazentin le Grand ●
Longueval ● Ginchy ●
Morval ●

TARA HILL ▲ SAUSAGE VALLEY
MAMETZ WOOD
TRÔNES WOOD
LEUZE WOOD

ALBERT Bécourt ● Fricourt ●
● Montauban
Guillemont ●
Combles ●

BERNAFAY WOOD
● Mametz
XXXX

Willow Stream
● Carnoy
● Maricourt
● Maurepas

Somme
Bouchavesnes ●

● Morlancourt
XXXX ● Curlu

● Bray
Omiecourt ●

Somme

PÉRONNE

Blaches ●

FR. 6 ARMY
FRONT LINE 1st JULY
● Flaucourt

● Dompierre

Barleux ●

● Fay
LINE AT 19th NOVEMBER

Foucaucourt ●

● Berny en Santerre
Villers Carbonnel ●

● Vermandovillers

Lihons ●
● Chaulnes

emerge and greet the oncoming attackers with a blizzard of fire. More than 1,000 machine-guns were in action on the Somme front on 1 July and their interlocking fields of fire presented an impassable barrier to the British infantry. It has been said that only bullet-proof soldiers could cross No Man's Land that day and it has to be added that the tactical instructions given to the infantry also played their part in the tragedy.

It is widely believed in Britain that the British infantry only used one tactical formation on 1 July. They got out of their trenches, filed through the gaps previously cut in their own wire, formed up in long lines, line abreast, and then in lines 12 miles long, with their rifles held at the 'high port', they advanced across No Man's Land to their deaths. This image is not entirely accurate, although this formation was widely employed and there was a good reason for it – control of the artillery support.

The serious shortage of reliable communications meant that there were no means of contacting or controlling the infantry beyond the front-line trench. This being so, the only way to control their essential artillery support was by observation, or by moving the fire forward, ahead of the advancing troops, in pre-set timed phases.

This need, to observe the effect of shellfire on the ground, deprived the infantry of two methods of attack commonly employed in future wars: the night attack and the protection of a smokescreen. Smoke shells were available but the decision on whether to use them was left to the divisional commanders. Some used smoke and some did not and it does not appear that any particular advantage went to those units that enjoyed smoke cover. Both Third Army divisions at Gommecourt used smoke; the 56th Division suffered 4,314 casualties and the 46th Division 2,455, so either smoke offered no particular advantage or other factors intervened. It is notable that Major-General Stuart-Wortley, commanding the 46th (North Midland) Division, was relieved of his command by Allenby on 5 July and sent back to Britain, allegedly (the court of inquiry failed to deliver a verdict) for failing to drive his men on hard enough on 1 July – and perhaps thereby sparing them further loss?[2]

As for night attacks, it was considered on 1 July that the troops lacked the training for night attacks and that daylight was necessary to allow the gunners a good view of their fire and the chance to keep their fall of shot safely ahead of the advancing infantry. Daylight was also needed so that the gunners could deliver a new form of fire support, later generally known as a 'creeping barrage', in which the shellfire was moved forward in timed stages, just ahead of the troops.

On 16 May, Haig and Rawlinson met again to discuss the attack and came to the joint decision that it would not be launched until the various corps commanders were fully convinced that the defences in their sectors had been sufficiently reduced. This was a good intention but there could be little doubt that the attack would go in on 1 July, whatever the state of the defences at that time, not least because the French were openly and understandably urging Haig to attack – and before that date if he could. This led to a growing amount of concern among the units tasked for the first attack because, in the weeks and days leading up to 1 July, it became increasingly apparent from the information coming in, from RFC observers and night reconnaissance patrols up to and into the enemy trenches, that the wire had not been cut adequately anywhere – with the possible exception of the right flank – and that in many places the deep German dugouts had not been touched.

On the day after that meeting with Haig, Rawlinson issued a pamphlet, 'Fourth Army Tactical Notes', which laid out the tactics he wanted his infantry to employ in the forthcoming battle. This called for an advance in extended line, or lines, each line 100 yards or so behind the line in front, with a space of two or three yards between each man. The idea here was to assist the artillery in their support task so that 'the artillery keeps their fire immediately in front of the infantry as they advance, battering down all opposition with a flurry of projectiles' – the first instruction for the 'creeping barrage' which was soon to become a standard Great War artillery tactic.

Not all the divisional, brigade or battalion commanders followed these Notes to the letter. Some moved their men out into No Man's Land on the previous night and had them lying within a few yards of the enemy wire when the barrage lifted next morning. Others had their men rush the enemy trenches, or advance across No Man's Land in open order, or had prepared shallow trenches – known as 'Russian saps' – set out in No Man's Land to shelter their men during the moments before the assault or during their advance.

General Rawlinson later estimated that whether a battalion succeeded or failed in the Somme attack came down to a matter of minutes. Three minutes to be exact – the time it took for the German infantry in their dugouts to realize that the bombardment had stopped, work out what that meant, and run up the stairs to their firing positions, carrying their machine-guns and boxes of ammunition. This may well be true; certainly in the days before the attack the Germans took to leaving only a couple of lookouts in their trenches and kept the bulk of their men safely below ground. When they emerged at 0730 hrs on 1 July, they saw before them the drifting shreds of smoke and dust from the shelling and beyond that long lines of heavily laden British infantry coming on slowly across No Man's Land.

'What ifs' are usually pointless after the event but, given the amount of ridicule deployed by historians in attacking the tactical methods employed on 1 July, it seems necessary to point out that everything done that day was done for a reason – and usually for a good reason. The orders given to the troops were not the result of stupidity or ignorance but attempts to cope with the hard and oft-repeated fact that there was no way of communicating with those troops once they had left their trenches. Hence the daylight attack, hence the general shortage of smoke, hence the advance in extended line, hence the 'creeping', or 'drifting', barrage.

However, Rawlinson's plan was based on artillery and that fact led on to the premise that by the time the infantry advanced there would be nothing on the far side of No Man's Land but dead bodies and empty trenches. In fact, there were more than 1,000 machine-guns waiting in those German dugouts and a mass of guns waiting to fire in the dips and folds of the ground beyond the Pozières ridge. Together these guns took an eerie toll of the advancing British infantry.

During the months before the opening of the combined offensive, the French share in the attack had shrunk inexorably, largely because of Verdun. Joffre had originally promised to commit 40 French divisions to the battle; on the day the Somme battle opened, the French share of the offensive had shrunk to 14 divisions compared to

16 British divisions; this fact disposes of one of the lesser British myths, that the French only played a minor part in the Somme offensive. On the first day of the Somme, the French divisions on the right also did far better than most of the British divisions.

The fact that the Somme battle had declined considerably both in weight and width also indicates that the main tactical idea arising from the defeats of 1915 – that to achieve a breakthrough an attack must be made on a wide front – had been tacitly abandoned. The Somme offensive would still be a major attack but on nothing like the scale envisaged by Joffre and Haig earlier in the year. However, two elements in the French Sixth Army would be of particular importance to the British in the early stages of the battle. The first was the assistance provided by French heavy guns positioned south of the Somme. These added their weight to the bombardment falling on the German defences opposite the British XIII Corps and helped it get forward towards Montauban. The second was the presence on the north bank of the Somme of the French XX Corps, lately engaged at Verdun, and now here to help, or hinder, the progress of the British attack on the Somme.

The artillery bombardment for the Somme battle started on 24 June. The first two days were devoted entirely to wire-cutting, though attempts were also made to find and register the positions of any German guns, which were staying ominously silent. The wire-cutting continued and the shelling mounted steadily over the next week, as more and more guns and mortars became engaged. This firing went on by day and night – 1,627,824 shells were fired in the preliminary bombardment on the Somme, stopping only to let the barrels cool, or the crews eat and rest, or to bring up more ammunition.[3] At night, infantry patrols went out to examine the enemy wire and report back on its condition.

These reports rarely brought much comfort to the infantry commanders. The weather was cloudy and rainy, which hampered the work of RFC observers, and that early decision – that the infantry would not go in until the wire was cut – was clearly not going to be kept. Indeed, when some battalion commanders reported to brigade and division that the wire on their front was still intact, they were told that they were 'scared' – which is probably true and hardly surprising;

if they were trapped by machine-guns in front of uncut wire, their men would be massacred.

Nor were the Germans entirely quiescent; British fighting patrols met German patrols in No Man's Land and reported that after dark the German trenches were 'full of men', up from deep dugouts and clearly willing to fight. On 27 June, General Haig moved to his advanced HQ at Beauquesne, 12 miles north-west of Albert and, on 28 June, the attack was postponed until 1 July, after heavy rain flooded the front-line trenches and made artillery observation impossible. So, slowly, the final hours and minutes ticked away.

The Germans certainly knew the attack was coming. The scale of the build-up could not be concealed and, although the Germans had lost control of the air over the Somme in the summer of 1916, enough of their aircraft succeeded in crossing the British lines to bring back news of extensive preparations in the country around Albert. They also had the advantage of higher ground and from their perches at Thiepval and the Pozières ridge they could see the gradual extension of the support trenches and feel the growing weight of the British artillery. Added to this was information from spies in neutral capitals, the interception of telephone messages and the public statement of a British Cabinet Minister asking workers in the ammunition factories to delay their summer holidays until after July. The Minister declined to give a specific reason but said his request 'should speak volumes'. Finally, there was that long-lasting barrage which, if it did little to cut the German wire, managed to alert the Germans to the impending attack.

As dawn broke on 1 July the gunfire rose in a final crescendo. Just before 0730 hrs the great mine went off at the Hawthorn Redoubt, followed by others at la Boisselle and at 15 other points along the German line. The British barrage lifted to the German support trenches – and now the race was on, between the lines of British infantry and the German machine-gunners now swarming from their dugouts to occupy their defensive positions. Two minutes later a curtain of German machine-gun fire interspersed with shell bursts was drawn across No Man's Land between the trenches.

*

How did this battle, like Verdun, become a battle of attrition? A change in purpose did not come about because one man wished it, as von Falkenhayn had wished at Verdun. The Allied generals eventually elected for attrition, partly because they saw no other way to gain any advantage but also because of all the other factors: the failure of peace efforts, the lack of an overall supreme commander and the growth of technology.

Bearing in mind the theme of this book – 1916 as a year of attrition on the Western Front – it has to be stressed that the Somme attack, unlike Verdun, was planned from the start as an *offensive* leading to a *breakthrough*. Even so, attacking on the Somme was almost certainly a strategic mistake. On the Somme, the Germans had an option denied to the French at Verdun, the choice of withdrawing to another position; there was plenty of space behind the German lines for such a withdrawal, should it become necessary, without surrendering any vital ground. In the event, the Germans chose to stand and fight on their long-prepared positions and on the first day alone these defenders took a heavy toll of British infantry. The British *Official History* is quite clear on this point:

> The British High Command had relied on the bombardment destroying the enemy's *matériel* defences and the morale of his troops. Confirmed in this belief by the information given by General Joffre as to the terrible effect of German fire at Verdun, their plan was framed, its tactics settled, and the troops trained, in the sure and certain hope that the infantry would only have to walk over No Man's Land and take possession.[4]

The *Official History* tends to be very sound on practical matters and its comments on the flaws in the initial attack seem fully justified. There were not enough guns and, as a result, their fire was too widely dispersed. Gas, so useful in other attacks, not least to deter the enemy gunners, was not employed in this bombardment, except for a small amount from French 75 mm guns. Many British guns were outranged by many German guns. The ammunition was all too often faulty, either failing to go off or sometimes exploding in the barrels of the guns. The weight of shot was not enough to penetrate the deep German dugouts except in the Montauban area, where French heavy guns, firing from across the Somme, contributed to the success on the right flank.

The *Official History* devotes several pages to a critique of infantry tactics, commenting that the large numbers attacking in the early hours of 1 July – 64 battalions, mostly in line – was of no advantage, since they simply offered a large target to the enemy guns. As a result, this 'extended line' formation was blown away in a matter of minutes, after which the survivors advanced, if at all, in small parties, dodging from crater to crater, a tactic which should arguably have been adopted from the start. This method, fire and movement, had been advocated by Haig, the cavalryman, but rejected by Rawlinson, the infantryman. The *Official History* comments favourably on the French infantry on the right:

> The French infantrymen, who thought for themselves and dis-obeyed instructions whenever they judged fit, though nominally advancing in lines, actually went forward in small packets, utilising cover, as could be seen from the British observation posts on Maricourt ridge.

It is curious to find an official military history suggesting that troops should disobey orders if they see fit, but the *Official History* has a point – though perhaps not the one it was making here. Once again, the question arises of that standard military technique, the 'appreciation of the situation', or 'Commander's Estimate' as it is now called, which every commander has to make before planning his attack. The generals were now two years into this war and it should have been – and indeed was – glaringly apparent that the methods being employed to attack the enemy lines, be they British, French or German, were simply not working. Increasing the scale of the attack by the current methods simply increased the number of casualties. The British casualties on the First Day of the Somme, at more than 60,000 killed, wounded and missing, were roughly the same as those for the entire Battle of Loos in the previous September – 50,380, or 60,392 if subsidiary attacks are included.

For these casualties, and for the standard procedure used in these attacks, the generals are exclusively blamed but, apart from this being fundamentally unfair, there is more to it than a failure of planning and tactics. First of all, politics intervened. It is possible to argue that the best course for the Allies in 1916 was to hold the line on the Western Front, fixing German troops there with limited attacks, while supplying troops, guns, artillery ammunition and training to the Russian armies on the Eastern Front through the northern ports of Murmansk and Archangel. Hindsight enables us to see that this strategy, which is not unlike the one adopted in the Second World War, might have enabled the Russians to defeat the Central Powers' armies . . . and might also have prevented the outbreak of the Russian Revolution.

It all sounds perfectly feasible now but at the time two factors militated against it. The first was that now-familiar difficulty, the lack of a supreme commander or a Combined Chiefs-of-Staff Committee which would take an overall, strategic view of the war. The second was the attitude of the French. They had a German Army on their soil and they wanted it removed, as quickly as possible, at any cost. The idea of waiting, of taking the long view and not doing everything in their own and their Allies' power to get rid of this intrusion, was anathema to the French people, political, civil and military.

The French attitude is understandable but, even so, waiting for the right time or the right kit is sometimes a very good idea. This is not hindsight; in other circumstances, later in the war, we hear generals and politicians, French as well as British, suggesting that attacks should wait until tanks are available in large numbers or, after the USA entered the war in 1917, until the Americans arrived.

The first factor, a failure of planning and tactics, has a more direct bearing on the conduct of the Somme campaign. It was clear, abundantly clear, that the present methods would not do, on whatever scale they were employed. Therefore new methods must be considered, in the shape of fresh ideas or new equipment.

This is where the appreciation of the situation, or Commander's Estimate, comes in. The 2000 issue of *British Defence Doctrine* states that this is 'a formal analysis of the environment, operational situation, mission, enemy and own courses of action conducted in preparation for forming a commander's intentions and concept of operations.' Another instruction, *The Fundamentals of Maritime Doctrine*, adds, 'The estimate is only a tool, aiding the commander to orchestrate the conduct of his campaign or operation. It is not an end in itself.'

If phrased differently, the appreciation, or estimate, was employed by the generals during the Great War, but the question that remains to be posed is — at what stage should that appreciation or estimate begin? The purpose of making an 'appreciation' is simply to clarify the problem and codify the commander's thinking into a logical form. What he has to do, what facts help or hinder him doing it, what courses of action lie open to him, what the enemy reaction may be in each case, which are the ones to adopt, and so on. All the relevant factors must be considered, for only then can he hope to work out a viable plan . . . but again, it has to be asked, at what point should the appreciation begin?

In practice, a general's appreciation usually begins when he is given his orders for a particular battle or campaign by some even more senior officer or by his political masters. Many historians seem to believe that generals dream up their own battles or campaigns, perhaps on a 'Things to do Today' basis, and can therefore be blamed when things go wrong. This is rarely the case; generals are ordered to start a campaign or undertake an engagement by their political masters — 'your orders are to liberate Belgium, relieve Kut, raid Zeebrugge, destroy the enemy field army . . . whatever' — and it is at that point that their planning usually begins.

However, it is also possible that a general, aided by his staff, could carry out an appreciation before being given firm orders to mount an operation, perhaps in response to being warned, formally or informally, of a superior's possible intentions. He might also carry out an appreciation in order to refine, or even influence, the tasks being laid on him. There may also be a situation, at the highest level, where a commander carries out an appreciation in order to give him a range of strategic choices to lay before his superiors or political masters — a process now known as a 'strategic estimate'. As before, the purpose of this appreciation is to take the widest possible view, weigh the influence of all the factors and reach a decision. It may be that the decision reached is that to attack this position at the present time, with the means currently available, would result in a disaster.

That situation was found all too frequently on the Western Front in 1914 and 1915 but the attacks went in anyway, based on the belief that more guns, more men, or a reshuffle of the tactical plan, would somehow win the day. Hindsight shows that until the tank and the aeroplane came along – and their true worth was appreciated and the right tactics developed – the Western Front defences were effectively impenetrable. For the moment, defensive technology – artillery, machine-guns, barbed wire and dugouts – dominated the battlefield, and would continue to do so until offensive technology – a combination of tanks, artillery and aircraft – was deployed to defeat it.

In the case of General Haig and the combined offensive on the Somme, his appreciation began when it was decided to launch a series of offensives in 1916, with the British taking part in an Anglo-French attack astride the Somme. All the plans prepared and considered by Haig and Rawlinson related to that strategic decision and, given the circumstances, it is hard to fault the plan they came up with.

The snag was that in the existing situation, no attack, however well planned and supported, could possibly succeed. Existing methods and equipment were simply not enough to cope with the German defences on the Western Front – and someone should have stated that fact plainly before the planning for the Somme offensive even began. Von Falkenhayn's plan for Verdun, however flawed in execution, was at least possible; he did not intend to gain ground, penetrate the enemy defences or take Verdun. He simply wanted to kill soldiers, to bleed the French Army to death. The Anglo-French Somme plan, even if it had not been disrupted and reduced by the Verdun offensive, was a far more risky business, with little chance of achieving its objectives without new tactical ideas and new equipment.

It might be argued that Haig and Rawlinson could not know this when they made their plan for the Somme. It can, therefore, also be argued that any criticism of their actions today smacks of hindsight. This argument does not stand up. First of all, the attacks of 1915 had been failures and to repeat them, with the same methods but on a larger scale, was a guarantee of larger losses. Generals are not paid to repeat a process that, on previous experience, probably leads to failure but to apply their intellect, their training and their experience to finding effective answers to the current problem. Wittering on about 'what else could they do?' only leads to the assumption that the senior Army commanders were incapable of any fresh thinking at all.

Secondly, even when they were baffled by the defensive use of the current technology for defence, offensive technology was available, notably the tank and the aircraft, if only someone had put this technology to use by devising fresh tactics for their employment on the battlefield. New tactics and new technology have to go together. New ideas on tactics really only needed a little imagination and more confidence on the part of the commanders about the tactical ability of their troops. New equipment, in the shape of the tank, was already in production; the first tanks were about to arrive in France as the Battle of the Somme opened.

The problem – and there is always a problem – relates to the matter of time. Had Haig waited until August to launch his Somme attack, it might be that he would then have decided to use the tanks in the initial phase, with incalculable results. But further delay, beyond 1 July, was impossible, firstly because of the situation at Verdun, secondly because Joffre would not hear of it.

After 1915, it should have been clear that 1916 was the year when a fresh look at the situation was essential. It can be accepted as reasonable that the conventional methods of attack, a combination of infantry and artillery and the looming presence of cavalry, was used in 1914 and 1915. If this combination failed, it can be argued that this was because the generals did not have enough artillery or infantry, or that these elements lacked training, or that the generals were faced with an entirely new situation – all of which is perfectly true.

One can accept that argument, up to a point, but there remains a limit on how long generals can continue with the old, conventional ways of warfare when they clearly do not work. Such evidence was there by 1916 – in the failures to gain ground and in the casualty lists. Also available was new equipment, the tank and the aircraft – kit that could make all the difference. As it was, another opportunity for new thinking – so easy after the event, so hard to do at the time or in the heat of battle – slipped away in the early months of 1916. During the battle, however, things did change and, in the weeks and months after the Somme offensive opened, three new elements were introduced to the British armies. First, night attacks. Secondly, the tank. Had this tactic and this kit been used with intelligence and skill, the story of 1916 might have been very different. But this was not all: the third element to appear in 1916 was attrition, a gift from General Joffre.

Notes

1 Fourth Army staff began to assemble on 5 February 1915 but the Army came into existence officially on 1 March.
2 See Middlebrook, *The First Day on the Somme*, p. 258.
3 *Official History*, 1916, vol. 5, p. 486.
4 Ibid., p. 485.

12

The First Days on the Somme
July–August 1916

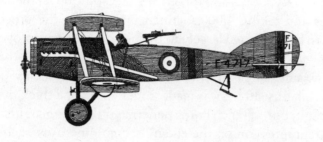

'Courage is sometimes the only substitute for the skill
that comes with experience.'
Lt-General Hunter Liggett, Commander, US First Army, 1917

After a seven-day artillery bombardment of the German line, the British infantry assault on the German positions north of the Somme began at 0730 hrs on 1 July 1916. A force of some 120,000 British soldiers of Fourth and Third Armies assaulted the German line between Maricourt and Gommecourt. Their attack was pressed home with great resolution – and at considerable cost. By the end of that day, 19,240 men had been killed outright and the total casualty figure, including the missing and those taken prisoner-of-war, amounted to 57,470 men.

It is not the purpose of this book to cover the actions along the Somme front that day in any detail. The purpose here is to discuss how the plans of Haig, Rawlinson, Allenby and their corps commanders contributed to this situation and what advantages the commanders could reap from the slender gains of that dreadful day. These gains were all on the right, or southern flank, where the British front faced north towards Fricourt, Mametz and Montauban. However, an explanation of the situation here should begin with the actions of the French Sixth Army, commanded by General Fayolle, which was mainly deployed south of the Somme, but had one corps, XX Corps, deployed north of the river.

On 1 July, XX Corps, still commanded by General Balfourier, who had led it at Verdun, attained all its objectives. South of the river, the divisions of XXV Corps also forged ahead, capturing all their 'first day' objectives and taking 4,000 German prisoners in the process. This success can be attributed largely to the heavy artillery deployed by the French – with 88 heavy batteries to 8 German batteries – before the infantry assault. Their fire destroyed most of the enemy positions, while the infantry attack was made under cover of a thick river mist.

As a result, both French corps penetrated the German first line but made little impression on the enemy second line. Any such advance would have left their left flank fully exposed, since beyond Maricourt the front line swung west and, although the British XIII Corps stayed in line with the French XX Corps to their right during the initial assault, from then on the two corps were heading in different directions, the French east, the British north and west, with the untaken villages of Guillemont and Combles as rocks on which to divide.

The British XIII Corps made a three-phase attack, first through the German front line to the village of Montauban, then through the village and up to the German second-line position on the ridge by Mametz. Here the corps was to pivot to the left, or north-west, and attack the German second-line position, but always keeping in touch with the French XX Corps on its right flank, a point to be noted for future reference.

On XIII Corps front, the preliminary bombardment had cut the German wire adequately and the advance across a narrow part of No Man's Land was accompanied by a strong artillery barrage. The corps gunners were also using a new technique; the corps orders state that 'the field artillery will creep back by short lifts', the first reference to a 'creeping barrage' on the Western Front. This 'creeping barrage', where the gunfire shifted forward as the infantry advanced, had to be controlled visually and therefore no smoke was laid to cover the infantry attack. The alternative was to control the movement of the guns by timed 'lifts', moving the fall of shot back a few hundred yards every few minutes; both methods, the timed and the visual, were employed on this day.

The orders at XIII Corps decreed that the infantry must wait until the barrage lifted, rather than shifting the barrage prematurely, which would give an alert enemy the chance to man his forward trenches and bring fire to bear on the advancing British infantry. In practice, the infantry advanced closely behind the exploding shells and were in the German front-line trenches before the barrage had fully lifted. Congreve's men were supported in their attack by the heavy guns of the French Sixth Army, firing across the river.

Congreve's corps contained the 30th, 18th and 9th (Scottish) Divisions, this last in reserve. The 18th Division was commanded by Major-General Sir Ivor Maxse, one of the finest of the divisional commanders, and one who, in his pre-attack training, had laid great stress on a rapid advance by the first waves and a careful clearing of the enemy positions by the follow-up waves – 'mopping-up' as it came to be called – partly to secure the ground, but mainly to stop any German defenders emerging from their deep dugouts and impeding the forward passage of reserves. This essential tactic was neglected, with dire results, by some of the divisions on Maxse's left. By this mixture of sound training and judgement, XIII Corps made good progress and by dusk its forward elements were on the Montauban ridge and digging in to resist the anticipated counterattacks.

West of Congreve's XIII Corps lay Lt-General Sir Henry Horne's XV Corps, which had a rather more difficult task. Its front was barred by the villages of Mametz and Fricourt and the width of their attack therefore encompassed two villages and the Fricourt village salient. This was a very strong position, a mixture of dugouts, fortified houses, deep cellars, trenches and wire, covered by machine-guns and artillery, at the point where the front lines turned north. XV Corps was charged with attacking on a 1,200-yard front and the only real advantage it had was that this position, though formidable, was inadequately manned, and much of the heavy artillery tasked to defend this part of the German line had been destroyed in the previous week. The Germans had only six battalions to defend this position but these troops were well dug in and fully alert when the British infantry attacked.

General Horne is one of the lesser known Great War generals. He left no memoirs and his papers have been destroyed so, apart from his actions, it is only possible to guess at what he had in mind for that day. General Horne was a gunner and therefore took a strong personal interest in the corps artillery. Here, too, it was decided that the guns must support the infantry during the attack; the phrase employed here is 'drift' – Horne's gunners were instructed to let their shells 'drift' forward at a timed rate that was not to exceed 50 yards a minute, which Horne calculated as the best speed his infantry could manage. In case this estimate was too pessimistic, the infantry were directed to wait if they reached an objective before the gunners could blast it. The idea here, as with XIII Corps, was that the guns should level a path for the infantry through the enemy positions. As an additional bonus to screen their advance, three mines were to be exploded under the enemy trenches immediately before the attack.

This 'drifting' barrage could have been a great help to the infantry, but soon after the attack began it became apparent that, far from being pessimistic, Horne's calculated timed advance rate of 50 yards a minute was far too high. The artillery barrage began to drift away from the infantry and the German defenders had time to reoccupy their positions and bring their automatic weapons into play. Not a great deal could be done about this for, again, lacking a decent battlefield radio, there was no way in which the gun batteries could be contacted and their fire brought back. As a result, the enemy were able to bring Horne's troops under a heavy and accurate fire.

The advance of XV Corps was made with two divisions 'up', the 7th and 21st Divisions leading the attack, with the 17th Division, less one brigade, in reserve. The 7th Division thrust led straight through Mametz. The 21st Division, a New Army formation, was tasked to take Fricourt, which would also be assaulted by the 50th Brigade of

17th Division, and then press on to Mametz Wood. Taking this strongly wired and well-defended position would have been a formidable task even if all had gone well but the loss of masking artillery brought heavy casualties from flanking machine-guns, which raked the infantry as they advanced. Although XV Corps made ground on the right flank, it was held at Fricourt in the centre. By the end of the day, the 7th Division had taken Mametz, reached the Willow Stream and linked up with the 18th Division in XIII Corps, but this had only been achieved at the cost of more than 8,000 men, more than half of them from the 21st Division.

The next Corps, to the left of XV Corps, was III Corps, commanded by Lt-General Sir W.P. Pulteney. His corps area straddled the Albert to Bapaume road, the axis of the Fourth Army advance, just before it led through the village of la Boisselle. The area offered a range of difficulties to the British attackers and some corresponding advantages to the German defenders, not least in good visibility from the Thiepval ridge.

The road to Bapaume came over the western ridge from Albert and descended into the valley now occupied by the rebuilt village of la Boisselle, and then straddled by the British front line. Communication trenches therefore came over this western ridge – Tara Hill – which was occupied by the support trench – the Tara–Usna Line – and zigzagged down to the front-line positions, under observation from the German lines all the way. The Germans were strongly ensconced in the village of la Boisselle, which lay within a few yards of the British front line and in a series of entrenchments, known as the 'Glory Hole' at the head of Sausage Valley, where the Lochnagar crater now lies and, on the left, in the village of Ovillers, which lay some 875 yards to the left of la Boisselle, at the head of a shallow re-entrant known as Mash Valley. The entire la Boisselle–Ovillers position, manned by four full infantry regiments, 12 battalions, was the usual complex mixture of trenches, dugouts, barbed-wire entanglements, fortified houses and cellars, all overlooked by interlocking machine-gun positions and artillery fire. This was the most formidable position on the southern section of the Fourth Army front and General Pulteney laid an elaborate plan to overcome it.

It seems likely that Pulteney gave his assault divisions too much to do: his corps task, to break through the German front line and advance two miles to the east, up to the German second-line position, must have seemed a daunting proposal in 1916; no British division had advanced anything like two miles since the Old Front Line was formed in the autumn of 1914. It hardly seems credible that III Corps commander could propose doing so on 1 July, especially when this task involved an advance on a 4,000-yard wide front and the taking of no less than six trench lines. That, however, was Pulteney's task, and he laid careful plans to carry it through.

To aid him in this undertaking, Rawlinson let Pulteney have all the guns he could spare for this vital attack astride the Albert–Bapaume road. More than 90 heavy guns were deployed on this front, where the final artillery concentration by 24 June reached one field gun for every 23 yards of front, and one heavy gun for every 40 yards of front. This was far more than the average along the front and sounds like a lot of artillery, but it was hardly sufficient for the task in hand. After several days of shelling, night patrols up to the German line in front of la Boisselle and in Mash Valley revealed the grim news that the wire was virtually untouched. Therefore, the guns were ordered to switch their fire from Ovillers and the German artillery and machine-gun positions behind the line, and concentrate instead on the German wire in front of it. On the assumption, a rather large assumption in the circumstances, that the infantry could get through the wire, the guns were to lay a carpet of shells in front of their advance and rake the German positions as the infantry went forward.

No one was in any doubt that success or failure on this part of the line depended on getting the infantry through the wire. As a further step to this end, two great mines had been laid in tunnels dug under the German lines, one overlooking the entrance to Mash Valley at la Boisselle and the other at the head of Sausage Valley. The Y-Sap crater at Mash Valley was filled in and ploughed over in the 1980s but the Sausage Valley crater, known as Lochnagar, created by the explosion of some 60,000 lbs of ammonal, has been preserved and still lies behind la Boisselle. As on XV Corps front, these mines had two purposes: firstly, to destroy the German positions and the men who held them and secondly, to throw up a great wall of soil and debris that would shelter the advancing British troops from direct rifle and machine-gun fire. At 0728 hrs on 1 July these mines exploded and two minutes later the attack went in.

The attack at la Boisselle and Ovillers was a total failure. Pulteney had been assured that his attack was viable because the German wire would have been cut, the German positions shattered by artillery, and the flanking machine-guns screened by the mine explosions. This happened, up to a point, but not for long and not sufficiently to allow the infantry a fair run at their objectives. The harsh fact was that the declared III Corps aim – to advance two miles to the German second-line position – was a pipedream and even a shorter advance equally impossible.

Until the flanking bastions at Thiepval had been reduced, the advance up Mash Valley could only be made by bullet-proof soldiers. This was further proof, if proof were necessary after 1915, that there was no current way of taking an interlinked defensive position without terrible losses, for even one machine-gun on the flank could savage the attacking troops and bring their advance to a halt. One of the accounts of the 8th Division infantry advancing up Mash Valley is of men 'leaning forward into the machine-gun fire, as into rain', and III Corps losses on 1 July were truly horrendous.

The 34th Division, attacking la Boisselle and Sausage Valley, lost 6,380 men, killed, wounded and missing, that morning, more than half of those who went over the top. The 8th Division suffered 5,121 casualties, and total III Corps casualties for the day were more than 11,000 . . . and all for nothing. At nightfall, the two villages of la Boisselle and Ovillers, respectively 110 yards and 880 yards from the start line, were still firmly in German hands. No Man's Land was carpeted with dead and wounded; it was not until the evening of 3 July that the last of the wounded were brought away. The corps attacking north of the Albert–Bapaume road had suffered even more severely and made no gains whatsoever . . . and the slaughter on the Somme had barely begun.

It is not necessary to continue this litany of loss up the British line to Gommecourt. The losses on the first day of the Somme were largely caused by miscalculation. At the start of the process that terminated when the infantry went over the top, Rawlinson had noted that success or failure on the Somme, as elsewhere, depended on the quantity, accuracy and reliability of the artillery. The infantry were therefore supported by more artillery than had previously been available and by unheard-of quantities of ammunition – 1,627,824 shells fell on the German defences in the seven days prior to the assault. This goes some way towards shifting the blame from the generals for, if the number of guns was insufficient for the task in hand, it still represented every gun they could find.

The guns were accurate but not accurate enough. During the preliminary bombardment the enemy refrained from using many of their batteries against the British guns and, when they sprang to life after 0730 hrs on 1 July, the weight of shot falling in No Man's Land came as a most unpleasant surprise. Rawlinson was unwise to distribute his artillery evenly along the entire front, with the small concentration at la Boisselle, and not concentrate it in particular spots to aid a breakthrough. This is an arguable point and suggestions on exactly where these particular spots might be are rather less easy to discover, but concentrating the artillery somewhere would have been a sensible move. Given that the British currently enjoyed air superiority over the front, it is also surprising that the RFC had not been able to detect more of the German batteries and bring them to the attention of the gunners.

Unlike the German attack at Verdun, the British attack on the Somme was made without the useful, some might say vital, element of surprise. The *Official History* comments: 'strategic surprise was to some extent secured', but it is hard to see what justified that statement.[1] In spite of the fact that British air superiority over the Somme front inhibited aerial reconnaissance, it is inconceivable that the German High Command did not know where, and roughly when, the attack was coming. There is also the matter of that long, seven-day bombardment, which gave them a full week to position reserves behind their front line, knowing that when the guns stopped the British infantry would come forward.

What any analysis of the first day on the Somme comes down to is the familiar lesson – that Western Front defensive positions could not be stormed and taken by any means currently open to the attacker. The British assault on the first day of the Somme was a classic example of a nineteenth-century attack, only with aircraft in the scouting role in the place of cavalry. The position had been pounded by heavy guns and the infantry had attacked in a manner that Pickett's Division at Gettysburg, some 50 years before, would have recognized and admired and they had been repulsed with loss, just as Pickett's attack had been, with the losses on 1 July expanded and compounded by the devastating power of modern weapons.

So the first day ended, with mounting casualty lists and the slow gathering of information on just how devastating the losses had been. When the extent of the damage was finally revealed, on 3 July, General Haig and his commanders still had to decide what to do next. Given that battle was raging at Verdun, it was impossible to call the Somme battle off, and there is no sign that Haig ever considered doing so; after all, he had seen grievous losses before, most recently at Loos. One suggestion he is said to have considered is halting the attacks on the Somme and switching his efforts to Messines but the logistical problems would seem to dismiss that option.

Haig was fully committed to an attack on the Somme. Therefore, what he had to do now was to find some ray of light in the pervading gloom, some way out of the current impasse. Such a ray was found on the right flank of the British attack, in the positions now held by XIII Corps and XV Corps where, it will be recalled, the attack had gone more or less according to plan and where Fricourt, which had held out on 1 July, was taken on 2 July. If Haig had to renew his attacks, the place to do so was on the right flank, with a push up and on to the Pozières ridge.

It is an axiom of warfare that a good officer never reinforces failure. To do so simply throws away more lives and a good general will avoid doing that. A commander's task, even in moments of defeat, is to find some way forward, some way out of the current catastrophe and when General Haig assembled his reports and looked at his maps on 2–3 July, he saw that all was not yet lost in this battle on the Somme. Yes, the first attack had been generally repulsed, but the small local successes on the right flank offered some tactical possibilities, if only they could be exploited. These possibilities largely related to the ground.

He who holds the high ground commands the battlefield. High ground offers observation points, shelter for the artillery, protection in dead ground from direct fire and concealment for the movement of troops. On the Western Front, high ground usually also offered better going, on drier ground than that normally available in the valleys or out on the plains. High ground was therefore well worth having and Haig, who had fought at Ypres in 1914 and 1915, was well aware of its importance. This being so, it would be most useful if he could take the Pozières ridge, which lies astride the Albert–Bapaume road and runs from Bazentin through Pozières, to Thiepval and the Ancre Valley. As Haig brooded over his maps in the hours after 1 July, he began to see the possibilities.

Two corps, XIII and XV, around Montauban, were already in position to strike north-west and get on to the Pozières ridge. Once on the ridge, the advancing XIII and XV Corps could first outflank and then roll up the German positions above the Ancre valley, where the British attack had been so bloodily repulsed on 1 July.

Meanwhile, the French XX Corps could develop its attack north-east, across the ground above the Somme and support the expanding British move towards the German second line. Seen on the ground or on the map, this plan looks plausible but Rawlinson did not agree with it. His first attack had failed but failure is to be expected in war and he wanted to try again. He intended to continue pressing on in the centre from la Boisselle, trying to force a way up the 'axis of advance', the road through Pozières. This was Rawlinson's first intention on 2 July but Haig promptly overruled him; frontal attacks were too costly in lives and, since they had one small success at Montauban, it made sense to exploit it and attack on the right flank. Arrangements to do that were in hand on 3 July, when Generals Joffre and Foch turned up at Haig's headquarters to discuss plans for the continuation of the Somme offensive.

The purpose of their visit was to discuss future arrangements for the battle but the discussions began with Joffre pointing out the importance of gaining ground at Thiepval. Haig demurred, pointing out that since the attack on his right flank had done well and gained ground, he proposed holding in the centre and pressing on with an advance up to Longueval . . . though this depended on the French XX Corps supporting this attack by pressing forward on the British right, towards Guillemont. When Joffre heard this proposal his well-known equanimity fractured into an explosion of rage.

Joffre did not want an attack on the right flank, he told Haig. He wanted an all-out attack on Thiepval – and he wanted it at once. He *ordered* Haig to attack Thiepval. He could not approve of an attack on the right, towards Longueval. While Haig and Foch stood wondering at this outburst, General Joffre forgot the true and delicate nature of the relationship between the Allied commanders and attempted to treat the British commander like a disobedient subordinate. In doing so he revealed the fundamental differences between the two Allies and at least one of the reasons why it proved so difficult to appoint a supreme allied commander.

The French, and especially the French generals, would not accept the British as equal partners in the war. The fact that without the help of Britain and her Empire they would already have lost the war and what remained of their national territory did not alter their belief in their own military superiority, or lead them into any feelings of gratitude towards their Anglo-Saxon allies. Indeed, when the French looked back on the events of 1914, 1915 and the first six months of 1916, and considered their British allies, their main feelings could be summed up as irritation and frustration.

According to the French version of the facts, one which the Francophile Henry Wilson had completely accepted, the British had failed to mobilize at once in August 1914, had arrived in position late, and had failed to bring every man they had at that time to the struggle, since there were only four infantry divisions in the original BEF, instead of the promised six. Since then, they had failed to produce a large supply of troops, had been reluctant to take advice – let alone orders – from Joffre and the assembly of military talent at GQG, and had been downright tardy in fielding their New Armies on the Somme, even while the French Army was being bled to death at Verdun.

And now, finally, having made a hash of the first Somme attack, General Haig was proposing to attempt an outflanking movement with a small part of his force, when the French wanted the British to hurl themselves at the German line again with everything they had, and continue a broad-front attack, regardless of loss, until they had engaged the Germans in an all-out, wide-front battle.

Joffre wanted – needed – such an all-out attack, in order to draw the pressure off Verdun. If the British attack succeeded, all well and good, but as long as it helped the French at Verdun, Joffre would be content. The important thing was to get the Germans fully involved on the Somme, which would force them to move troops from Verdun. It is, of course, arguable that the arrival of Haig's troops on the Pozières ridge, in a position to roll up the entire German line along the Ancre, would have proved equally galvanizing to the German generals, but imagination was not General Joffre's strong point. That was speculation, an all-out attack was real, immediate, essential . . . and the only way to take the heat off Verdun.

Haig was made of sterner stuff than his predecessor, Field Marshal Sir John French. When Joffre's rant had finished, Haig explained calmly that he, and he alone, was responsible for the actions of the British Army and that, since he had decided to exploit the gains on the right flank and push up to Longueval, he fully intended to do so. Standing up to the French usually paid dividends, albeit briefly, and so it was here. Joffre assured Haig that he knew this was an 'English' battle and responded warmly to Haig's conciliatory comment that they shared a common aim – the defeat of Germany – and towards that aim their countries marched together.

Unfortunately, before the meeting ended, the two sides had compromised. Having won his point, Haig agreed to press forward where possible in the centre and the French agreed to support the movement of the British right wing on Longueval. A French aide-de-camp produced medals and, after they had been distributed to Haig's staff, the French departed.

What Joffre wanted on the Somme was not a tactical battle. As he saw it, the attempt at a breakthrough had failed and now, as so often before, the task of breaking the enemy line would get even harder.

Therefore, since it was probably impossible to break through the enemy line, the next best thing was to attack all along the line, and engage the enemy in a battle that would force him to remove divisions from the Verdun front – not because he had lost a lot of territory, but because the cost of retaining it had cost a lot of men. In short, Joffre wanted Haig to engage the enemy in a battle of attrition that would suck more and more German divisions on to the Somme front.

In fact, as we have seen, the German attack at Verdun had already reached its peak with the failure of the assault on 23 June. There was one final, desperate attempt at a breakthrough, an assault on the French line on the right bank at Fort Souville on 10 July, but that too failed miserably, under a storm of shrapnel put down by the French 75s. On 14 July, after four days of fighting, the Germans were back where they had been on 10 July and the German advances on the Verdun front were over.

The high-water mark of the German attack at Verdun occurred on 14 July. The battle would continue but from then on it would take the form of a slow German retreat, again with a painful contest for every yard of ground as the enemy were driven back. The four months since the battle began had cost the French Army more than 280,000 men, and the Germans about 250,000 . . . and these grim totals would grow on both sides.

On the Somme front, the slaughter was just getting under way. After the meeting with Joffre and Foch on 3 July, it would be pleasant to record that Haig then proceeded to execute his declared intention and move on Longueval and the Pozières ridge with the French covering his flank at Guillemont, as promised, but it was not that easy. It will be recalled that the French had insisted that one French corps, XX Corps, was positioned on the north bank of the Somme. Inevitably, though Haig indeed ordered further, and fruitless, attacks in the centre around Thiepval, French support for an advance on the right failed to materialize. Indeed, in spite of Joffre's promise of 3 July, the French flatly refused to support any move towards Guillemont. Unless they did so it was impossible for XIII Corps to advance, for this would have exposed its right flank to the German second line.

The only way the British could advance on to the Pozières ridge was if the French came forward as well, to cover their open flank as they wheeled north. In the hope that the French would keep their word, Haig prepared further attacks all along the line, with a push towards Thiepval in the centre and a thrust up the Ancre valley on the left. He also decided to rearrange the command structure, charging Rawlinson and Fourth Army with the battle south of the Albert–Bapaume road, and bringing in Lt-General Sir Hubert Gough and his Reserve Army, soon to be renamed Fifth Army, to handle the battle north of that axis. These arrangements made, both generals renewed the attack in the centre.

Gough ordered attacks up Mash Valley towards Ovillers and across the Ancre valley towards Thiepval. Both of these attacks were beaten off with loss. Rawlinson's attempts to take la Boisselle also failed; la Boisselle was not taken until 4 July, a gain of perhaps 220 yards in four days of constant fighting. The problem, as the Germans had found when attacking at Verdun, was that the defences had interlocking fields of fire. It was virtually impossible to advance towards Ovillers and Thiepval, up the Mash Valley, unless and until the defences of la Boisselle had been quelled; equally, any attack on la Boisselle was inhibited by fire that could be brought down from Ovillers and the high ground beyond, at Thiepval.

While Gough was beating his head against the defences of Thiepval and Ovillers, Rawlinson was facing similar difficulties south of the road. His main task was to get on to the Pozières ridge and so up to the German second line. The most direct route lay via la Boisselle but, before he could get beyond that, he must clear his front by capturing Mametz Wood and the village of Contalmaison. He attacked these positions on 7 July, only to be beaten off. Part of this failure, in the attack on Mametz Wood, was blamed, correctly, on the poor handling of the 38th (Welsh) Division. Three days later the divisional commander, Major-General Ivor Phillips, a personal friend of the War Minister, Lloyd George, was relieved of his command. Three days later, another divisional commander, Major-General T.D. Pilcher of the 17th (Northern) Division, was also sacked. Meanwhile, the battering of the German line continued. Contalmaison fell on 10 July and by 12 July Fifth Army (still called Reserve Army at this time) had penetrated the western outskirts of Ovillers. On that day Mametz Wood was finally taken by Fourth Army and so, slowly and painfully, the British line inched forward.

In view of the pessimistic accounts that usually define the Somme battle, it is interesting to note that in the summer of 1916 confidence in the outcome of the campaign was widespread among the Entente leadership. On 17 July Haig wrote: 'There must be no question of discussing peace terms. We must dictate peace terms to the Germans.' On 9 August, Sir William Robertson, the CIGS, wrote: 'The general situation is now better than it has been since the beginning of the war. The Entente are winning on all fronts and losing nowhere.'² This view seems to have been shared in Berlin for, at the end of August, Chancellor von Bethmann-Hollweg told the King of Bavaria that if the Entente did not ask for peace by the end of the autumn, Germany would be obliged to seek terms.

As the battle wore on and lengthened into months, however, opinions changed. Speaking in the House of Commons on 11 October 1916, C.P. Trevelyan said: 'It is not everybody who is blind to the real meaning of the abominable phrase, a war of attrition. They know that rubbing away is not all on one side. It was all very well when the attrition was all on the other side at the time of Verdun, when the principle "attrition" was hundreds of thousands of Germans; but part of the attrition is now hundreds of thousands of British lives.'

By then the Battle of the Somme had been going on for more than three months and there were grounds for such pessimism but, during the summer months, the probable outcome of the offensive had still not been revealed and besides, the battle could claim some strategic successes. To begin with, the Germans had broken off their attacks at Verdun and were now in retreat. This had led to dissension among the German command, the Crown Prince had finally parted company with von Knobelsdorf, who had been sent to command an Army Corps in the east, and the Kaiser had asked Field Marshal von Hindenburg for his advice.

When news of this conversation between his rival and the Supreme War Lord got to the ears of von Falkenhayn, he promptly tendered his resignation: 'The summoning of a subordinate, without previous reference to him . . . was a sign that he no longer possessed the absolute confidence of the Supreme War Lord. He therefore begged to be relieved of his appointment.' His resignation was accepted and the High Command therefore passed to Field Marshal von Hindenburg, who became Chief of the General Staff on 29 August. Accompanied by his colleague, General Erich Ludendorff, the First Quartermaster-General, von Hindenburg made an immediate visit to Verdun and at once ordered the cessation of all attacks. By that time the losses of the two sides at Verdun had reached more than half a million men, killed, wounded and missing – 315,000 French and 281,000 German – and the battle was still not over.

The partnership of von Hindenburg and Ludendorff was one of the strangest and most effective of the war but such partnerships were not unusual. Haig had Robertson, Foch had Weygand, Joffre had de Castelnau – but in these cases one man was a support or a prop for the other. Not so Hindenburg and Ludendorff. They were full partners; their talents complemented each other. Although von Hindenburg was the senior officer and the appointed head, Ludendorff was the de facto commander of operations in the field and neither made a move without the support of the other.

Their partnership was unusual because they were not at all alike. Von Hindenburg was 62 when the war began and had already retired from the Army to the family estates in East Prussia, where the Hindenburgs were archetypal *Junkers*, an aristocratic but impoverished country family. Von Hindenburgs had served in the armies of Prussia for centuries and the present incumbent had fought in the Austro-Prussian War of 1866 and the Franco-Prussian War of 1870–71. Having retired with the rank of General, von Hindenburg had been recalled in 1914 and sent to command the Eighth Army on the Eastern Front, taking with him, as Chief of Staff, his close associate General Ludendorff. Their successes in stemming the Russian advances had contributed greatly to their joint reputation and, when von Falkenhayn was found wanting, only this pair were considered as a replacement.

Their appointment began with a small problem of protocol. When they came west, von Hindenburg was appointed Chief of the Imperial

General Staff and Ludendorff was offered the title of Second Chief of the Imperial General Staff. Ludendorff declined this title, saying that he was second to nobody – and promptly invented the title of First Quartermaster-General. Ludendorff was always an outsider among the Prussian officer corps and may therefore have needed to clarify his position.

Just to begin with, he was not a 'von', and was completely without aristocratic connections. He came from a family of merchants and rose to high command partly on ability and partly by catching the eye of the Kaiser. He had shown considerable expertise in various staff appointments and had drawn praise from both von Schlieffen and the younger Moltke, who had appointed him Chief of the Operations Section at General Staff Headquarters before the outbreak of war. After the outbreak, Ludendorff had obtained a field command and had proved his ability in action by besieging and taking the Belgian city of Liège.

Whatever his title, Ludendorff was effectively von Hindenburg's Chief-of-Staff, an appointment that, as von Knobelsdorf had demonstrated, offered considerable scope for men of determination and ability in the German Army. This was not a subservient position. Von Hindenburg recognized his colleague's capacity for hard work and his intellectual abilities and knew that Ludendorff was a devoted advocate of the attack. 'The offensive is the most effective means of making war; the attack alone is decisive,' he wrote. 'History proves it; it is the symbol of authority.' The two men had proved this doctrine in the mobile warfare of the Eastern Front; now they were appointed to command on the Western Front, where they would find conditions very different.

Von Hindenburg and Ludendorff had not seen the Western Front since 1914; since Tannenburg, they had been fully occupied in the east, where advances or retreats of hundreds of miles were not uncommon, and it is fair to say that their first sight of the Western Front, *circa* 1916, horrified them. They would have closed down the Verdun fighting immediately and concentrated on the Somme battle but they had counted without the aggression of General Nivelle, who was still determined to push the Germans back. In doing so, he offered the German generals a chance to kill more French soldiers and the fact that this would also kill more German soldiers was somehow overlooked; the French were still attacking and the German artillery was killing them in quantity.

On the French side of the line, Pétain was finding it increasingly impossible to restrain Nivelle and Mangin. They persisted in mounting attacks against the German line, with the result that the number of French casualties soon moved ahead of the German total. Attrition, once the aim only of von Falkenhayn, was spreading like a virus among the commanders, and the infection gradually spread to Pétain. From the end of August and throughout September, he began to bring up guns from all over the French front, preparing for a major counter-offensive in October, an all-out attack supported by an overwhelming amount of artillery, and one that would drive the Germans back to their original positions. While that devastating onslaught was being prepared, the fighting on the Somme continued.

A new phase of the campaign of the Battle of the Somme began on 14 July with the Battle of Bazentin, when General Rawlinson put in an attack against the German second line at Longueval–Delville Wood, using four divisions from the two right-flank Corps, the 3rd and 9th (Scottish) from XIII Corps and the 7th and 21st from XV Corps . . . and attacked at night.

In the Second World War and in many subsequent wars, right down to the Falklands War of 1982, major attacks have frequently been mounted at night. Many attacks – Arnhem and Walcheren in 1944, for example – were launched in daylight, but night attacks were by no means uncommon and were not actually new, even in 1916. Garnet Wolseley had attacked the Egyptian positions at Tel-el-Kebir by night in 1882, but night attacks usually involved small forces and needed careful planning; night attacks on a large scale were known to be difficult. On the other hand, night attacks provided concealment for both the final preparations and the opening phases of an attack and daylight for the reorganization phase and, from 1916, for any available air support to help beat off counterattacks. The Great War had not yet seen any major night attacks, so Rawlinson's decision to launch a night attack on 14 July, only two weeks after the opening débâcle, introduced a useful tactical innovation to British attacks on the Western Front and was therefore widely regarded as extremely risky.

The main reason for previously denying attacking troops the concealment of darkness, or the daylight protection of smoke, was the ongoing problem of communications. In their previous battles, the British had preferred to attack at dawn, using darkness to cover the final movement of troops, while the French preferred to attack in mid-morning, being prepared to sacrifice the cover of darkness for the benefits of daylight observation. These preferences are understandable but both had proved costly and Rawlinson believed that the cover of night was essential for his attack on 14 July.

The prime reason for this decision was tactical and related to the ground. Even after working their way forward on to the higher ground at Contalmaison and north of Mametz Wood, Rawlinson's men still had around one mile of open ground to cover before reaching the German second line at Longueval. It was abundantly clear that there was no way the infantry could cross that ground in daylight. But a night attack, if not exactly revolutionary, was still fraught with difficulties in 1916.

The first problem lay in guiding tens of thousands of laden men up to the assault position, or start line, without detection by the enemy and Haig, for one, felt that this difficulty was insurmountable. The men would go forward and get lost, one thing would lead to another, chaos would reign and dawn would find the four assault divisions blundering about in the open, fully exposed to the waiting German machine-guns. Rawlinson, on the other hand, felt that the staff work of the assault divisions was fully up to the task and, as was usual in these circumstances, Haig let him go ahead.

Rawlinson's preparations received their first setback on 8 July, when Foch informed him that the French XX Corps on his right would not support this attack, as previously promised. Rawlinson's views are not recorded but he did not let this rebuff deter him and, on 11 July, he presented his plan to General Haig. One advantage of a night attack was surprise; if his divisions had that, then the absence of the French on their flank would not be too serious.

Four divisions, mustering some 22,000 men, would make a night advance, uphill, to a start line within striking distance of the German trenches on a narrow front, between Bazentin-le-Petit, Longueval and Delville Wood. The present front line was not straight, so the extent of the advance would vary from division to division, from more than 1,300 yards to less than 550 yards, but when all the troops were on the start line their battalions would be between 330 and 550 yards of the German line.

Rawlinson had also decided to use surprise in his artillery preparation. At 0324, about an hour before dawn, the German line would be blasted by a 'hurricane' bombardment from 1,000 guns, as at Verdun, but much shorter. This bombardment would last just five minutes and then the troops would go in, full tilt. Since this bombardment fell on a very narrow front of some two miles, the concentration of fire was devastating.

Rawlinson's night attack on 14 July displayed a number of tactical innovations and some sensible tactics, at least in Western Front terms. The wire was well cut and, when the attack went in, the troops entered the German line without undue difficulty; such was the speed of their advance that the enemy barrage fell behind them, in No Man's Land. The advance continued for some hours, the troops mopping up the enemy support and reserve trenches and dugouts as they went forward and, by 1100 hrs, the leading elements were on the edge of Delville Wood and the ruins of Longueval, having made contact with Maxse's 18th Division on their right. They had also obtained a position on the Pozières ridge and had expanded their front to 6,000 yards . . . a great achievement in this battle and a stepping stone for further advances.

Then matters began to go awry. German resistance stiffened and reserves failed to come up swiftly or in adequate quantity, not least because the enemy artillery was now concentrating on the approach routes. The gradual slowing down of the advance had resulted in failure to take High Wood, a vital piece of ground on the outskirts of Longueval. High Wood might have been taken on 14 July and the 2nd Indian Cavalry Division had been tasked to come forward at speed and take it but, to keep this division out of the initial battle and away from shellfire, it had been held back at Morlancourt, four miles south of Albert.

This was well behind the front line and, when the cavalry was finally ordered forward, it swiftly became tangled in the heavy traffic heading to the front and slowed by the shell-torn ground and the wounded coming to the rear. It was not until the early afternoon that the cavalry shook itself free of all this and began to canter up towards High Wood and not until early evening that it was in position to attack. By that time the wood was firmly in German hands and machine-gun fire swiftly emptied saddles and brought the cavalry's advance to a halt.

The 14 July night attack, so well planned and executed, therefore petered out. The fighting for Delville Wood, High Wood and Longueval went on for weeks before these positions finally fell, and the process of taking them ate up thousands of lives. This set the pattern for the summer fighting, a grinding process that consumed men for every yard of ground taken. The South African Brigade earned great glory at terrible cost in Delville Wood while High Wood became a byword for slaughter, its capture costing the lives of more than 6,000 men.

On 23 July the newly arrived 1st and 2nd Australian Divisions, which had shown their mettle at Gallipoli and had come to join Gough's army, opened their war on the Western Front with an attack on Pozières. This attack replicated parts of Rawlinson's recent tactics, in that the infantry worked its way to within about 200 yards of the German line before the assault, and took the German position within minutes. Then, as elsewhere, the breach was closed off and the battering process began again, eating up lives. So it went on throughout August and into early September. Then, on 15 September 1916, the war saw yet another innovation when the British, still seeking a breakthrough, employed tanks at the Battle of Flers-Courcelette.

Notes

1 *Official History*, 1916, vol. 5, p. 484.
2 Letter to the Duke of Connaught, quoted in French, *British Strategy and War Aims*, p. 210.

13

The Autumn Battles – Verdun and the Somme

September–November 1916

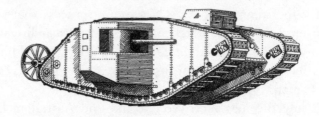

The opportunity for success on the Somme rapidly
passed. The battle . . . became a ding-dong struggle of
attrition, in spite of the experience gained on July 1 and
duly applied. General Joffre, in this respect at any rate,
had got his way.'
Official History, 1916, vol. 5, p. 493

The story of the tank begins in 1914. How this new weapon was
developed illustrates the fact that the problems confronting the
generals on the Western Front were not unappreciated, at least by the
more inventive minds, even in the first days of the war. Since the basic
elements of track, armour plate and internal combustion engine
already existed, the tank was assembled rather than invented, but
credit for the idea of a tracked armoured fighting vehicle, or AFV, can
be given to Lt-Colonel E.D. Swinton, an officer of the Royal

Engineers, in September 1914, barely a month into the war.

Although a serving officer, Swinton had been sent to the Western Front as an official war correspondent. He covered the latter stages of the retreat from Mons and stayed on after the battle of the Marne to see the creation of that 400-mile long defence line, composed of wire, dugouts, machine-guns and artillery, that came to be the Western Front. This line clearly created problems for any attacking troops and thinking on how it might be breached led Swinton to rough out some ideas for a tracked armoured vehicle based on an existing agricultural machine, the Holt Caterpillar Tractor. This in itself was a departure, for current military opinion still averred that the Western Front could be breached by conventional means – artillery, infantry, cavalry, used in the correct combination. While the commanders were trying to find that combination in 1915, the development of the tank continued.

Knowing that any practical development would need finance and official backing, Swinton sent his idea to Lt-Colonel Sir Maurice Hankey, then Secretary to the War Council, a man with access to the powers-that-be. Hankey read Swinton's outline and added some further elaboration to overcome some of the more obvious objections; one of these was Swinton's estimate that to develop these machines would take up to a year . . . and surely the war could not possibly last that long?

On Christmas Day 1914, Hankey wrote a memorandum to the Prime Minister, Herbert Asquith, which began by explaining the course of events on the Western Front, where the First Battle of Ypres had just ended. Hankey was a Royal Marines officer and he laid out his memorandum in military terms, describing the ground and the defences and stating plainly that in this situation the Allies were left with only two choices: to go round the Western Front defences, or to go through them.

A year later, at the end of 1915, both of these methods had been tried. The outflanking choice had led to Gallipoli, while numerous attempts to break through the defences of the Western Front with infantry and artillery had endowed northern France with a quantity of graveyards. Even so, it was now abundantly clear that the decisive battlefield in this war lay on the Western Front and that that front had somehow to be broken. To do that, said Hankey, the armies needed an Armoured Fighting Vehicle – the tank.

Swinton and Hankey suggested the tasks an armoured fighting vehicle must perform but the credit for developing the basic idea into what became the first tank must go to Winston Churchill, then First Lord of the Admiralty. The name 'tank' was chosen for security reasons: when the first, shrouded models of the AFV were taken about Britain under tarpaulins, curious observers were told that they were simply 'water tanks' and the name stuck. Churchill saw Hankey's memorandum and gave the project his full support. Thus, in the early days of 1915, when the first tank prototypes were under development, they were simply troop-carrying vehicles known as 'landships' and were funded by the Admiralty under its 'Landships' Committee.

However, after the failure of the Dardanelles expedition Churchill was obliged to resign from the Admiralty and AFV development might have collapsed had the project not been taken up in the middle of 1915 by the new Minister of Munitions, David Lloyd George. In the meantime the AFV idea had been developed on lines originally proposed by Swinton: a petrol-engined, armoured tractor, armed with machine-guns and some two-pounder guns, capable of crossing muddy, shell-pitted ground and breaking through barbed-wire entanglements.

Swinton produced his design in June 1915. A Joint Committee was formed later that month, responsibility for this new weapon was handed over to the Department of the Master General of the Ordnance and from then on its development speeded up considerably. A full-sized working prototype, called 'Tritton', was ordered and later christened 'Little Willie'. Little Willie was born in August 1915 but by the time it crawled into the open a month later it had grown considerably and was renamed 'Big Willie'.[1] Big Willie continued to grow throughout the winter of 1915–16.

When Big Willie was finally shown to the Government ministers and senior Army officers on the trial grounds at Hatfield in February 1916, the embryo had become a formidable machine, 31ft long, 8ft high, 13ft wide and weighing 28 tons, carrying a crew of eight – in considerable discomfort – and machine-guns or a six-pounder gun, mounted on sponsons between the body-embracing tracks. When fully manned and loaded, Big Willie could manage a top speed of two miles per hour and could cross a wide range of obstacles, including muddy fields and wide trenches, at least in the peaceful fields of England.

Reactions to this new marvel varied. Colonel Swinton was entranced and suggested that the Army should order 3,000 of them at once. Lord Kitchener, the Secretary of State for War, was rather less impressed and suggested that 40 might do to start with. In the event, just 150 of these Mark 1 vehicles were ordered and put into production at Lincoln. This decision was made on 11 February 1916 and production of the first batch of Mark 1 machines began at once.

The advent of the tank on the battlefield could not now be long delayed but there was still much to do before it could make its debut. The machines had to be built, spare parts ordered and organized, servicing manuals written, men trained to man, fight and maintain these vehicles, and a whole new range of military textbooks prepared, explaining how this new weapon was to be used and where it fitted into the British Army's scale of equipment and battle plans.

Designing and producing a new weapon of war is only part of the exercise. A weapon, however revolutionary, does not exist on its own. It has to slot in with existing weapons, methods and formations and these formations – infantry, cavalry, artillery – have to know exactly what this weapon can and cannot do. In peacetime, this work normally takes place at special schools or on the annual all-arms manoeuvres, but the tank appeared in the middle of a major war and many of the steps in its tactical development were inhibited by the need to keep its existence secret. The tank could not be allowed out for field trials with UK-based divisions, or taken on manoeuvres where a number of mechanical and operational drawbacks would have become apparent. As far as the tank was concerned, all was theory until the tanks went into battle.

This fact was appreciated and, as a first step towards the development of a tank doctrine, Lt-Colonel Swinton was appointed to set up and train the infant tank force. As part of this task, many field commanders, brigadier-generals and above, currently serving in France, were brought back to Britain, sworn to secrecy, shown the new weapon and invited to comment. Their reaction was very positive indeed; within weeks the generals were agitating for the speedy construction of a quantity of tanks and their equally speedy introduction to the battlefields of France.

Swinton was determined to resist this pressure for fast deployment. Quite apart from the day-to-day work of developing and testing the tanks and training men in how to drive and fight in them, Swinton was busy developing a series of 'Tactical Notes', outlining his thoughts about the weapon and how it should be used. Considering that the tank had been first proposed as a means of supporting the infantry, it is strange but encouraging that Swinton's first and main proposal was that the tanks should not be tied to the infantry at all.

In the fullness of time Swinton's proposal would prove all too correct, as the German blitzkrieg tactics of the Second World War were to demonstrate, but Swinton's ideas were over-ruled in 1916, not least by the fact that the first tank was simply too slow and cumbersome for use in the 'armoured cavalry' role he envisaged. These arguments over deployment and role were not academic; they affected every aspect of tank development and had to start with a decision on what sort of weapon the tank actually *was*. Was it simply an armoured, mobile gun, capable of keeping up with the infantry as they moved across country and helping them through the enemy wire, or was it really something new, armoured cavalry, capable of breaking the opposing defences wide open, or exploiting the breach made by artillery and infantry and, by its mobility, restoring open warfare to the battlefield? Depending on the view taken and the answer arrived at, everything about the tank, its size, speed, armour, manning, deployment and tactical role, would be dictated, and so the machine would be developed.

At this time no thought had been given to the question of co-operation between tanks and infantry for mutual support and defence, though this too would be difficult until the infantry had a battlefield radio or the tank had a telephone. The need for such co-operation would soon become apparent on the battlefield as the enemy developed ways to cope with this new weapon – and would eventually require the creation of another new arm, lorried and later armoured infantry, carried in vehicles like the modern Warrior personnel carrier and trained to fight alongside tanks.

At the time the tank was seen purely as an 'infantry support' weapon, designed to cope with the defences of the Western Front, and it was in that role that the first tanks – manned by the Heavy Section of the Machine Gun Corps – advanced across the fields of Picardy to open the Battle of Flers-Courcelette, just before dawn on 15 September 1916.

The decision to employ tanks at the Battle of Flers-Courcelette has caused considerable controversy in military circles down the years and is often cited by his critics as the prime example of General Haig's stupidity. According to the tank 'experts' of 1916 – notably the military pundit, Major-General Fuller and his disciples – tanks should not have been employed at all at this time because there were not enough of them and the ground was unsuitable. Fuller maintained that the tanks should have been kept back, in secret, until they were available in quantity and then launched at the enemy in a surprise attack over good ground. Then they would have achieved that long-sought-after breakthrough, with all the benefits that would follow.

This is a persuasive argument – if one chooses to take the popular route chosen by so many historians and consider the particular situation out of context. In the context of the military situation on the Somme front in September 1916, Haig's decision to use the tanks at Flers is at least arguable, and probably correct.

First of all, there were no tank 'experts' in 1916. Fuller's claims were all theory. The tank was an experimental weapon, one that had never been tested in war. Lacking any chance to test it on field trials, it made good sense to employ it at Flers and see if all the claims made for it were true, before committing scarce productive capacity to the production of more machines and diverting officers and men to the creation of a new military arm. Indeed, in their 1919 history of the Tank Corps, the authors refer to the Battle of Flers-Courcelette as 'essentially experimental'.[2]

As for the point about the ground being 'unsuitable', if the ground had been firm and dry, free from mud and shell holes, even wheeled vehicles could have made their way forward – armoured cars had been employed on the Western Front in 1914 and had been dispensed with because they were restricted to roads or firm ground. One of the great advantages claimed for the tank was that, as a tracked vehicle, it could make its way over shell-pitted, muddy ground – and if it could not do that, what use was it?

Finally, on the question of surprise, the tank was already in France by the summer of 1916 and by September winter was coming on. If the tanks were not employed at Flers in mid-September, they could probably not be employed before the spring of 1917 and the secret could certainly not be kept that long. Such practical points apart, it is necessary to put the Flers battle in the wider context of the Somme campaign. The decision to commit the tanks at Flers-Courcelette was a matter of judgement and to take a view of that judgement it is necessary to consider the context in which the decision was taken.

By mid-September 1916, the Battle of the Somme had been going on for two and a half months. Gains had been negligible, losses horrendous and the infantry could make little progress over muddy ground, laced with barbed wire and covered by artillery and machine-guns. Now there was this new and wonderful weapon, the tank, which, it was claimed, could defy mud and shell-torn ground, silence machine-guns and field artillery and crush down wire . . . the perfect answer to the continual problem of helping the infantry through the wire.

Haig has been soundly criticized for incompetence in using the tanks at Flers but consider what would have been said if he had failed to use them at Flers to help his infantry get ahead, and this attack had ended in bloody failure like so many others? Then that other popular accusation made against Haig, that he was callous about casualties, would have had fresh fodder to feed on. On the issue of using tanks at Flers, Haig was damned if he did and damned if he did not.

Even taking the long view, the tank was still an experimental weapon and it made good sense to try it out in battle – the only place where the effectiveness or failure of a new weapon will be fully revealed – and find out there if all the claims of its supporters were true.

Matters had not been quiet on the Somme battlefield since Rawlinson's night attack in July, two months before Flers. The fighting had been continuous, though the front line itself had barely moved. From the south, Fourth Army front now ran from its junction with the French just west of Combles, past the north side of Delville Wood and on to the Albert–Bapaume road, where Gough's Fifth, or Reserve, Army was engaged. The village of Flers lay 1,650 yards east of Delville Wood on the right-hand side of the road and on the left-hand side, but 880 yards from it, lay the village of Courcelette. The distance between the two villages of Flers and Courcelette was about four miles and this was the front of attack, on the axis of the Bapaume road, between these two villages and across the flat and open ground behind the Pozières ridge.

The attacking force was given a number of objectives or 'lines' – Green, Brown, Blue and Red – the last of which, the Red Line, included the villages of Gueudecourt and Morval. If these could be taken, then Flers and Courcelette would end up well inside the British lines, after an advance of some two and a half miles on a four-mile front. The attack began at 0620 hrs on the morning of 15 September and employed all the painfully learned lessons of the last two and a half months, plus a small number of tanks.

As in July, Rawlinson's staff work was impeccable. To prevent this attack petering out in stalemate, Rawlinson took care to ensure that his reserves could get forward, allocating certain roads behind the front line for their exclusive use. Other roads were reserved for ambulances coming back with the wounded or field artillery moving forward. Sappers and pioneers were detailed for road repair work and for filling in shell craters, and to help the tanks beat the mud, certain areas of No Man's Land and the enemy line were left unshelled to prevent the craters causing problems.

More guns were employed, always more guns; in the case of Flers-Courcelette, one heavy gun for every 30 yards of front and one field gun for every 10 yards, twice as many as on 1 July. Moreover, these guns were manned by skilled, experienced gunners, well able to handle creeping barrages and counter-battery fire and keeping in constant contact with observers of the RFC flying above the battlefield. The British Army was learning how to fight the 'all-arms' battle by this stage of the war; no longer would the brunt be left to the infantry. Before the assault, the enemy line was subjected to three days of bombardment from half a million shells, gas and shrapnel as well as high explosive. Four full corps would take part in this battle, III Corps, XIV Corps, XV

Corps from Rawlinson's Fourth Army, plus the Canadian Corps from Gough's Fifth Army, which was charged with taking Courcelette. The infantry of these corps would be supported by the 40-plus tanks that finally made it to the battlefield – accounts vary on how many actually crossed the start line. The tanks operated in 'penny packets', with just one or two machines attached to each of the assault battalions – another cause of later complaint from tank 'experts'.

The Battle of Flers-Courcelette was a considerable if limited success. Those tanks that made it to the start line proved useful but the various inadequacies of the Mark 1, particularly a lack of engine power and thin armour, soon became all too evident to the tank crews – and that vital need for tank and infantry co-operation had not been realized by anyone at that time.

At the Battle of Flers-Courcelette, 49 tanks were committed and 32 made it to the start line. Of that number, nine broke down with mechanical failure, five sank in the mud, ran into tree stumps or otherwise 'ditched', nine fell behind the infantry they were tasked to support but did some good work, and nine went ahead of the infantry and caused alarm and despondency among the enemy. For a first attempt it was a good effort and it became clear that when the operational snags had been overcome, the British had a weapon that, in time, could break the Western Front wide open. During that waiting time, traditional methods still applied.

Even so, the first sight of these terrible machines, lumbering towards their positions, took the Germans completely unawares and, for a time at least, caused considerable panic. The famous communiqué that 'A tank is walking up the high street of Flers with the British Army cheering behind it' was an exaggeration, but the spirit it captures is not far from the truth. At Flers the war appeared, briefly, to be moving again. High Wood fell, Flers was taken, Martinpuich was in British hands, the Canadians had Courcelette. By the end of the day 6,600 yards of the German first line and 4,400 yards of the second line were in British hands – taken and held.

The new-fangled tanks had been in action and had proved their worth. Yes, the present machines were under-powered, too thinly armoured, needed better weapons and some kind of infantry support;

there should also have been more of them; but from then on tanks were to play a growing part in the Western Front battles, and before long British troops were reluctant to go into an attack without them. In all the odium the British generals have attracted, it should be noticed that it was the British, not the French or the Germans, who created the tank and brought it into action and in so doing changed the face of war.

The advent of the tank did not, unfortunately, do a great deal to help further movement on the Somme front or reduce the rising number of casualties. Moreover, the attack at Flers quickly stalled, not least because the French Sixth Army, on Rawlinson's right, could make no progress at all, failed to take the important village of Combles and called off its attack on the evening of 15 September. Although the fighting continued in the autumn rain, there was now a brief pause before another major attack went in – a pause in which this story can return to Verdun.

Imagery is important to the chronicler of Verdun, for the reality is hard to grasp at a distance. The battle at Verdun can best be imagined as some monstrous ball game, in which two teams of giants push a boulder to and fro across impossible terrain. For months the Germans had pushed the French south, towards Verdun; now the French were pushing the Germans back to the north, towards their start-line positions of 21 February. The entry fee in this contest for a worthless piece of terrain was a great number of lives.

Nivelle's star was in the ascendant, and soaring. In mid-September, President Poincaré arrived in Verdun to present the municipality with a range of awards and decorations, including a Military Cross from Britain and the French Croix de Guerre. This event might have signalled the formal end of the battle but Nivelle and Mangin had other plans; they still wanted to retake Fort Douaumont and were preparing their forces for another push up the right bank of the Meuse. The aim of Nivelle, Mangin, and indeed Pétain, was now to retake the ground lost between February and July, in effect to replay those disastrous months but in the other direction.

Pétain had been sucked into the planning for this offensive and, during September and October, he prepared for a set-piece battle: no instant, responsive onslaught, but a carefully planned offensive using eight divisions and more than 600 guns, of which more than half were heavy howitzers, including two Schneider-Creusot railway mounted guns of 400 mm calibre to shatter the carapaces of the German-occupied forts.

Once again the key factor was artillery. The French gunners had also been carefully trained in laying down a creeping barrage ahead of the infantry, while the three infantry divisions tasked to make the first attack were trained in their work on a specially constructed replica of the Verdun battlefield laid out near Bar-le-Duc. The French and German guns had never stopped shelling but from mid-September the weight of shot coming from the French side increased day by day. This barrage, helped by incessant autumn rains, soon reduced the German trenches to muddy ditches, while the old, battered *Stollen* of the previous winter gradually filled with water.

Nivelle aimed to support the infantry attack with a massive creeping barrage following a concentrated bombardment in the hours before the infantry went in, and the usual heavy artillery fire in the time before that. Preparations went on for a month, during which more than a quarter of a million shells fell on ·this section of the Verdun front and many of the German batteries were silenced by the weight of shot falling on their positions. This bombardment culminated on 23 October, when 400 mm shells landed on Fort Douaumont, crashing through to destroy a number of casemates and set fire to stores and ammunition. As a result, fearing an explosion, most of the German garrison withdrew from the fort on the night of 23 October, leaving behind a single platoon which was still inside the fort when the French infantry attacked on the following day.

Thick mist aided the attackers and Fort Douaumont, ·which had been fought over for eight months, fell in four hours. The attack on 24 October was a triumph; on that day alone Mangin's troops, inevitably spearheading the advance, advanced for more than two miles, a victory celebrated as the greatest French triumph since the Battle of the Marne. Their nerves shattered by six days of shellfire, weakened by six days without food – no ration carriers could get forward through that daily blizzard of steel – the German troops fell back, hesitated, and then took to their heels. With the fort, the French recaptured the village of Douaumont – or the few piles of bricks where that village had once stood – and most of the ground taken by the German Fifth Army since February. This victory did not, however, end the battle. Nivelle and Mangin now had their eyes on Fort Vaux, which was abandoned by the Germans on 2 November and occupied by the French later that day.

The final action of the Verdun battle took place on 15 December, when Mangin's men attacked yet again on a six-mile front on the right bank, around Louvemont and Bezonvaux, pushing on for two and a half miles north of Fort Douaumont and capturing a large number of field guns the Germans were unable to extricate from the mud and more than 10,000 prisoners – another clear victory for the French and one acknowledged as such by the Germans.

'I now know for the first time what it is to lose a battle,' wrote Crown Prince Wilhelm in his memoirs. 'Doubts as to my own competence, self-commiseration, bitter feelings, unjust censures, passed in quick succession through my mind and lay like a heavy burden on my soul, and I am not ashamed to confess it was some time before I recovered my mental stability and my firm confidence in ultimate victory.'

These counter-offensives since October cost the French Army another 47,000 men but, for the moment at least, none of that mattered. Victory can excuse a multitude of casualties and with Douaumont and Vaux recaptured and the Germans driven back to the positions of February, who could deny that the Battle of Verdun had ended in victory for the French? France rejoiced and her citizens allowed themselves to believe that more victories must surely follow.

The credit for this victory went to General Robert Nivelle. Back in March, he had declared that he 'had the formula' and it now appeared that he had indeed worked out a way to drive the Germans back, even from their most strongly held positions, and without the need of tanks. His reputation soared yet again and, when the time came to find a new Commander-in-Chief for the French Armies, other contenders, like Pétain, were soon overlooked. While the French rejoiced at their autumn successes and united in their praise of Robert Nivelle, the

British generals and their forces on the Somme were slowly sinking into the autumn mud.

At the end of September, while Nivelle was preparing for the fresh assault at Verdun, Rawlinson's line lay astride Flers, with the Fifth/Reserve Army line taking in Courcelette on the left and the French Sixth Army on his right. Joffre pressed Haig to keep attacking, hinting yet again that the British were not pulling their weight, though in July and August alone the British had lost 190,000 men on the Somme, compared to 80,000 French, the first day accounting for much of this total on the British side.

Even so, fresh attacks were ordered but Rawlinson decided that, before he sent his infantry forward again in mid-September, the enemy position should receive a further pounding from his artillery. The eight days after Flers-Courcelette saw a continuation of the offensive, a mixture of artillery bombardments and infantry attacks, with no help from the tanks, but when this attack was called off on 23 September, the British troops had not moved far from the positions they had reached by the evening of 15 September.

More battering followed and, by the end of the month, the British had driven a salient into the German line up the Bapaume road and now lay before the village of Le Sars, close to the prehistoric burial mound of the Butte de Warlencourt; casualties in the fighting on 23–26 September alone exceeded 8,000 men. The Butte de Warlencourt was as far as the British armies were to get but two more months of severe fighting, much of it on the left flank, lay ahead before the Battle of the Somme ended . . . or, more exactly, was called off. In all but killing terms, the battle ended in the last days of September and the main reason it ended was mud.

The veterans of the Somme have gone now but while they lived they talked incessantly of the mud of the Somme, mud which permeated everything, clogged rifles, flowed like lava into dugouts and trenches, sucked off boots, drowned wounded men and horses and made movement either impossible or a tremendous physical effort. To fight on the Somme was bad enough; to also fight the mud of the Somme was simply too much.

The failure of these recent attacks, following the wonderful success

– at least in Western Front terms – of the 15 September attack, was a considerable disappointment. The fighting went on all along the Somme front in October and November and into December but now it was a new kind of fighting. Haig was still launching attacks, and still talking of a breakthrough, but the aim of the Somme battle was no longer an attempt at a breakthrough to Bapaume but an attempt to write down the strength of the German field army and kill German soldiers – in other words, attrition.

The Battle of Flers-Courcelette was Haig's last effective attack in 1916 and it was at some time shortly after this point, in early October 1916, that the nature of the battle changed. This was partly due to the weather. Autumn had arrived and with it the rains, turning the battle-field into a quagmire. Haig, Rawlinson and Gough must have known that the campaigning season, and the term was still apposite in 1916, was effectively over, but still the battle continued. Flers-Courcelette was followed by the Battle of Morval, which began on 25 September and lasted three days until the evening of 28 September. It was followed by the Battle of the Transloy Ridges in the first half of October, a constant series of attacks, in ever-worsening weather. The territorial gains in these repeated attacks were at best minimal, yet even while they were going on, Haig was in conference with Rawlinson and Gough, discussing plans for an attack in November, aimed at the city of Cambrai, which lay twenty miles behind the German lines.

One can only wonder if the generals were serious . . . or mad. In all but slaughter, the Battle of the Somme was over by early October, and to continue past that point was madness indeed, but this side of Haig's character, his stubbornness combined with a seemingly incurable optimism, is one that even his supporters find difficult to defend: an inability to realize that the law of diminishing returns applied on the battlefield. It was a character flaw rather than a professional one, and stems from the fact that behind Haig's Lowland Scots façade lay an optimist. On the Somme in the autumn of 1916, and at Passchendaele a year later, Haig persisted in attacks beyond the point of reasoned calculation, attacks that drove up the casualty figures for no useful gain . . . except to drive up the casualty figures on the other side – and the word for this kind of action is attrition.

This accusation has to be qualified by the admission that it can be equally fatal to break off an attack too soon. At First Ypres in 1914, when Haig was commanding I Corps, the British were saved from defeat when the Germans broke off their attack just at the point where they might have brushed Haig's depleted corps aside and pushed on into Ypres. The decision on when to break off an attack, like the decision to launch it, is one requiring careful calculation and fine judgement. That said, Haig's judgement in fighting on into the early winter of 1916, when he could have stopped after Flers, is a clear error. At Passchendaele a year later, the matter is more debatable, for had Haig stopped the attacks in October he would have left his soldiers in a swamp, under the eyes and guns of the German defenders on the Passchendaele ridge. On the Somme, his decisions were less inhibited by such factors.

By the onset of winter in 1916, however, the doctrine of attrition had gripped all the armies on the Western Front. When the generals of three competing armies all adopt the same doctrine, it seems reasonable to ask if they were not right to do so, and whether any sensible reasons can be found to support their decision. The short answer is, *none whatsoever* . . . so why did they do it? To answer that question we must go back to the start of the year.

Von Falkenhayn's original, stated intention at Verdun was 'to bleed the French Army to death', and thereby deprive the arch-enemy, Britain, of her principal ally, France. This was a flawed doctrine for a number of reasons but, even had it been valid as a workable intention, the fact remains that, as the casualty figures swiftly illustrated, the Germans lost as many men as the French at Verdun, which rendered the whole affair a particular failure.

Granted, Germany had more men than France but not more than France and the British Empire combined. Germany also had more enemies to fight and needed all her manpower to do so. For the Germans, engaging in a battle of attrition was at best short-sighted, a fact that von Hindenburg and Ludendorff realized as soon as they took over. It might also be argued that the battle at Verdun tore the heart out of the French Army and led to the mutinies of 1917, which is probably true, at least up to a point, but that hardly excuses the other point, that Verdun failed in its declared intention. The collapse of morale in the French Army arose not because of the German attack at Verdun but because the French generals, specifically Nivelle, also adopted the doctrine of attrition, and fought with *cran* and *élan*, instead of intelligence.

One small advantage of a divided high command is that, for a while at least, it prevented the British command subscribing to this dire doctrine. It was during the final phase of the Somme battle that the chill madness that already had overtaken von Falkenhayn, Joffre and Nivelle finally gripped Haig and his army commanders. Put starkly, a breakthrough on the Somme had proved impossible and the tanks were not yet available to force one. The choices before General Haig after Flers were the sensible one – to wait until the tanks were available in sufficient numbers, with improved machines, well-trained crews and suitable tactics, and attack in the spring – or to carry on fighting, replacing the aim of a breakthrough with the aim of writing down the German field army, at whatever cost to the British Army.

Heretofore, whatever their differences over tactics, on the possibilities of a breakthrough, or the merits of 'bite and hold', the British generals had always tried to use their brains as well as the power of their armies, to attack with guile as well as with courage and skill. As the battles of 1915 had demonstrated, none of this went far enough; they were still tinkering with conventional methods, trying to find 'the formula', like Robert Nivelle and, perhaps because they were too close to the problem, failing to realize that conventional methods would not work in an entirely new situation. In many of their attacks courage was more evident than either of the other two assets and, sometime in October 1916, Haig abandoned the notion of a breakthrough on the Somme and joined his peers in France and Germany in committing his soldiers to a battle of attrition.

It can be said in his defence that Haig would gladly have called off all attacks when the October rain turned the Somme into a swamp but that he was urged to continue by Joffre and Foch, who wanted him to join them in a second battle of attrition, both on the Somme and at Verdun, to wear down the front-line divisions of the German field armies on those fronts before the winter forced the armies to break off their attacks. Joffre certainly urged Haig to follow this course of action, pressing the point until there was another small skirmish at Haig's HQ on 19 October, at which Joffre was yet again reminded that the British Armies were not his to command. This may have been a factor, for ultimately Haig usually tried to fall in with Joffre's wishes, but it appears that Haig needed very little urging to continue his offensive. In terms of what he set out to achieve, the Somme battles had been a failure, and something had to be retrieved from the position or heads would probably roll. The fate of Sir John French, who had failed in the previous September at Loos – but had not lost anything like so many men in the process – cannot have passed unnoticed by General Haig in the autumn of 1916.

Haig was a competent general and far from callous but his character had the faults of his virtues. In all his battles, Haig never seems to have appreciated that there came a time when he had obtained or achieved all he could hope for and that to press on would either throw away his success to date or result in terrible losses. This inner conviction was reinforced by Haig's alter ego, Lt-General Gough of the Reserve, or Fifth, Army, the last general to ever suggest calling off an attack, who was commanding a section of the Somme battle and was more than willing to order fresh attacks.

So it was after the Battle of Flers. By the end of September, the British line had driven a large salient into the German position south of the Bapaume road, with its tip near the village of Le Sars at the Butte de Warlencourt. That was as far as Rawlinson's men could go and their losses in getting that far had been appalling. Fourth Army's part in the Battle of the Somme ended here and further attacks were therefore called off. The effort was promptly switched to Gough's forces north of the Albert–Bapaume road and along the Ancre valley, where little gain of any kind had been made since 1 July, in spite of constant attacks and a steady drain in lives.

On 1 October, Gough ordered the Canadian Corps, under the command of Lt-General Sir Julian Byng, to seize a German position, Regina Trench, on the Thiepval ridge, as part of a general push up the Ancre by Fifth Army (as it became on 30 October). The Canadians pressed home their attack with great courage and resolution but, after three weeks of fighting for this one position, they had little to show for it but a casualty list approaching 24,000 men . . . and an abiding suspicion of General Sir Hubert Gough, who they rightly believed had pushed them too far. The next battle, the Battle for the Ancre Heights, went on for a further two weeks, until 11 November, and achieved very little in deteriorating weather.

Two days after it ended, all-out fighting was renewed, this time on the north bank of the Ancre, with another attack which lasted until 19 November – the Battle of Ancre – and this battle finally brought the Battle of the Somme to an end. On 12 November, Haig had told Gough that this attack need not proceed if the cost was likely to be high but losses did not deter General Gough. On the evening of 14 November he ordered his army to prepare for a further push on the Ancre but, when a copy of this order reached Haig, then attending another Inter-Allied Conference in Paris, the Commander-in-Chief ordered Gough to wait until he returned. Gough did not wait: the attack against Beaucourt duly went in and the village was taken . . . in ruins and four months after its proposed capture on 1 July.

Gough asked Haig to let him push on and clear the rest of the Ancre valley and Haig reluctantly agreed. This attack, the last of the Somme battle, went in on 18 November, when the British line was finally established at Beaumont-Hamel, another of the objectives for 1 July. These successive attacks on the Ancre in October and November were simply re-runs of the battles that took place here in the first days of July; they even had the same objectives: Beaumont-Hamel, the Hawthorn Redoubt, Grandcourt, Thiepval. The weather was atrocious, the mud almost bottomless, the suffering of the men almost beyond endurance, the losses almost beyond computation. The cost of Gough's recent advance was the addition of another 23,274 names to the casualty list – appalling, but a drop in the ocean of blood that had been shed on these fields in the last four months . . . and all for nothing.

No tactical or strategic gain was made on the Somme front that was worth the cost in lives. Even had the British and French achieved their breakthrough on the Somme, the Germans had plenty of room to manoeuvre and, unlike the French at Verdun, no national interest in staying where they were. During the winter of 1916–17 the Germans simply withdrew to the Hindenburg Line, east of the Somme battlefield, and it all had to be done again. The battles at Verdun and the Somme, planned with such care and promising such gains, had in the end achieved only one thing: like the battles of 1914 and 1915, they had killed a great number of soldiers. Some historians have claimed that these battles, especially the Somme, also destroyed the fighting strength of the German field army, not least by killing so many German NCOs – but even if that were true, the losses on the Allied side were equally terrible.

Total casualties on the Somme, killed, wounded and missing, come to some 1,300,000 men, British, French and German. The British share in this total includes the losses incurred by the Empire and Commonwealth troops, from Australia, Canada, India, South Africa and New Zealand, and amounts to some 400,000 men. The French lost 200,000 men on the Somme, to add to the more serious losses of Verdun. German losses on the Somme came to more than 600,000 men, killed, wounded and missing – though most of the 'missing' were in fact killed. In other words, the overall German losses on the Somme alone equal those of the combined British and French losses; rarely has the declared aim of attrition been so clearly refuted. As for Verdun, while the estimates vary, the most widely accepted figure is 377,231 French and 337,000 German – a total of more than 700,000 men.

It has been said that while the death of one man is a tragedy, the death of a million men is a statistic. It is true that recounting month after month of shellfire, infantry attacks, gas attack, chaos and confusion, of battles where millions of men fight it out and shed their lives for a few yards of muddy ground, is a process that eventually begins to numb the senses. Surely, comes the thought, there must have been a better way to manage things than this.

Notes

1 Colonel Cave of the Western Front Association tells me that Big Willie was also known as HMLS (His Majesty's Land Ship) *Centipede*.
2 *The Tank Corps*, Major Clough Williams Ellis and A. Williams Ellis, London, 1919.

14

Recriminations December 1916

'1916 would, in a rational world, have been a good year to
have ended the war, along the lines of exhaustion.'
Alistair Horne, Preface, *Verdun: The Price of Glory*

On 15 November 1916, even before the Western Front campaigns
of that disastrous year finally ended, General Joffre and General
Haig met again at Chantilly to discuss their plans for 1917. On that
day, Nivelle's army retook the shattered villages of Louvemont and
Bezonvaux, thereby moving the French front line back to well north
of Verdun and putting Fort Douaumont more than two miles inside
the French lines. On the Somme front, the British were still
battering their way up the Ancre valley or were firmly stuck in the
mud before the Butte de Warlencourt. Over the next few weeks, as
the barrage faded from the offensive's all-out, shattering roar to the
usual daily muttering of the guns, the most general reaction was
relief.

Verdun was safe, a victory of sorts could be claimed on the Somme;
so at the end of a year that had begun with such high hopes and come

so close to catastrophe, it seemed that everything had finally worked out well. Only when the pressure eased on the battle fronts did the nations have time to look around, count the cost, and find people to blame. Among those singled out for particular criticism were General Joffre and General Haig and if either man assumed that he would be allowed to carry on as before after the Somme and Verdun, the events of the next few weeks would swiftly disabuse him. For 1916 had been a disaster and heads must roll.

Comparing Great War casualty figures is never easy, for the opposing armies calculated their losses on a different basis. For example, German casualty returns did not include the less seriously wounded who were treated in their corps area. All British wounded were included in the casualty returns, even if they were treated in a regimental aid post (RAP) or at dressing stations and then returned to duty. This factor tended to increase the total of British casualties, which were dreadful enough.

By any calculation, the human cost of the eight-month battle at Verdun was close to 700,000 men and the Battle of the Somme cost even more. The Entente generals tried to excuse the death toll by editing their original intentions and by declaring that their entire aim had been to wear out the enemy forces, not to gain ground or achieve a breakthrough. In the case of the French generals, their declared aim was to defend Verdun and since Verdun had not fallen they could, for a brief while, claim a victory. Sir Douglas Haig had rather less excuse; he got round the problem by altering the objectives of the campaign.

On 23 December 1916, for example, General Sir Douglas Haig wrote his official despatch on the Somme battle. This despatch appeared in the *London Gazette* on 29 December and provides an interesting postscript to the year. The first point to note is the name Haig gives to what, then and now, is called 'The Battle of the Somme'. Although British commanders had been naming their battles after the nearest fortress, town or locality for centuries – hence the Battles of Agincourt, Salamanca or the Crimea – Haig chose to call his recent campaign north of the Somme and in the *département* of the Somme simply 'The Wearing-Out Battle'.

'Wearing out' is an accurate translation of the French word *usure*, and *usure* is another word for attrition. *Usure* was the word widely employed by General Joffre in the early part of 1916, when he was urging Haig to make a series of attacks before the main offensive, in order to wear out the German reserves. Haig had rightly declined that suggestion, wishing to conserve his force for the main offensive . . . but when that offensive stalled after Flers-Courcelette, he went over to a campaign of attrition. Now he was attempting to claim that this was his intention all along.

In his despatch, General Haig stated that the aims of the battle were three-fold:

1. To relieve the pressure on Verdun.
2. To assist our allies in the other theatres of war by stopping any further transfer of troops from the Western Front.
3. To wear down the strength of the forces opposed to us.[1]

It can be said that Sir Douglas Haig's armies had succeeded in the first two aims when the troops went over the top on 1 July but these three aims, and especially the last one, were emphatically *not* the declared objectives of the combined offensive on the Somme before the battle started. The aim of the Somme offensive was a breakthrough and confirmation of this fact comes, among others, from General Foch, who records in his memoirs that General Joffre had planned:

An Allied offensive on a scale hitherto never attempted. His idea was an attack along the whole front, from Arras to the valley of the Oise, beginning in the early days of July, the British advancing north of the river, the French south of that river. The general plans for that offensive were agreed upon in the course of an Inter-Allied Conference held at Chantilly on February 14.

There is no mention here of a battle of attrition. Foch adds that the French share of this offensive would be confined to the Northern Group of Armies – the Second, Third and Sixth Armies – which he then commanded. This commitment was quickly reduced after the opening of the Verdun battle but Foch's original plan for the French share in the combined offensive – the Battle of the Somme – was sent out on 16 March, three weeks *after* the Battle of Verdun had started. There is therefore no evidence, even on the French side, to support the aims declared in Haig's despatch . . . and it is worth adding that although the *Official History* states plainly: 'The Somme offensive had no strategic object except attrition', this volume was not published until 1932 and may benefit from hindsight.[2]

The aims stated in the December 1916 despatch may have been 'added benefits' resulting from the offensive but the offensive did not open, and certainly was not planned, with any of these aims in mind. The original aims were first stated in the letter sent to Haig by Joffre on 30 December 1915, which mentions a 'powerful offensive' and are given in detail on 12 April in the form of Haig's GHQ instructions to Fourth Army, which stated that its attack would form part of 'a general offensive in close co-operation with the French'. The Fourth Army instructions then go into great detail and call for a general advance of about one and a half miles on a 25,000-yard front on the first day, with the aim of achieving a *breakthrough* into open country beyond the German third line astride Flers.

There is nothing in any of this, at any level, about either a 'wearing-out battle' or the need to relieve the pressure on Verdun. If the main aim of the 1916 offensive was to relieve German pressure on Verdun, as Haig implies in his despatch, it is strange that the 'wearing-out battle' did not start until July, four and a half months after the Verdun battle opened. Neither did this aim appear in the GHQ instruction which was issued in mid-April, seven weeks after the opening attack at Verdun, when the desperate situation there must have been completely apparent to all concerned.

It would appear, therefore, that in his official despatch General Haig listed what his force had actually achieved and chose to ignore what it had set out to achieve. This is at least partly legitimate, for it is reasonable to record the actual events of the past campaign and give credit where it is due. Whether it is equally legitimate not only to ignore the original objectives of the battle but actually to substitute new ones is far more debatable.

At the start of the year, President Poincaré of France had stated that the French High Command had lost its belief in the possibility of a breakthrough, stating in his memoirs that 'a war of attrition . . . must be carried out by our [France's] Allies, England, Russia, even Italy'. The French aim in 1916 was to wear out the German armies and they expected their allies to bear the brunt of this activity. This intention was thwarted by von Falkenhayn's attack at Verdun but the French decision to defend the city, *coûte que coûte*, was to cost both sides a great many lives. As a result of these losses and the further losses on the Somme, none of the commanding generals survived 1916 unscathed.

Von Falkenhayn had gone by the end of the summer, his hair prematurely white, his career in tatters. The casualty toll at Verdun had provided useful ammunition to his enemy von Bethmann-Hollweg and the final blow to his reputation came at the end of August when Romania entered the war on the Entente side, an event von Falkenhayn had stated could not possibly take place before the autumn. On the day after Romania entered the war, von Falkenhayn resigned his post at GHQ and went to the Balkans, where he commanded the Ninth Army in a well-conducted campaign against the Romanians. He died at Potsdam, near Berlin, in 1922.

The next to go was General Joffre. Nivelle's rise in popular esteem coincided with the eclipse of his old commander, on whom the ire of France now began to focus. With Nivelle as a possible replacement, Joffre's grip on the high command began to slip, a process that had begun as far back as June, with those rumblings of discontent in the Chamber of Deputies over the dismounting of guns from the Verdun forts. The ever-rising toll of casualties at Verdun since then had been compounded by the further bloodbath of the Somme and when the territorial gains in both battles were measured against the cost per yard in lives, these rumblings grew even louder. Nor was there any way in which Joffre could avoid a large share of the blame.

The combined offensive on the Somme had been his idea from start to finish and, when Haig had attempted to vary the original plan on 2 July and mount a tactical battle along the Montauban–Pozières ridge, Joffre was the first to insist that the plan must be worked out to the letter, regardless of loss, with attacks all along the Franco-British line.

Joffre's reputation as the victor of the Marne staved off his critics for a while but, by the autumn of 1916, his time was over. He could not be simply dismissed – *limogé* – like so many other French generals since the war began, but he could be booted upstairs. On 27 December 1916, he was promoted to the rank of Marshal of France and left his headquarters at Chantilly for the obscurity of a small office at the École de Guerre in Paris. Joffre died, almost forgotten, in 1931.

With Joffre gone, the post of Commander-in-Chief was open and various French generals, notably Foch and Pétain, felt they had earned the right to occupy it. However, the failure on the Somme also led to the temporary eclipse of General Foch, and General Pétain, whatever he had achieved at Verdun, had not become more popular with the politicians, who were well aware that he held them in contempt. The post of Commander-in-Chief of the French Armies therefore went to Robert Nivelle, the only general to emerge from 1916 with an enhanced, not to say inflated, reputation.

If the French Government had deliberately intended to inflict further torment and loss on their long-suffering soldiers they could hardly have done better than appoint General Nivelle to the post of Commander-in-Chief. Nivelle's qualifications for high command were scarcely apparent at the time and have long since disappeared but, at the end of 1916, Nivelle was famous and had given conclusive proof of his apparent abilities as the man who had retaken the Verdun position. He had then gone on to declare that what had been done at Verdun could be done elsewhere, an optimistic statement that went down very well with his political masters.

Politicians are notoriously prone to listen to people who tell them what they want to hear and Nivelle, charming, confident, sprightly, was telling them that there was a way to break the German grip on the Western Front and achieve victory without terrible losses. The fact that all he had achieved at Verdun was to retake ground previously lost, and to retake it at great cost, was somehow overlooked in the enthusiasm his pronouncements generated. As a result, both President Poincaré and the new Prime Minister of Great Britain, David Lloyd George, were willing, indeed anxious, to hear him. So the stage was set for more tragedy on the Chemin des Dames in 1917, where

General Nivelle succeeded in doing something that three years of war and the armies of Germany had so far failed to do; he broke the heart and spirit of the French Army.

Nivelle was appointed Commander-in-Chief in December 1916. On 20 December, he had a fateful meeting with the new British Prime Minister, David Lloyd George, who had replaced Asquith, another casualty of 1916, in November. As a result of the Somme death toll, David Lloyd George had become disillusioned with the British generals and especially with General Haig, and was very doubtful if Haig or his generals would ever achieve anything in battle, except at an unacceptable cost in lives.

It was at the Calais Conference in February 1917 that Lloyd George backed the French proposal that, from 1 March 1917, General Nivelle should exercise full authority over the British Armies in France for all matters connected with military operations, the strength and boundaries of their operational areas, and the allocation of supplies and reinforcements – a proposal that would place the five British Armies in France under Nivelle's direct command. This startling suggestion failed to go through and although the various steps which followed cannot be covered here, the compromise solution was that Nivelle should take command, but for one campaign only, the spring offensives of 1917. That campaign began in April 1917 with the Canadian Corps attack at Vimy, which was an outstanding success and was followed by attacks by Allenby on the Scarpe and at Arras, which went reasonably well.

Nivelle's attack on the Aisne and along the Chemin des Dames later that month was a total disaster. Nivelle had promised the politicians that if his attack did not succeed within 48 hours he would break it off. It did not succeed but Nivelle did not break it off. In the first week of his offensive, the French lost 96,000 men – far more than in the first week at Verdun – but Nivelle kept up the pressure until the French Army broke into open mutiny. It could be said that Verdun, which made Nivelle's name and gained him high promotion, also played a part in the tragedies of 1917; Alistair Horne's comment: 'The superb triumph at Douaumont was to father France's greatest disaster of the war,' seems entirely true.[3]

In spite of those shattering losses, Nivelle's attacks on the Chemin des Dames continued into May, when regiment after regiment of the French Army mutinied and refused to attack. Robert Nivelle had finally driven the *poilus* too far; these mutinies, which began on 29 April, two weeks into Nivelle's offensive, went on for months. Nivelle was duly sacked and vanished into obscurity, to be replaced by Pétain, who remained in command of the French Armies until the end of the war.

The failure of the Somme offensive had also damaged the reputation of General Foch but his time in the limelight came later, after the German March offensive in 1918, when he became Allied Commander-in-Chief on the Western Front, co-ordinating the actions of the French, British and US Armies in the months leading up to the final victory. He became a Marshal of France and died, full of honours, in 1929.

General Pétain lived longer and died disgraced. In 1940, following the defeat of France by Nazi Germany, he became the Head of State and headed the Vichy Government that collaborated with the Germans until the end of the war. As the Germans withdrew into Germany in 1944 they took Pétain with them but he returned to France in 1946, when he was put on trial for his life and sentenced to death. The sentence was commuted to life imprisonment – Pétain was then 90 – on the Île de Yeu on the Atlantic coast until his release in 1951; he died one month later and the request of the Great War veterans, the *Ceux de Verdun*, that his body should be buried with his soldiers on the Verdun battlefield was refused.

Douglas Haig remained Commander-in-Chief of the British Armies in France until the end of the war but his reputation was blasted by the death toll on the Somme and took a further beating in 1917, after the losses of Passchendaele. Only now, more than 80 years after the Great War ended, has Haig's reputation begun to recover. This seems only fair, for many of the attacks on his character and reputation seem misguided. Haig was neither callous nor incompetent; he fought a long, hard and ultimately successful war with considerable skill.

Nevertheless, there remains an element of culpability in his actions that will not be easily erased. The generals were not *entirely* to blame for the losses of the Great War, as the public has come to believe, but they were not entirely blameless either. Haig was an intelligent, sensible general, at least in Great War terms, a man who could learn from experience, and yet some of his actions on the Somme fly in the face of commonsense and show that his talents, if real, were still limited.

On the Somme, as at Passchendaele in 1917, Haig displayed either a reluctance or an inability to realize, at some point in the battle, say in early October, that he had no more to gain from this offensive and that to press on was simply to nullify the gains made so far by inflating the casualty figures. Haig should have taken the time to evaluate this offensive, his first as Commander-in-Chief. By the end of September it should also have been apparent that he had a war-winning weapon in his hands – the tank. The tank had not done all the experts claimed for it but it clearly had potential and, given time, could be a war-winner.

The point here is that Haig had time. Winter was coming on and the tank could not be used again until the spring. In fact, tanks were not employed again until April 1917, when they took part in the Battle of Arras. To call off the Somme offensive in October would therefore have been sensible and completely justified. If we accept the aims stated in his despatch, as the British Government apparently did, Haig's 1916 campaign had been a total success, with all his aims achieved. This being so, what was there left to fight for?

Historians should not 'play general', for generalship is not their trade, but it must have been obvious after Flers-Courcelette that there was now an alternative to wasteful, frontal infantry attacks on the enemy wire. Haig had always wanted to achieve a breakthrough. Now he had the tank which, if available in quantity, improved in performance and properly handled, would probably give him one. Haig certainly appreciated the potential of the tank; after Flers he stated that 'wherever the tanks advanced we took our objectives and where they did not advance, we failed.' He followed this up with a request for 1,000 tanks, as soon as possible. If he appreciated what the tanks could do and ordered a large number for his armies, why did he not wait for them to arrive?

It would take time to deliver this quantity of machines, time to train the crews and mull over the lessons of Flers-Courcelette but again, Haig had time. That time – the coming winter – could have been utilized in building more and better tanks, in absorbing and applying the many lessons of the Somme, and in training the men in both tank tactics and in night fighting, thereby using the machines and the tactics that had paid good dividends in some stages of the Somme battle.

Had Haig waited, or been allowed to wait, his situation could only have improved. More *matériel* was becoming available all the time, more guns, more aircraft, more tanks, more ammunition, and if all these assets had been assembled in the coming spring, much might have been accomplished. As it was, Haig elected to press on with the battle into the autumn mud and justified that decision later by changing the battle's purpose.

The Somme began as an offensive; it ended as a battle of attrition. It would take another war before the combination of tanks and aircraft could create the conditions for rapid, fast-moving campaigns, those blitzkriegs which would do away with the stalemate typical of the Western Front. This time was not yet; the tanks of the Great War were too slow and the aircraft lacked an adequate performance for blitzkrieg tactics, even had those tactics been thought of, but the potential was there had someone in authority had the wit to see it . . . and in that lack of vision we see the greatest failure of all. The High Command, both military and political, failed to realize the nature of the war in which they were engaged and continued in that failure, that lack of vision, even when the piles of corpses were too high to ignore. Perhaps they were too close to the problem and therefore failed to see a way round it.

One has to beware of the dangers of hindsight. Douglas Haig cannot be ranked as one of the Great Captains of history but that is no reason to overlook the problems which confronted him during his time in command, or forget that it was Haig's armies, working to Haig's plans, that defeated the German armies in the last months of 1918: even General Foch conceded that. From the end of 1916, Haig's existing problems with the Germans and the French were to be compounded by fresh problems with his new political master,

Prime Minister Lloyd George.

David Lloyd George simply did not like General Haig – the root of their antipathy was no more complicated than that. The two men were not remotely alike, in background, attributes, character or experience; there was no common ground on which they could meet. As a result, from the moment of Lloyd George's coming to power until the end of the war, Haig was obliged to fight his battles with part of his mind fixed on the reaction at home, knowing that the Prime Minister did not trust him or have any confidence in his military abilities.

Lloyd George could not sack Haig; he was too popular, too well respected and too well connected for that – and besides, who would replace him? Even so, Lloyd George was quite determined that Haig would not again be able to engage in battles of attrition and devoted his considerable energies to querying Haig's plans and then denying him the reinforcements that would enable him to launch another offensive on the scale of the Somme. However, this did not prevent another bloodbath at Passchendaele – the Third Battle of Ypres – in the summer and autumn of 1917, another battle that went on far too long.

And yet the British Armies did not break or mutiny in 1917 as the French Armies did, though those French mutinies put an additional burden on the British Army. As that year ended in general gloom, Europe could look forward to another year of war and an ever-rising scale of loss. In April 1917, Germany's unrestricted submarine offensive would be resumed and in that month, thanks to the submarine offensive and the 'Zimmerman Telegram', which revealed Germany's attempts to involve the USA in war with Mexico, the Great War expanded yet again with the entry into the conflict of the United States.

Entering the war finally ended the many US attempts at mediation, unsuccessful as they were. At the end of 1916 the United States again attempted to negotiate a peace and another year of pointless slaughter should have concentrated minds on that purpose. After President Wilson was re-elected in November 1916, he again sent Colonel House to sound out the possibilities for a settlement in Europe. The losses of 1916 had certainly made an impression on the German side, for at a conference at Pless in January 1917, von Hindenburg is on record as saying: 'Things cannot go on as they are. The war must be brought to an end by the use of all means, and as soon as possible.' The snag, as usual, was on what terms?

When invited to state her terms for peace, Germany again demanded possession of the Belgian Congo, the heart of Mittelafrika and, again, the French industrial area of Briey-Longwy. The Belgian state could be recreated but would remain under German supervision and the Belgians must cede the city of Liège to Germany, which would also retain Alsace and Lorraine. Austria-Hungary, where the Emperor Franz Josef had recently died and been replaced by his son, the Emperor Carl, would, of course, absorb Serbia and gain certain territories in Italy. The list of demands left the Entente Powers in no doubt that Germany intended to gain at the conference table whatever had so far been unattainable on the battlefield.

There was no room for manoeuvre on the Entente side either, for here too war aims had been declared or discovered. France demanded Alsace and Lorraine and full reparations from Germany, covering the entire costs of the war. Britain demanded the destruction of the German Fleet. Other aims included the division of the Austro-Hungarian Empire into its two component parts, while the Italians required Austria to cede territory in the Tyrol and around Trieste. Finally, all the Entente Powers, Britain, France, Italy, Romania and Serbia, had greedy eyes fixed on various parts of the Turkish Empire.

While these attitudes persisted, there was no hope of the parties even meeting, let alone coming to some agreement. The losses of 1916 had taught the two sides nothing and the war would go on, but the basic problem was that no real basis for peace existed. The combatant nations could not even agree on the causes of the war, on who started it, or on what their true war aims were. Fundamentally, they did not know what they were fighting about.

Most of the European nations, and the United States, laid the blame for starting the war on Germany, but that was not how the Germans saw it. They attributed their actions in 1914 to dire necessity, to 'encirclement', and to the Franco-Russian mobilization, which had presented them with the problems of 'encirclement' in stark military terms. The German Government continued to maintain this point even at the 1919 Peace Conference at Versailles, when the German delegation took strong exception to Article 231 of the Treaty which insisted that Germany acknowledge the blame for 'causing all the loss and damage to which the Allied and Associate Governments have been subjected as a consequence of the war imposed on them by the aggression of Germany and her Allies.'

Germany was eventually forced to accede to Article 231 but her leaders never saw it as a correct definition of their motives. This view – that Germany was not responsible for the outbreak of war – was maintained for the next two decades, during the Weimar Republic and the Third Reich, and was only finally refuted by the extensive researches made into the Wilhelmine archives at Potsdam by Professor Fritz Fischer, research which proved beyond any reasonable doubt that Germany had been planning a major European war for years and saw the Sarajevo incident, and the subsequent reactions of Austria-Hungary and Serbia, as a chance to start it.

The end of every year is a time for reflection and, at the end of 1916 as in 1915, there was a great deal to reflect on. The year had begun with high hopes and had seen two cataclysmic battles on the Western Front alone, but what had been achieved, what steps had been taken towards ending the war or achieving victory? There was a growing sense that the war should be ended as soon as possible, by getting the parties around a conference table. Here again though, what sort of bargain could be struck when the parties' assets were not equal?

Germany had territorial assets to bargain with at a peace conference, but what had the Entente got to put on the table? Except a million more skulls, and the prospect of even more slaughter in the years ahead, either at the front or from starvation at home as the Allied blockade continued, the Entente powers had nothing to bargain with but death and terror. After the bloodbaths of 1916, Germany still held all of Belgium and most of northern France and, in the east, Russia was on the brink of revolution. Nor had German successes ended; in December 1916 the German Army entered Bucharest, the capital of Romania.

It was this success which inspired von Bethmann-Hollweg, a constant advocate of a negotiated settlement, to suggest to the Kaiser that Germany could now offer terms to the Entente Powers without this gesture being interpreted as a sign of weakness. The generals of the High Command did not object to this proposal, and the Kriegsmarine was even in favour of it, knowing that if the Entente rejected German terms, the Kaiser and his Chancellor could no longer prevent them introducing unrestricted submarine warfare.

The one hope for a peaceful settlement at the end of 1916 lay in the United States of America, where President Woodrow Wilson had just been re-elected for a further four-year term. America had influence in the war, partly because of her financial and economic muscle, partly because of her rich and untapped store of fighting men. While neither side would openly solicit, or attempt to prevent, America's military intervention, the Entente Powers were still hoping that the United States would be provoked by German militarism and the actions of the German submarine fleet into entering the war on their side.

Fear of American involvement was certainly a potent factor at this time; throughout 1916 the Kaiser had been kept back from permitting unrestricted submarine warfare for fear that the inevitable sinking of US vessels would indeed bring the USA into the war on the side of the Entente, although the neutrality lobby in the USA, which wanted the USA to stay out of the war, and the German *bund*, which wanted the USA to support Germany, were both still strong and vocal. The United States could still, for the moment, claim to be a disinterested party, anxious to restore peace to a war-torn continent and put an end to this senseless slaughter.

President Wilson's emissaries and ambassadors had been constant advocates of peace but, by the end of 1916, persuasion having failed, Wilson tried more direct methods, ordering that US banks were no longer to grant war credits to any of the belligerent powers, an action that almost brought Britain, the Entente's paymaster, to the brink of bankruptcy. Wilson's principal emissary, Colonel House, was the one who finally succeeded in getting the belligerents to declare their war aims, but none of this edged any of the belligerents an inch nearer the conference table.

The general feeling among the Entente nations at the end of 1916 seemed to be that unless Europe returned to the status quo ante, the terrible loss of life in the previous three years had been for nothing.

Exactly the same argument could be deployed by the Central Powers; they too wanted something out of this war, some return for the sacrifice of their young men, and they wanted it in the shape of territorial concessions and guaranteed frontiers.

No one seemed able to accept that the war had been a terrible mistake and that ending it, on any reasonable terms, which must include the German evacuation of France and Belgium, was far less costly than letting it continue. No one had expected the war to last this long or be so terrible, and plenty of people on either side, including some among the German commanders, knew that the war must be ended. This argument failed to convince the contestants and, since no agreement could be reached and no basis for a compromise found, the war would go on. It would also be fought as one of attrition because, in the end, the only way to stop it was not by limiting the suffering, but by increasing it . . . not by saving soldiers' lives, but by killing as many soldiers as possible.

Finally, it is necessary to summarize the main causes inhibiting military success in the field. It can be argued that the various armies ended up with a policy of attrition for three fundamental reasons. First of all, there was the absence of a Supreme Command. This was true on both sides of the line; von Falkenhayn saw no reason to inform, never mind consult, the commander of the Austrian armies, Field Marshal Conrad von Hötzendorf, on his intention to attack Verdun, the main German campaign in 1916. The two men cordially disliked each other and the German attitude to the Austrian armies bordered on contempt. As a result, the advantages of interior lines and of pursuing a joint policy in the east, one which could have resulted in the crushing of Russia, and the essential restoration of a single-front war, were never taken up. The failure here is remarkable, for the need to avoid a war on two fronts was the entire purpose of the Schlieffen Plan, itself the only plan for total victory in 1914. The war came back to the Western Front in 1918 as a result of the Russian Revolution, not because of strategic or political action on the part of the Central Powers.

The Entente generals got on much better and met more frequently but they too were largely fighting separate wars. What was needed, as in the Second World War, was a Combined Chiefs-of-Staff Committee, to conduct the *strategic* business of the war. Such a committee could have viewed the struggle on a continental, if not global scale, allocating the appropriate assets where they would do the most good and co-ordinating the various campaigns to stretch the Central Powers' resources to the limit. This kind of overview hardly happened, even within the United Kingdom, as General Sir William Robertson, the CIGS, relates in his memoirs:

> Finally, in addition to the ministerial heads of the two fighting services and the Secretary of State for India, there were other Ministers who considered themselves qualified and entitled, as members of the Cabinet, to have a controlling voice in the operations undertaken.
>
> It thus came about by the end of 1914 that while the Secretary of State for War was aiming at decisive results on the Western Front, the First Lord of the Admiralty was advocating the seizure of the Dardanelles and Constantinople; the Secretary of State for India and the Indian Government were conducting a campaign in Mesopotamia; the Secretary of State for the Colonies was concerned with operations in various parts of Africa; and the Chancellor of the Exchequer was impressing upon his colleagues the strategical advantages to be gained by transferring the main British military effort from the Western Front to the Balkan peninsula and Syria. A more deplorable state of affairs can surely never have existed in the conduct of any war.[4]

Matters improved over time but not much, and on the broader canvas of the Entente, not at all. Joffre's conferences at Chantilly were steps in the right direction but they really took the Entente commanders little farther than the conference room. Where and with what force the war should be fought was left to the various national commanders and it was not until the Franco-British armies were in extremis in 1918 that a supreme commander, Foch, was appointed to co-ordinate the armies on the Western Front. This failure to prepare a strategy for the entire war can largely be laid at the door of the politicians, who in the Second World War laid out the main objectives and at a series of conferences at Casablanca, Tehran, Quebec and Yalta, to control the overall direction of the war. That policy, so obvious now, so useful then, was totally neglected between 1914 and 1918.

The second flaw was a military one, a failure to appreciate the impact of science and industrialization on military technology and the conduct of war. The problem was not the existence of such technology – aircraft, tanks, poison gas, wire, machine-guns – but a failure to think through the implications of such technology, how it might be employed to better effect, not least by developing proper tactics for its employment in attack and defence. This failure can be laid at the door of the generals who can also be blamed for a lack of vision.

The final, fatal failure was a general one – a failure to realize that this war was not like any previous war. In size, in geographic spread, in the use of technology, in sheer killing power, in the way it was fought and in the way it quickly veered away from the reasons for which it was allegedly entered into, this war was totally different from all that had gone before. This fact became obvious quite early on but that realization did not lead to the obvious conclusion – that since this was not the sort of conflict the nations envisaged before it began, the sooner it was ended the better. The failure to take action can be laid at the door of governments.

The late Barbara Tuchman, an American historian and the author of some fine books on the Great War, has written that while the human race has made great progress in many fields of endeavour – science, medicine, the arts – since the siege of Troy to the present day, it has made no discernible progress whatsoever in the field of government. She adds that nations will frequently adopt policies which are not only dangerous to their national well-being, but which are seen and known to be dangerous even before they are undertaken.[5] The events of 1916 give ample proof of this observation. For the nations to permit their commanders to enter into a war of attrition, in spite of the current domination of the battlefield by defensive technology, was at best madness.

And so the war was fought with new weapons and old ideas and the result was a slaughter exceeding that of any previous war. In just four years, about 9,300,000 soldiers died on the battlefields of the Great

War; 3,600,000 from the nations comprising the Central Powers and 5,700,000 from the nations of the Entente. As in the Second World War, Russia lost the most with 2,300,000 dead, followed by Germany with 2,036,897 and then France with 1,900,000. British and Empire dead totalled 956,000, of whom 704,000 came from the United Kingdom, about 12.5 per cent of all the men mobilized. Italy lost 450,000 dead and the USA 126,000.

And then there were the wounded. Germany had more than 5,000,000 men maimed in the war, Britain close to 3,000,000. These are only the battlefield totals, for the pain and loss went much deeper. By 1919, Germany had more than 500,000 war widows and more than 1,000,000 fatherless children. If the totals vary, other nations could produce similar statistics.[6] These totals are awesome but how many must suffer before a nation accepts that the cost of war is too high? It seemed during the Great War that sooner or later some nation would buckle, a fear expressed by Lloyd George in November 1916:

> As the war drags on its weary and bloodstained path, the sacrifices and sufferings must necessarily increase, and the gloom cast by the appalling losses over the country will become darker. Food will become scarcer and costlier, the burdens of taxation heavier. Efforts will be made by powerful neutrals to patch up a peace on what would appear to be specious terms and there is a real danger that people will listen . . . last of all there is a danger which one hardly likes to contemplate, of one of the four great Allies being offered terms which seem better than an indefinite prolongation of the horrors of war. No alliance has ever borne the strain of a protracted war without breaking.

Not for the last time, Lloyd George was wrong. The Entente did not break and Russia collapsed from internal troubles, not from any wish to abandon her allies.

The battles on the Western Front, especially Verdun and the Somme, were battles that continued because they could not be called off and so they spread their deadly contagion into the hearts and souls of the belligerent nations. War has its own dynamic and that dynamic had taken full charge by the end of 1916. The fighting would therefore continue until there was nothing left to fight over and nothing left to fight with, and until one side gained the victory. That time would come in 1918, when the German March offensive failed, when Haig and Foch and the American armies were driving the German Army back in full retreat, when German women and children were dying of starvation caused by the British naval blockade, when mutiny swept the German Navy and Communist mobs roamed the streets of German cities, and the Kaiser, the Supreme War Lord, fled into exile. Perhaps that kind of collapse was inevitable; the Second World War ended in much the same way and only the atomic bomb has prevented a further world-wide conflagration. The nations knew what they were doing by 1916, even perhaps in 1915, for in June of that year Lord Curzon wrote:

> The war seems to be resolving itself largely into a question of killing Germans. For this purpose, viewing the present methods and instruments of war, one man seems to be about the equivalent of another and one life taken to involve another life. If then two million, or whatever, more of Germans have to be killed at least the corresponding number of Allied soldiers will have to be sacrificed to achieve that object; I say at least because if we contemplate an advance into Germany, the proportion will be gravely deflected against the allies.

Lord Curzon had access to the corridors of power, and the coming of attrition must have been as obvious to others as it was to him. The Great War remains an outstanding tragedy because those in government, on both sides of the battle line, knew the costs of continuing the war; the chances to end it were constantly on offer, not least from the United States, yet nothing was done.

Alistair Horne's remark, which opens this chapter, seems to be entirely accurate but the will to end the war did not exist in 1916. Victory came in 1918 because the Central Powers had been defeated in the field but the peace of November 1918 was deeply flawed by the Treaty of Versailles in 1919, a treaty largely dictated by the French and with terms so harsh that it led to another European war 20 years later. Why civilized nations could not – cannot – find a better way to organize their affairs remains a mystery but the events of 1916 provide abundant lessons on what can happen when reason fails.

Notes

1 *Sir Douglas Haig's Despatches*, p. 20.

2 *Official History*, *1916*, vol. 5, Military Operations France and Belgium, p. 31.

3 *The Price of Glory, Verdun*, *1916*, p. 321.

4 *Soldiers and Statesmen*, p. 160.

5 Barbara Tuchman, *The March of Folly*, Foreword,

6 From Holgar Herwig, *The First World War, Germany and Austria-Hungary, 1914–1918*.

Bibliography

What follows is only a small selection of the books consulted and leaves out the well-known and indispensable works of Martin Middlebrook and Lyn Macdonald with which everyone interested in the Western Front will be familiar. For tracking some of these down I am especially grateful to the staff of the London Library and for help with the German text to the late Colin Fox of the Western Front Association.

Addison, C., *Politics from Within, 1911–1918*, Herbert Jenkins, 1924

Asprey, Robert B., *The German High Command at War*, Morrow & Co., 1991

Balfour, M., *The Kaiser and His Times*, Cresset Press, 1964

Barnett, Correlli, *The Swordbearers: Studies in Supreme Command in the First World War*, Hodder & Stoughton, 1963

Baynes, John, *Far From a Donkey, The Life of General Sir Ivor Maxse*, Brassey's, 1995

Behrend, Arthur, *As from Kemmel Hill*, Eyre & Spottiswood, 1963

Bethmann-Hollweg, Theobald von, *Reflections on the World War*, Thornton Butterworth, 1922

Bidwell, R.G., *Gunners at War*, Arms & Armour Press, 1970

Blake, Robert, *The Private Papers of Douglas Haig, 1914–1919*, Eyre & Spottiswoode, 1952

Boraston, J.H. (ed.), *Sir Douglas Haig's Despatches (December 1916–April 1919)*, J.M. Dent, 1919

British Commission for Military History, *Look to your Front: Studies in the First World War*, Spellmount, 1999

British Official History: History of the Great War, vol. 5, 1916, Brigadier-General Sir James Edmonds, Macmillan & Co., 1932

British Official History: The War in the Air, vol. 2, H.A. Jones, The Clarendon Press, 1928

Brown, Malcolm, *Verdun, 1916*, Tempus Books, 1999

Brüchmuller, Colonel Georg, *Die Artillerie beim Angriff Stellungskrieg*, Offen Worte Verlag, 1926

Carver, Field Marshal Lord, *The War Lords*, Weidenfeld & Nicolson, 1976

Charteris, Brigadier-General J., *At GHQ*, Cassell, 1931

Clark, Alan, *The Donkeys*, Hutchinson, 1961

Clausewitz, C. von, *On War*, Pelican, 1968

Cooper, Bryan, *The Ironclads of Cambrai*, Souvenir Press, 1967

Duncan, G.S., *Douglas Haig As I Knew Him*, Allen & Unwin, 1966

Falkenhayn, General, Erich von, *General Headquarters, 1914–1916*, Hutchinson, 1919

Farrar-Hockley, General A. H., *The Somme*, Batsford, 1964

Fischer, Fritz, *Germany's Aims in the First World War*, London, 1967

Foch, Marshal Ferdinand, *The Memoirs of Marshal Foch*, trans. Bentley Mott, Heinemann, 1931

French, David, *British Strategy and War Aims, 1914–1916*, Allen & Unwin, 1956

Gardner, Brian, *The Big Push, The Somme 1916*, Sphere Books, 1968

Gardiner, A.G., *The War Lords*, Dent, Toronto, 1915

Gilbert, Martin, *The First World War*, Weidenfeld & Nicolson, 1994

Gooch, Joseph, *The Plans of War: The General Staff and British Military Strategy, 1900–1916*, Routledge, Kegan Paul, 1974

Gough, General Sir Hubert, *The Fifth Army*, Hodder & Stoughton, 1931

Griffiths, Paddy, *Battle Tactics of the Western Front, The British Army's Art of Attack, 1916–1918*, Yale, 1996

Hankey, Lord, *The Supreme Command, 1914–1918*, 2 vols, Allen & Unwin, 1961

Hardach, Gerd, *The First World War 1914–1918*, Allen Lane, 1977

Harris, J.P., *Men, Ideas and Tanks, 1903–1939*, Manchester University Press, 1995

Henig, Ruth, *The Origins of the First World War*, Routledge, 1989

Holmes, Professor Richard, *War Walks*, BBC Publications, 1996

Horne, Alistair, *The Price of Glory, Verdun 1916*, Penguin, 1993

Hughes and Siegelman, ed., *Leadership and Conflict, 1914–1918*, Pen & Sword, 2000

James, Lawrence, *Imperial Warrior: The Life and Times of Field Marshal Viscount Allenby*, Weidenfeld & Nicolson, 1993

Keegan, John, *The First World War*, Hutchinson, 1998

Kennedy, Paul (ed.), *The War Plans of the Great Powers*, Allen & Unwin, 1979

Kilduff, Peter, *Germany's First Air Force, 1914–1918*, Arms & Armour Press, 1991

Liddell Hart, B.H., *History of the First World War*, Cassell, 1970

— *Reputations*, Cassell, 1928

— *The Tanks*, 2 vols, Cassell, 1950

Ludendorff, General Erich, *My War Memories*, Hutchinson, 1919

Macksey, Kenneth, *The Encyclopaedia of Weapons and Military Technology*, Penguin, 1993

— *Why the Germans Lose at War*, Greenhill Books, 1997

Marshall-Cornwall, J., *Haig as Military Commander*, Batsford, 1973

Neillands, Robin, *The Great War Generals on the Western Front*, Robinson, 1998

Norris, Geoffrey, *The Royal Flying Corps, A History*, Frederick Muller, 1965

Prior, Robin and Wilson, Trevor, *Command on the Western Front*, Blackwell, 1992

Puleston, William Dilworth, *High Command in the World War*, Charles Scribner's Sons, 1934

Reicharchiv, *Der Weltkrieg*, Berlin, 1925

Simkins, Peter, *Kitchener's Army, The Raising of the New Armies, 1914–1916*, Manchester University Press, 1988

Sixsmith, Major General E.K.G., *British Generalship in the Twentieth Century*, Arms & Armour Press, 1976

Stone, Norman, *The Eastern Front, 1914–1917*, Hodder & Stoughton, 1975

Taylor, A.J.P., *The First World War*, Hamish Hamilton, 1963

Terraine, John, *The Western Front, 1914–1918*, Hutchinson, 1964

— *Douglas Haig, the Educated Soldier*, Hutchinson, 1963

— *White Heat, The New Warfare*, Sidgwick & Jackson, 1982

Tuchman, Barbara, *The Guns of August*, Papermac, 1962

— *The Zimmerman Telegram*, Papermac, 1958

Whitehouse, Arch, *The Years of the Sky Kings*, Macdonald, 1960

Index